Just The
facts101
Textbook Key Facts

Israe
Regulations and Procedures Handbook

by cram101
Texbook NOT Included

Table of Contents

Index: Answers

Just The Facts101

Exam Prep for

Israel Customs, Trade Regulations and Procedures Handbook

Just The Facts101 Exam Prep

eAIN 464111

Foundations of Business

A business, also known as an enterprise, agency or a firm, is an entity involved in the provision of goods and/or services to consumers. Businesses are prevalent in capitalist economies, where most of them are privately owned and provide goods and services to customers in exchange for other goods, services, or money.

:: Business terms ::

A ________ is a short statement of why an organization exists, what its overall goal is, identifying the goal of its operations: what kind of product or service it provides, its primary customers or market, and its geographical region of operation. It may include a short statement of such fundamental matters as the organization`s values or philosophies, a business`s main competitive advantages, or a desired future state—the "vision".

Exam Probability: **Medium**

1. *Answer choices:*

(see index for correct answer)

- a. strategic plan
- b. Personal selling
- c. organizational capital
- d. Mission statement

Guidance: level 1

:: Telecommunication theory ::

In reliability theory and reliability engineering, the term ________ has the following meanings.

Exam Probability: **Low**

2. *Answer choices:*

(see index for correct answer)

- a. Trellis
- b. Exformation
- c. Availability
- d. Trellis modulation

Guidance: level 1

:: Asset ::

In financial accounting, an _________ is any resource owned by the business. Anything tangible or intangible that can be owned or controlled to produce value and that is held by a company to produce positive economic value is an _________. Simply stated, _________ s represent value of ownership that can be converted into cash . The balance sheet of a firm records the monetary value of the _________ s owned by that firm. It covers money and other valuables belonging to an individual or to a business.

Exam Probability: **Medium**

3. *Answer choices:*

(see index for correct answer)

- a. Current asset
- b. Fixed asset

Guidance: level 1

:: Materials ::

A __________, also known as a feedstock, unprocessed material, or primary commodity, is a basic material that is used to produce goods, finished products, energy, or intermediate materials which are feedstock for future finished products. As feedstock, the term connotes these materials are bottleneck assets and are highly important with regard to producing other products. An example of this is crude oil, which is a __________ and a feedstock used in the production of industrial chemicals, fuels, plastics, and pharmaceutical goods; lumber is a __________ used to produce a variety of products including all types of furniture. The term " __________ " denotes materials in minimally processed or unprocessed in states; e.g., raw latex, crude oil, cotton, coal, raw biomass, iron ore, air, logs, or water i.e. "...any product of agriculture, forestry, fishing and any other mineral that is in its natural form or which has undergone the transformation required to prepare it for internationally marketing in substantial volumes."

Exam Probability: **High**

4. *Answer choices:*

(see index for correct answer)

- a. Solid surface
- b. Raw material
- c. Samuel Peal
- d. Materials World

Guidance: level 1

:: Management ::

In organizational studies, __________ is the efficient and effective development of an organization`s resources when they are needed. Such resources may include financial resources, inventory, human skills, production resources, or information technology and natural resources.

Exam Probability: **High**

5. *Answer choices:*

(see index for correct answer)

- a. Pareto analysis
- b. Business process improvement
- c. Resource management
- d. Earned value management

Guidance: level 1

:: Reputation management ::

__________ or image of a social entity is an opinion about that entity, typically as a result of social evaluation on a set of criteria.

Exam Probability: **Low**

6. *Answer choices:*

(see index for correct answer)

- a. BrandYourself
- b. Reputation
- c. Hilltop algorithm
- d. EigenTrust

Guidance: level 1

:: Money ::

In economics, _________ is money in the physical form of currency, such as banknotes and coins. In bookkeeping and finance, _________ is current assets comprising currency or currency equivalents that can be accessed immediately or near-immediately . _________ is seen either as a reserve for payments, in case of a structural or incidental negative _________ flow or as a way to avoid a downturn on financial markets.

Exam Probability: **Low**

7. *Answer choices:*

(see index for correct answer)

- a. Green money
- b. Metallism
- c. Love of money
- d. Fungibility

Guidance: level 1

:: Land value taxation ::

_________ , sometimes referred to as dry _________ , is the solid surface of Earth that is not permanently covered by water. The vast majority of human activity throughout history has occurred in _________ areas that support agriculture, habitat, and various natural resources. Some life forms have developed from predecessor species that lived in bodies of water.

Exam Probability: **High**

8. *Answer choices:*

(see index for correct answer)

- a. Harry Gunnison Brown
- b. Prosper Australia
- c. Georgism
- d. Land

Guidance: level 1

:: Generally Accepted Accounting Principles ::

In business and accounting, _________ is an entity's income minus cost of goods sold, expenses and taxes for an accounting period. It is computed as the residual of all revenues and gains over all expenses and losses for the period, and has also been defined as the net increase in shareholders' equity that results from a company's operations. In the context of the presentation of financial statements, the IFRS Foundation defines _________ as synonymous with profit and loss. The difference between revenue and the cost of making a product or providing a service, before deducting overheads, payroll, taxation, and interest payments. This is different from operating income .

Exam Probability: **Medium**

9. *Answer choices:*

(see index for correct answer)

- a. Long-term liabilities
- b. Gross sales
- c. Profit
- d. Cash method of accounting

Guidance: level 1

:: Debt ::

__________ is when something, usually money, is owed by one party, the borrower or __________ or, to a second party, the lender or creditor. __________ is a deferred payment, or series of payments, that is owed in the future, which is what differentiates it from an immediate purchase. The __________ may be owed by sovereign state or country, local government, company, or an individual. Commercial __________ is generally subject to contractual terms regarding the amount and timing of repayments of principal and interest. Loans, bonds, notes, and mortgages are all types of __________. The term can also be used metaphorically to cover moral obligations and other interactions not based on economic value. For example, in Western cultures, a person who has been helped by a second person is sometimes said to owe a " __________ of gratitude" to the second person.

Exam Probability: **Medium**

10. *Answer choices:*

(see index for correct answer)

- a. Legal liability
- b. Perpetual subordinated debt
- c. Compulsive buying disorder
- d. Debt relief

Guidance: level 1

:: Business ::

A __________ is a mathematical object used to count, measure, and label. The original examples are the natural __________ s 1, 2, 3, 4, and so forth. A written symbol like "5" that represents a __________ is called a numeral. A numeral system is an organized way to write and manipulate this type of symbol, for example the Hindu–Arabic numeral system allows combinations of numerical digits like "5" and "0" to represent larger __________ s like 50. A numeral in linguistics can refer to a symbol like 5, the words or phrase that names a __________ , like "five hundred", or other words that mean a specific __________ , like "dozen". In addition to their use in counting and measuring, numerals are often used for labels , for ordering , and for codes . In common usage, __________ may refer to a symbol, a word or phrase, or the mathematical object.

Exam Probability: **High**

11. *Answer choices:*

(see index for correct answer)

- a. Equality impact assessment
- b. Operating agreement
- c. Number
- d. Sustainopreneurship

Guidance: level 1

:: Real estate ::

__________ s serve several societal needs – primarily as shelter from weather, security, living space, privacy, to store belongings, and to comfortably live and work. A __________ as a shelter represents a physical division of the human habitat and the outside .

Exam Probability: **High**

12. *Answer choices:*

(see index for correct answer)

- a. Building
- b. Rent strike
- c. CMC Group
- d. Property ladder

Guidance: level 1

:: Generally Accepted Accounting Principles ::

In accounting, _________ is the income that a business have from its normal business activities, usually from the sale of goods and services to customers. _________ is also referred to as sales or turnover.Some companies receive _________ from interest, royalties, or other fees. _________ may refer to business income in general, or it may refer to the amount, in a monetary unit, earned during a period of time, as in "Last year, Company X had _________ of $42 million". Profits or net income generally imply total _________ minus total expenses in a given period. In accounting, in the balance statement it is a subsection of the Equity section and _________ increases equity, it is often referred to as the "top line" due to its position on the income statement at the very top. This is to be contrasted with the "bottom line" which denotes net income .

Exam Probability: **Low**

13. *Answer choices:*

(see index for correct answer)

- a. Revenue
- b. Net realizable value
- c. Generally accepted accounting principles
- d. French generally accepted accounting principles

Guidance: level 1

:: Private equity ::

_________ is a type of private equity, a form of financing that is provided by firms or funds to small, early-stage, emerging firms that are deemed to have high growth potential, or which have demonstrated high growth . _________ firms or funds invest in these early-stage companies in exchange for equity, or an ownership stake, in the companies they invest in. _________ ists take on the risk of financing risky start-ups in the hopes that some of the firms they support will become successful. Because startups face high uncertainty, VC investments do have high rates of failure. The start-ups are usually based on an innovative technology or business model and they are usually from the high technology industries, such as information technology , clean technology or biotechnology.

Exam Probability: **High**

14. *Answer choices:*

(see index for correct answer)

- a. Venture capital
- b. World Business Angels Association
- c. Business Development Company
- d. Junk bond

Guidance: level 1

:: ::

__________ or accountancy is the measurement, processing, and communication of financial information about economic entities such as businesses and corporations. The modern field was established by the Italian mathematician Luca Pacioli in 1494. __________, which has been called the "language of business", measures the results of an organization`s economic activities and conveys this information to a variety of users, including investors, creditors, management, and regulators. Practitioners of __________ are known as accountants. The terms "__________" and "financial reporting" are often used as synonyms.

Exam Probability: **Low**

15. *Answer choices:*

(see index for correct answer)

- a. Accounting
- b. imperative
- c. interpersonal communication
- d. information systems assessment

Guidance: level 1

:: Generally Accepted Accounting Principles ::

Expenditure is an outflow of money to another person or group to pay for an item or service, or for a category of costs. For a tenant, rent is an _________ . For students or parents, tuition is an _________ . Buying food, clothing, furniture or an automobile is often referred to as an _________ . An _________ is a cost that is "paid" or "remitted", usually in exchange for something of value. Something that seems to cost a great deal is "expensive". Something that seems to cost little is "inexpensive". " _________ s of the table" are _________ s of dining, refreshments, a feast, etc.

Exam Probability: **High**

16. *Answer choices:*

(see index for correct answer)

- a. Contributed capital
- b. Deprival value
- c. Gross sales
- d. Goodwill

Guidance: level 1

:: Debt ::

_________ is the trust which allows one party to provide money or resources to another party wherein the second party does not reimburse the first party immediately , but promises either to repay or return those resources at a later date. In other words, _________ is a method of making reciprocity formal, legally enforceable, and extensible to a large group of unrelated people.

Exam Probability: **Medium**

17. *Answer choices:*

(see index for correct answer)

- a. Credit
- b. Bad debt
- c. Floating charge
- d. Paid outside closing

Guidance: level 1

:: Management ::

The term _________ refers to measures designed to increase the degree of autonomy and self-determination in people and in communities in order to enable them to represent their interests in a responsible and self-determined way, acting on their own authority. It is the process of becoming stronger and more confident, especially in controlling one`s life and claiming one`s rights. _________ as action refers both to the process of self- _________ and to professional support of people, which enables them to overcome their sense of powerlessness and lack of influence, and to recognize and use their resources. To do work with power.

Exam Probability: **Low**

18. *Answer choices:*

(see index for correct answer)

- a. Statistical process control
- b. Certified management consultant
- c. I-VMS
- d. Change advisory board

Guidance: level 1

:: Employment ::

__________ is a relationship between two parties, usually based on a contract where work is paid for, where one party, which may be a corporation, for profit, not-for-profit organization, co-operative or other entity is the employer and the other is the employee. Employees work in return for payment, which may be in the form of an hourly wage, by piecework or an annual salary, depending on the type of work an employee does or which sector she or he is working in. Employees in some fields or sectors may receive gratuities, bonus payment or stock options. In some types of __________, employees may receive benefits in addition to payment. Benefits can include health insurance, housing, disability insurance or use of a gym. __________ is typically governed by __________ laws, regulations or legal contracts.

Exam Probability: **High**

19. *Answer choices:*

(see index for correct answer)

- a. Forced retention
- b. Liaison job
- c. Make-work job

- d. delayering

Guidance: level 1

:: Accounting terminology ::

_________ is a legally enforceable claim for payment held by a business for goods supplied and/or services rendered that customers/clients have ordered but not paid for. These are generally in the form of invoices raised by a business and delivered to the customer for payment within an agreed time frame. _________ is shown in a balance sheet as an asset. It is one of a series of accounting transactions dealing with the billing of a customer for goods and services that the customer has ordered. These may be distinguished from notes receivable, which are debts created through formal legal instruments called promissory notes.

Exam Probability: **Medium**

20. *Answer choices:*

(see index for correct answer)

- a. Statement of financial position
- b. Cash flow management
- c. managerial accounting
- d. double-entry bookkeeping

Guidance: level 1

:: Competition (economics) ::

_________ arises whenever at least two parties strive for a goal which cannot be shared: where one`s gain is the other`s loss .

Exam Probability: **Low**

21. *Answer choices:*

(see index for correct answer)

- a. Level playing field
- b. Wantrapreneur
- c. School choice
- d. Currency competition

Guidance: level 1

:: E-commerce ::

_________ is the activity of buying or selling of products on online services or over the Internet. Electronic commerce draws on technologies such as mobile commerce, electronic funds transfer, supply chain management, Internet marketing, online transaction processing, electronic data interchange , inventory management systems, and automated data collection systems.

Exam Probability: **Medium**

22. *Answer choices:*

(see index for correct answer)

- a. Supply chain attack
- b. Webjet
- c. Ven
- d. Piano Media

Guidance: level 1

:: Analysis ::

_________ is the process of breaking a complex topic or substance into smaller parts in order to gain a better understanding of it. The technique has been applied in the study of mathematics and logic since before Aristotle , though _________ as a formal concept is a relatively recent development.

Exam Probability: **Medium**

23. *Answer choices:*

(see index for correct answer)

- a. Configurational analysis
- b. Narrative logic
- c. DESTEP
- d. Analysis

Guidance: level 1

:: Stochastic processes ::

__________ in its modern meaning is a "new idea, creative thoughts, new imaginations in form of device or method". __________ is often also viewed as the application of better solutions that meet new requirements, unarticulated needs, or existing market needs. Such __________ takes place through the provision of more-effective products, processes, services, technologies, or business models that are made available to markets, governments and society. An __________ is something original and more effective and, as a consequence, new, that "breaks into" the market or society. __________ is related to, but not the same as, invention, as __________ is more apt to involve the practical implementation of an invention to make a meaningful impact in the market or society, and not all __________ s require an invention. __________ often manifests itself via the engineering process, when the problem being solved is of a technical or scientific nature. The opposite of __________ is exnovation.

Exam Probability: **Medium**

24. *Answer choices:*

(see index for correct answer)

- a. Stochastic resonance
- b. Innovation
- c. Balance equation
- d. Brownian excursion

Guidance: level 1

:: Stochastic processes ::

_________ is a system of rules that are created and enforced through social or governmental institutions to regulate behavior. It has been defined both as "the Science of Justice" and "the Art of Justice". _________ is a system that regulates and ensures that individuals or a community adhere to the will of the state. State-enforced _________ s can be made by a collective legislature or by a single legislator, resulting in statutes, by the executive through decrees and regulations, or established by judges through precedent, normally in common _________ jurisdictions. Private individuals can create legally binding contracts, including arbitration agreements that may elect to accept alternative arbitration to the normal court process. The formation of _________ s themselves may be influenced by a constitution, written or tacit, and the rights encoded therein. The _________ shapes politics, economics, history and society in various ways and serves as a mediator of relations between people.

Exam Probability: **Low**

25. *Answer choices:*

(see index for correct answer)

- a. G/G/1 queue
- b. Branching random walk
- c. Law
- d. Doob decomposition theorem

Guidance: level 1

:: Scientific method ::

In the social sciences and life sciences, a _________ is a research method involving an up-close, in-depth, and detailed examination of a subject of study , as well as its related contextual conditions.

Exam Probability: **High**

26. *Answer choices:*

(see index for correct answer)

- a. Causal research
- b. Preference test
- c. explanatory research
- d. Case study

Guidance: level 1

:: Decision theory ::

Within economics the concept of _________ is used to model worth or value, but its usage has evolved significantly over time. The term was introduced initially as a measure of pleasure or satisfaction within the theory of utilitarianism by moral philosophers such as Jeremy Bentham and John Stuart Mill. But the term has been adapted and reapplied within neoclassical economics, which dominates modern economic theory, as a _________ function that represents a consumer`s preference ordering over a choice set. As such, it is devoid of its original interpretation as a measurement of the pleasure or satisfaction obtained by the consumer from that choice.

Exam Probability: **Medium**

27. *Answer choices:*

(see index for correct answer)

- a. Nominal group technique
- b. Utility
- c. Choice-supportive bias
- d. Decision tree

Guidance: level 1

:: Evaluation ::

_________ solving consists of using generic or ad hoc methods in an orderly manner to find solutions to _________ s. Some of the _________ -solving techniques developed and used in philosophy, artificial intelligence, computer science, engineering, mathematics, or medicine are related to mental _________ -solving techniques studied in psychology.

Exam Probability: **Medium**

28. *Answer choices:*

(see index for correct answer)

- a. SPECpower
- b. Common Criteria Testing Laboratory

- c. Integrity
- d. Encomium

Guidance: level 1

:: Business ::

The seller, or the provider of the goods or services, completes a sale in response to an acquisition, appropriation, requisition or a direct interaction with the buyer at the point of sale. There is a passing of title of the item, and the settlement of a price, in which agreement is reached on a price for which transfer of ownership of the item will occur. The seller, not the purchaser typically executes the sale and it may be completed prior to the obligation of payment. In the case of indirect interaction, a person who sells goods or service on behalf of the owner is known as a _________ man or _________ woman or _________ person, but this often refers to someone selling goods in a store/shop, in which case other terms are also common, including _________ clerk, shop assistant, and retail clerk.

Exam Probability: **Low**

29. *Answer choices:*

(see index for correct answer)

- a. GoCardless
- b. Operating subsidiary
- c. Disadvantaged business enterprise
- d. Sales

Guidance: level 1

:: Market research ::

__________ is "the process or set of processes that links the producers, customers, and end users to the marketer through information used to identify and define marketing opportunities and problems; generate, refine, and evaluate marketing actions; monitor marketing performance; and improve understanding of marketing as a process. __________ specifies the information required to address these issues, designs the method for collecting information, manages and implements the data collection process, analyzes the results, and communicates the findings and their implications."

Exam Probability: **Low**

30. *Answer choices:*

(see index for correct answer)

- a. Sociomapping
- b. Nielsen VideoScan
- c. Competitive intelligence
- d. Early adopter

Guidance: level 1

:: Goods ::

In most contexts, the concept of _________ denotes the conduct that should be preferred when posed with a choice between possible actions. _________ is generally considered to be the opposite of evil, and is of interest in the study of morality, ethics, religion and philosophy. The specific meaning and etymology of the term and its associated translations among ancient and contemporary languages show substantial variation in its inflection and meaning depending on circumstances of place, history, religious, or philosophical context.

Exam Probability: **Medium**

31. *Answer choices:*

(see index for correct answer)

- a. Goods and services
- b. Veblen good
- c. Substitute good
- d. Yellow goods

Guidance: level 1

:: Bribery ::

_________ is the act of giving or receiving something of value in exchange for some kind of influence or action in return, that the recipient would otherwise not offer. _________ is defined by Black`s Law Dictionary as the offering, giving, receiving, or soliciting of any item of value to influence the actions of an official or other person in charge of a public or legal duty. Essentially, _________ is offering to do something for someone for the expressed purpose of receiving something in exchange. Gifts of money or other items of value which are otherwise available to everyone on an equivalent basis, and not for dishonest purposes, is not _________. Offering a discount or a refund to all purchasers is a legal rebate and is not _________. For example, it is legal for an employee of a Public Utilities Commission involved in electric rate regulation to accept a rebate on electric service that reduces their cost for electricity, when the rebate is available to other residential electric customers. Giving the rebate to influence them to look favorably on the electric utility`s rate increase applications, however, would be considered _________.

Exam Probability: **Medium**

32. *Answer choices:*

(see index for correct answer)

- a. Holyland Case
- b. Cockerham bribery case
- c. Cunningham scandal
- d. Global Corruption Barometer

Guidance: level 1

:: Statistical terminology ::

__________ is the ability to avoid wasting materials, energy, efforts, money, and time in doing something or in producing a desired result. In a more general sense, it is the ability to do things well, successfully, and without waste. In more mathematical or scientific terms, it is a measure of the extent to which input is well used for an intended task or function . It often specifically comprises the capability of a specific application of effort to produce a specific outcome with a minimum amount or quantity of waste, expense, or unnecessary effort. __________ refers to very different inputs and outputs in different fields and industries.

Exam Probability: **Medium**

33. *Answer choices:*

(see index for correct answer)

- a. Fair coin
- b. Efficiency
- c. Percentile rank
- d. Probability distribution function

Guidance: level 1

:: Mathematical finance ::

In economics and finance, __________ , also known as present discounted value, is the value of an expected income stream determined as of the date of valuation. The __________ is always less than or equal to the future value because money has interest-earning potential, a characteristic referred to as the time value of money, except during times of negative interest rates, when the __________ will be more than the future value. Time value can be described with the simplified phrase, "A dollar today is worth more than a dollar tomorrow". Here, `worth more` means that its value is greater. A dollar today is worth more than a dollar tomorrow because the dollar can be invested and earn a day`s worth of interest, making the total accumulate to a value more than a dollar by tomorrow. Interest can be compared to rent. Just as rent is paid to a landlord by a tenant without the ownership of the asset being transferred, interest is paid to a lender by a borrower who gains access to the money for a time before paying it back. By letting the borrower have access to the money, the lender has sacrificed the exchange value of this money, and is compensated for it in the form of interest. The initial amount of the borrowed funds is less than the total amount of money paid to the lender.

Exam Probability: **Medium**

34. *Answer choices:*

(see index for correct answer)

- a. Future value
- b. QuantLib
- c. Implied repo rate
- d. Present value

Guidance: level 1

:: Business ::

_________ is the activity of making one`s living or making money by producing or buying and selling products . Simply put, it is "any activity or enterprise entered into for profit. It does not mean it is a company, a corporation, partnership, or have any such formal organization, but it can range from a street peddler to General Motors."

Exam Probability: **Low**

35. *Answer choices:*

(see index for correct answer)

- a. Auckland Chamber of Commerce
- b. Business
- c. Planned obsolescence
- d. Certified Business Continuity Professional

Guidance: level 1

:: Business models ::

A _________ is "an autonomous association of persons united voluntarily to meet their common economic, social, and cultural needs and aspirations through a jointly-owned and democratically-controlled enterprise". _________ s may include.

Exam Probability: **Medium**

36. *Answer choices:*

(see index for correct answer)

- a. Meta learning
- b. Subsidiary
- c. Cooperative
- d. Very small business

Guidance: level 1

:: Marketing ::

_________ is the percentage of a market accounted for by a specific entity. In a survey of nearly 200 senior marketing managers, 67% responded that they found the revenue- "dollar _________ " metric very useful, while 61% found "unit _________ " very useful.

Exam Probability: **Medium**

37. *Answer choices:*

(see index for correct answer)

- a. Market share
- b. Customer dynamics
- c. Brandjacking
- d. Promo

Guidance: level 1

:: Business law ::

A __________ is an arrangement where parties, known as partners, agree to cooperate to advance their mutual interests. The partners in a __________ may be individuals, businesses, interest-based organizations, schools, governments or combinations. Organizations may partner to increase the likelihood of each achieving their mission and to amplify their reach. A __________ may result in issuing and holding equity or may be only governed by a contract.

Exam Probability: **High**

38. *Answer choices:*

(see index for correct answer)

- a. European Patent Convention
- b. Negative option billing
- c. Free agent
- d. Partnership

Guidance: level 1

:: ::

__________ is the administration of an organization, whether it is a business, a not-for-profit organization, or government body. __________ includes the activities of setting the strategy of an organization and coordinating the efforts of its employees to accomplish its objectives through the application of available resources, such as financial, natural, technological, and human resources. The term " __________ " may also refer to those people who manage an organization.

Exam Probability: **High**

39. *Answer choices:*

(see index for correct answer)

- a. corporate values
- b. Management
- c. empathy
- d. co-culture

Guidance: level 1

:: Management ::

_________ is the process of thinking about the activities required to achieve a desired goal. It is the first and foremost activity to achieve desired results. It involves the creation and maintenance of a plan, such as psychological aspects that require conceptual skills. There are even a couple of tests to measure someone's capability of _________ well. As such, _________ is a fundamental property of intelligent behavior. An important further meaning, often just called " _________ " is the legal context of permitted building developments.

Exam Probability: **High**

40. *Answer choices:*

(see index for correct answer)

- a. Main Street Manager
- b. Planning
- c. Performance indicator
- d. Reverse innovation

Guidance: level 1

:: Globalization-related theories ::

_________ is the process in which a nation is being improved in the sector of the economic, political, and social well-being of its people. The term has been used frequently by economists, politicians, and others in the 20th and 21st centuries. The concept, however, has been in existence in the West for centuries. "Modernization, "westernization", and especially "industrialization" are other terms often used while discussing _________ . _________ has a direct relationship with the environment and environmental issues. _________ is very often confused with industrial development, even in some academic sources.

Exam Probability: **Low**

41. *Answer choices:*

(see index for correct answer)

- a. Economic Development
- b. post-industrial
- c. postmodernism

Guidance: level 1

:: Packaging ::

In work place, _________ or job _________ means good ranking with the hypothesized conception of requirements of a role. There are two types of job _________ s: contextual and task. Task _________ is related to cognitive ability while contextual _________ is dependent upon personality. Task _________ are behavioral roles that are recognized in job descriptions and by remuneration systems, they are directly related to organizational _________, whereas, contextual _________ are value based and additional behavioral roles that are not recognized in job descriptions and covered by compensation; they are extra roles that are indirectly related to organizational _________. Citizenship _________ like contextual _________ means a set of individual activity/contribution that supports the organizational culture.

Exam Probability: **High**

42. *Answer choices:*

(see index for correct answer)

- a. Record sleeve
- b. Plastic bag
- c. Obi
- d. Egg carton

Guidance: level 1

:: ::

_________ is the means to see, hear, or become aware of something or someone through our fundamental senses. The term _________ derives from the Latin word perceptio, and is the organization, identification, and interpretation of sensory information in order to represent and understand the presented information, or the environment.

Exam Probability: **High**

43. *Answer choices:*

(see index for correct answer)

- a. Perception
- b. functional perspective
- c. open system
- d. interpersonal communication

Guidance: level 1

:: Marketing ::

A _________ is an overall experience of a customer that distinguishes an organization or product from its rivals in the eyes of the customer. _________ s are used in business, marketing, and advertising. Name _________ s are sometimes distinguished from generic or store _________ s.

Exam Probability: **High**

44. *Answer choices:*

(see index for correct answer)

- a. Channel conflict
- b. Next-best-action marketing
- c. Adobe Target
- d. Foreign market entry modes

Guidance: level 1

:: Banking ::

A _________ is a financial institution that accepts deposits from the public and creates credit. Lending activities can be performed either directly or indirectly through capital markets. Due to their importance in the financial stability of a country, _________ s are highly regulated in most countries. Most nations have institutionalized a system known as fractional reserve _________ ing under which _________ s hold liquid assets equal to only a portion of their current liabilities. In addition to other regulations intended to ensure liquidity, _________ s are generally subject to minimum capital requirements based on an international set of capital standards, known as the Basel Accords.

Exam Probability: **Medium**

45. *Answer choices:*

(see index for correct answer)

- a. Europeans for Financial Reform

- b. International Academy of Retail Banking
- c. Prize-Linked Savings Account
- d. Bank

Guidance: level 1

:: Management ::

The __________ is a strategy performance management tool – a semi-standard structured report, that can be used by managers to keep track of the execution of activities by the staff within their control and to monitor the consequences arising from these actions.

Exam Probability: **High**

46. *Answer choices:*

(see index for correct answer)

- a. Balanced scorecard
- b. Dynamic enterprise modeling
- c. Sensemaking
- d. Situational crisis communication theory

Guidance: level 1

:: Industry ::

_________ describes various measures of the efficiency of production. Often , a _________ measure is expressed as the ratio of an aggregate output to a single input or an aggregate input used in a production process, i.e. output per unit of input. Most common example is the labour _________ measure, e.g., such as GDP per worker. There are many different definitions of _________ and the choice among them depends on the purpose of the _________ measurement and/or data availability. The key source of difference between various _________ measures is also usually related to how the outputs and the inputs are aggregated into scalars to obtain such a ratio-type measure of _________ .

Exam Probability: **Medium**

47. *Answer choices:*

(see index for correct answer)

- a. Cleaner
- b. Production line
- c. Productivity
- d. Prefabrication

Guidance: level 1

:: Fraud ::

In law, __________ is intentional deception to secure unfair or unlawful gain, or to deprive a victim of a legal right. __________ can violate civil law , a criminal law , or it may cause no loss of money, property or legal right but still be an element of another civil or criminal wrong. The purpose of __________ may be monetary gain or other benefits, for example by obtaining a passport, travel document, or driver`s license, or mortgage __________, where the perpetrator may attempt to qualify for a mortgage by way of false statements.

Exam Probability: **High**

48. *Answer choices:*

(see index for correct answer)

- a. Deceptive advertising
- b. Insurance fraud
- c. Essay mill
- d. Visa fraud

Guidance: level 1

:: Public relations ::

__________ is the public visibility or awareness for any product, service or company. It may also refer to the movement of information from its source to the general public, often but not always via the media. The subjects of __________ include people , goods and services, organizations, and works of art or entertainment.

Exam Probability: **Low**

49. *Answer choices:*

(see index for correct answer)

- a. Cunningham Communication
- b. Lawfare
- c. Public affairs
- d. David Landis

Guidance: level 1

:: ::

Business is the activity of making one`s living or making money by producing or buying and selling products . Simply put, it is "any activity or enterprise entered into for profit. It does not mean it is a company, a corporation, partnership, or have any such formal organization, but it can range from a street peddler to General Motors."

Exam Probability: **Medium**

50. *Answer choices:*

(see index for correct answer)

- a. Firm
- b. interpersonal communication

- c. imperative
- d. personal values

Guidance: level 1

:: Stock market ::

__________ is a form of corporate equity ownership, a type of security. The terms voting share and ordinary share are also used frequently in other parts of the world; " __________ " being primarily used in the United States. They are known as Equity shares or Ordinary shares in the UK and other Commonwealth realms. This type of share gives the stockholder the right to share in the profits of the company, and to vote on matters of corporate policy and the composition of the members of the board of directors.

Exam Probability: **Low**

51. *Answer choices:*

(see index for correct answer)

- a. Common stock
- b. Intermarket analysis
- c. Clientele effect
- d. Automated trading system

Guidance: level 1

:: Management accounting ::

__________ s are costs that change as the quantity of the good or service that a business produces changes. __________ s are the sum of marginal costs over all units produced. They can also be considered normal costs. Fixed costs and __________ s make up the two components of total cost. Direct costs are costs that can easily be associated with a particular cost object. However, not all __________ s are direct costs. For example, variable manufacturing overhead costs are __________ s that are indirect costs, not direct costs. __________ s are sometimes called unit-level costs as they vary with the number of units produced.

Exam Probability: **Medium**

52. *Answer choices:*

(see index for correct answer)

- a. Variable cost
- b. Certified Management Accountant
- c. Dual overhead rate
- d. Direct material total variance

Guidance: level 1

:: Classification systems ::

__________ is the practice of comparing business processes and performance metrics to industry bests and best practices from other companies. Dimensions typically measured are quality, time and cost.

Exam Probability: **High**

53. *Answer choices:*

(see index for correct answer)

- a. Ecological land classification
- b. International Code of Nomenclature for algae, fungi, and plants
- c. Benchmarking
- d. Physics and Astronomy Classification Scheme

Guidance: level 1

:: Market research ::

__________, an acronym for Information through Disguised Experimentation is an annual market research fair conducted by the students of IIM-Lucknow. Students create games and use various other simulated environments to capture consumers' subconscious thoughts. This innovative method of market research removes the sensitization effect that might bias peoples answers to questions. This ensures that the most truthful answers are captured to research questions. The games are designed in such a way that the observers can elicit all the required information just by observing and noting down the behaviour and the responses of the participants.

Exam Probability: **Low**

54. *Answer choices:*

(see index for correct answer)

- a. Cambashi
- b. Multistage sampling
- c. Early adopter
- d. INDEX

Guidance: level 1

:: Legal terms ::

An __________ is an action which is inaccurate or incorrect. In some usages, an __________ is synonymous with a mistake. In statistics, " __________ " refers to the difference between the value which has been computed and the correct value. An __________ could result in failure or in a deviation from the intended performance or behaviour.

Exam Probability: **Medium**

55. *Answer choices:*

(see index for correct answer)

- a. Error
- b. Blunt instrument

- c. Mitigation
- d. Affray

Guidance: level 1

:: Economic globalization ::

__________ is an agreement in which one company hires another company to be responsible for a planned or existing activity that is or could be done internally,and sometimes involves transferring employees and assets from one firm to another.

Exam Probability: **Low**

56. *Answer choices:*

(see index for correct answer)

- a. global financial
- b. Outsourcing

Guidance: level 1

:: Marketing ::

__________ comes from the Latin neg and otsia referring to businessmen who, unlike the patricians, had no leisure time in their industriousness; it held the meaning of business until the 17th century when it took on the diplomatic connotation as a dialogue between two or more people or parties intended to reach a beneficial outcome over one or more issues where a conflict exists with respect to at least one of these issues. Thus, __________ is a process of combining divergent positions into a joint agreement under a decision rule of unanimity.

Exam Probability: **Low**

57. *Answer choices:*

(see index for correct answer)

- a. Profit chart
- b. Negotiation
- c. Price premium
- d. Affective design

Guidance: level 1

:: Marketing ::

__________ or stock is the goods and materials that a business holds for the ultimate goal of resale .

Exam Probability: **Medium**

58. *Answer choices:*

(see index for correct answer)

- a. Bricks and clicks
- b. Market information systems
- c. Private label
- d. Nia effect

Guidance: level 1

:: Unemployment ::

In economics, a _________ is a business cycle contraction when there is a general decline in economic activity. Macroeconomic indicators such as GDP , investment spending, capacity utilization, household income, business profits, and inflation fall, while bankruptcies and the unemployment rate rise. In the United Kingdom, it is defined as a negative economic growth for two consecutive quarters.

Exam Probability: **Medium**

59. *Answer choices:*

(see index for correct answer)

- a. Recession
- b. Male unemployment
- c. Employment-to-population ratio
- d. Organization Workshop

Guidance: level 1

Management

Management is the administration of an organization, whether it is a business, a not-for-profit organization, or government body. Management includes the activities of setting the strategy of an organization and coordinating the efforts of its employees (or of volunteers) to accomplish its objectives through the application of available resources, such as financial, natural, technological, and human resources.

:: ::

A _________ is an individual or institution that legally owns one or more shares of stock in a public or private corporation. _________ s may be referred to as members of a corporation. Legally, a person is not a _________ in a corporation until their name and other details are entered in the corporation's register of _________ s or members.

Exam Probability: **High**

1. *Answer choices:*

(see index for correct answer)

- a. deep-level diversity
- b. Shareholder
- c. hierarchical
- d. empathy

Guidance: level 1

:: Operations research ::

_________ is a method to achieve the best outcome in a mathematical model whose requirements are represented by linear relationships. _________ is a special case of mathematical programming .

Exam Probability: **High**

2. *Answer choices:*

(see index for correct answer)

- a. Vehicle routing problem
- b. Behavioral operations research
- c. Linear programming
- d. Potentially all pairwise rankings of all possible alternatives

Guidance: level 1

:: Budgets ::

A _______ is a financial plan for a defined period, often one year. It may also include planned sales volumes and revenues, resource quantities, costs and expenses, assets, liabilities and cash flows. Companies, governments, families and other organizations use it to express strategic plans of activities or events in measurable terms.

Exam Probability: **Low**

3. *Answer choices:*

(see index for correct answer)

- a. Budget
- b. Zero-based budgeting
- c. Participatory budgeting
- d. Railway Budget

Guidance: level 1

:: Industrial relations ::

_________ or employee satisfaction is a measure of workers` contentedness with their job, whether or not they like the job or individual aspects or facets of jobs, such as nature of work or supervision. _________ can be measured in cognitive , affective , and behavioral components. Researchers have also noted that _________ measures vary in the extent to which they measure feelings about the job . or cognitions about the job .

Exam Probability: **Low**

4. *Answer choices:*

(see index for correct answer)

- a. Injury prevention
- b. Job satisfaction
- c. Industrial violence
- d. European Journal of Industrial Relations

Guidance: level 1

:: ::

The __________ officer or just __________ , is the most senior corporate, executive, or administrative officer in charge of managing an organization especially an independent legal entity such as a company or nonprofit institution. CEOs lead a range of organizations, including public and private corporations, non-profit organizations and even some government organizations . The CEO of a corporation or company typically reports to the board of directors and is charged with maximizing the value of the entity, which may include maximizing the share price, market share, revenues or another element. In the non-profit and government sector, CEOs typically aim at achieving outcomes related to the organization`s mission, such as reducing poverty, increasing literacy, etc.

Exam Probability: **Low**

5. *Answer choices:*

(see index for correct answer)

- a. empathy
- b. Chief executive
- c. interpersonal communication
- d. open system

Guidance: level 1

:: Organizational behavior ::

__________ is the state or fact of exclusive rights and control over property, which may be an object, land/real estate or intellectual property. __________ involves multiple rights, collectively referred to as title, which may be separated and held by different parties.

Exam Probability: **Medium**

6. *Answer choices:*

(see index for correct answer)

- a. Ownership
- b. Organizational citizenship behavior
- c. Affective events theory
- d. Organizational justice

Guidance: level 1

:: Management ::

__________ is the identification, evaluation, and prioritization of risks followed by coordinated and economical application of resources to minimize, monitor, and control the probability or impact of unfortunate events or to maximize the realization of opportunities.

Exam Probability: **Medium**

7. *Answer choices:*

(see index for correct answer)

- a. Real property administrator
- b. Middle management
- c. Quality control
- d. Knowledge ecosystem

Guidance: level 1

:: Organizational theory ::

__________ refers to both a body of non-elective government officials and an administrative policy-making group. Historically, a __________ was a government administration managed by departments staffed with non-elected officials. Today, __________ is the administrative system governing any large institution, whether publicly owned or privately owned. The public administration in many countries is an example of a __________, but so is the centralized hierarchical structure of a business firm.

Exam Probability: **High**

8. *Answer choices:*

(see index for correct answer)

- a. Decentralization
- b. Bureaucracy
- c. Team effectiveness
- d. Team Service Management

Guidance: level 1

:: Production and manufacturing ::

__________ consists of organization-wide efforts to "install and make permanent climate where employees continuously improve their ability to provide on demand products and services that customers will find of particular value." "Total" emphasizes that departments in addition to production are obligated to improve their operations; "management" emphasizes that executives are obligated to actively manage quality through funding, training, staffing, and goal setting. While there is no widely agreed-upon approach, TQM efforts typically draw heavily on the previously developed tools and techniques of quality control. TQM enjoyed widespread attention during the late 1980s and early 1990s before being overshadowed by ISO 9000, Lean manufacturing, and Six Sigma.

Exam Probability: **High**

9. *Answer choices:*

(see index for correct answer)

- a. Hydrosila
- b. Total quality management
- c. Advanced Manufacturing Software
- d. Changeover

Guidance: level 1

:: Management ::

A __________ is a method or technique that has been generally accepted as superior to any alternatives because it produces results that are superior to those achieved by other means or because it has become a standard way of doing things, e.g., a standard way of complying with legal or ethical requirements.

Exam Probability: **Medium**

10. *Answer choices:*

(see index for correct answer)

- a. Concept of the Corporation
- b. Best practice
- c. Business relationship management
- d. Project management

Guidance: level 1

:: Business ::

The seller, or the provider of the goods or services, completes a sale in response to an acquisition, appropriation, requisition or a direct interaction with the buyer at the point of sale. There is a passing of title of the item, and the settlement of a price, in which agreement is reached on a price for which transfer of ownership of the item will occur. The seller, not the purchaser typically executes the sale and it may be completed prior to the obligation of payment. In the case of indirect interaction, a person who sells goods or service on behalf of the owner is known as a _________ man or _________ woman or _________ person, but this often refers to someone selling goods in a store/shop, in which case other terms are also common, including _________ clerk, shop assistant, and retail clerk.

Exam Probability: **Low**

11. *Answer choices:*

(see index for correct answer)

- a. E-lancing
- b. Sales
- c. 24/7 service
- d. EPG Model

Guidance: level 1

:: Electronic feedback ::

__________ occurs when outputs of a system are routed back as inputs as part of a chain of cause-and-effect that forms a circuit or loop. The system can then be said to feed back into itself. The notion of cause-and-effect has to be handled carefully when applied to __________ systems.

Exam Probability: **Medium**

12. *Answer choices:*

(see index for correct answer)

- a. feedback loop
- b. Feedback

Guidance: level 1

:: ::

A __________ is a research instrument consisting of a series of questions for the purpose of gathering information from respondents. The __________ was invented by the Statistical Society of London in 1838.

Exam Probability: **Medium**

13. *Answer choices:*

(see index for correct answer)

- a. imperative

- b. functional perspective
- c. corporate values
- d. Questionnaire

Guidance: level 1

:: ::

In mathematics, a _________ is a relationship between two numbers indicating how many times the first number contains the second. For example, if a bowl of fruit contains eight oranges and six lemons, then the _________ of oranges to lemons is eight to six . Similarly, the _________ of lemons to oranges is 6:8 and the _________ of oranges to the total amount of fruit is 8:14 .

Exam Probability: **Medium**

14. *Answer choices:*

(see index for correct answer)

- a. Ratio
- b. hierarchical perspective
- c. surface-level diversity
- d. levels of analysis

Guidance: level 1

:: ::

_________ consists of using generic or ad hoc methods in an orderly manner to find solutions to problems. Some of the problem-solving techniques developed and used in philosophy, artificial intelligence, computer science, engineering, mathematics, or medicine are related to mental problem-solving techniques studied in psychology.

Exam Probability: **High**

15. *Answer choices:*

(see index for correct answer)

- a. similarity-attraction theory
- b. Problem solving
- c. cultural
- d. functional perspective

Guidance: level 1

:: Systems theory ::

A _________ is a set of policies, processes and procedures used by an organization to ensure that it can fulfill the tasks required to achieve its objectives. These objectives cover many aspects of the organization`s operations . For instance, an environmental _________ enables organizations to improve their environmental performance and an occupational health and safety _________ enables an organization to control its occupational health and safety risks, etc.

Exam Probability: **High**

16. *Answer choices:*

(see index for correct answer)

- a. Management system
- b. transient state
- c. decentralized system
- d. equifinality

Guidance: level 1

:: Occupational safety and health ::

_________ is a chemical element with symbol Pb and atomic number 82. It is a heavy metal that is denser than most common materials. _________ is soft and malleable, and also has a relatively low melting point. When freshly cut, _________ is silvery with a hint of blue; it tarnishes to a dull gray color when exposed to air. _________ has the highest atomic number of any stable element and three of its isotopes are endpoints of major nuclear decay chains of heavier elements.

Exam Probability: **Low**

17. *Answer choices:*

(see index for correct answer)

- a. Chlorine
- b. Lead
- c. Canadian Registered Safety Professional
- d. Wildfire

Guidance: level 1

:: Workplace ::

A __________ is a process through which feedback from an employee`s subordinates, colleagues, and supervisor, as well as a self-evaluation by the employee themselves is gathered. Such feedback can also include, when relevant, feedback from external sources who interact with the employee, such as customers and suppliers or other interested stakeholders. __________ is so named because it solicits feedback regarding an employee`s behavior from a variety of points of view . It therefore may be contrasted with "downward feedback" , or "upward feedback" delivered to supervisory or management employees by subordinates only.

Exam Probability: **Medium**

18. *Answer choices:*

(see index for correct answer)

- a. Feminisation of the workplace
- b. labour turnover
- c. Discrimination based on hair texture
- d. 360-degree feedback

Guidance: level 1

:: Project management ::

A _________ is a professional in the field of project management. _________s have the responsibility of the planning, procurement and execution of a project, in any undertaking that has a defined scope, defined start and a defined finish; regardless of industry. _________s are first point of contact for any issues or discrepancies arising from within the heads of various departments in an organization before the problem escalates to higher authorities. Project management is the responsibility of a _________. This individual seldom participates directly in the activities that produce the end result, but rather strives to maintain the progress, mutual interaction and tasks of various parties in such a way that reduces the risk of overall failure, maximizes benefits, and minimizes costs.

Exam Probability: **Low**

19. *Answer choices:*

(see index for correct answer)

- a. Task
- b. Scope
- c. Project manager

- d. Schedule

Guidance: level 1

:: Human resource management ::

An organizational chart is a diagram that shows the structure of an organization and the relationships and relative ranks of its parts and positions/jobs. The term is also used for similar diagrams, for example ones showing the different elements of a field of knowledge or a group of languages.

Exam Probability: **High**

20. *Answer choices:*

(see index for correct answer)

- a. Organization chart
- b. Appreciative inquiry
- c. Focal Point Review
- d. Organizational behavior and human resources

Guidance: level 1

:: Organizational theory ::

_________ comprises the actual output or results of an organization as measured against its intended outputs .

Exam Probability: **Medium**

21. *Answer choices:*

(see index for correct answer)

- a. Organizational theory
- b. Participatory organization
- c. The three circles model
- d. Network-centric organization

Guidance: level 1

:: Production and manufacturing ::

_________ is a theory of management that analyzes and synthesizes workflows. Its main objective is improving economic efficiency, especially labor productivity. It was one of the earliest attempts to apply science to the engineering of processes and to management. _________ is sometimes known as Taylorism after its founder, Frederick Winslow Taylor.

Exam Probability: **Low**

22. *Answer choices:*

(see index for correct answer)

- a. Capacity planning
- b. Scientific management
- c. Fixed position assembly
- d. Factory Instrumentation Protocol

Guidance: level 1

:: ::

In business strategy, _________ is establishing a competitive advantage by having the lowest cost of operation in the industry. _________ is often driven by company efficiency, size, scale, scope and cumulative experience .A _________ strategy aims to exploit scale of production, well-defined scope and other economies , producing highly standardized products, using advanced technology.In recent years, more and more companies have chosen a strategic mix to achieve market leadership. These patterns consist of simultaneous _________ , superior customer service and product leadership. Walmart has succeeded across the world due to its _________ strategy. The company has cut down on exesses at every point of production and thus are able to provide the consumers with quality products at low prices.

Exam Probability: **Medium**

23. *Answer choices:*

(see index for correct answer)

- a. similarity-attraction theory
- b. personal values

- c. hierarchical
- d. Cost leadership

Guidance: level 1

:: Human resource management ::

_________ is the corporate management term for the act of reorganizing the legal, ownership, operational, or other structures of a company for the purpose of making it more profitable, or better organized for its present needs. Other reasons for _________ include a change of ownership or ownership structure, demerger, or a response to a crisis or major change in the business such as bankruptcy, repositioning, or buyout. _________ may also be described as corporate _________ , debt _________ and financial _________ .

Exam Probability: **High**

24. *Answer choices:*

(see index for correct answer)

- a. Restructuring
- b. Employment testing
- c. Employee value proposition
- d. Mechanical aptitude

Guidance: level 1

:: ::

In sales, commerce and economics, a __________ is the recipient of a good, service, product or an idea - obtained from a seller, vendor, or supplier via a financial transaction or exchange for money or some other valuable consideration.

Exam Probability: **High**

25. *Answer choices:*

(see index for correct answer)

- a. Customer
- b. empathy
- c. process perspective
- d. open system

Guidance: level 1

:: Business law ::

A __________ is an arrangement where parties, known as partners, agree to cooperate to advance their mutual interests. The partners in a __________ may be individuals, businesses, interest-based organizations, schools, governments or combinations. Organizations may partner to increase the likelihood of each achieving their mission and to amplify their reach. A __________ may result in issuing and holding equity or may be only governed by a contract.

Exam Probability: **High**

26. *Answer choices:*

(see index for correct answer)

- a. Jurisdictional strike
- b. Ladenschlussgesetz
- c. Partnership
- d. Industrial relations

Guidance: level 1

:: Business planning ::

_________ is an organization`s process of defining its strategy, or direction, and making decisions on allocating its resources to pursue this strategy. It may also extend to control mechanisms for guiding the implementation of the strategy. _________ became prominent in corporations during the 1960s and remains an important aspect of strategic management. It is executed by strategic planners or strategists, who involve many parties and research sources in their analysis of the organization and its relationship to the environment in which it competes.

Exam Probability: **Low**

27. *Answer choices:*

(see index for correct answer)

- a. Business war games
- b. operational planning
- c. Joint decision trap
- d. Strategic planning

Guidance: level 1

:: ::

_________ refers to the overall process of attracting, shortlisting, selecting and appointing suitable candidates for jobs within an organization. _________ can also refer to processes involved in choosing individuals for unpaid roles. Managers, human resource generalists and _________ specialists may be tasked with carrying out _________, but in some cases public-sector employment agencies, commercial _________ agencies, or specialist search consultancies are used to undertake parts of the process. Internet-based technologies which support all aspects of _________ have become widespread.

Exam Probability: **High**

28. *Answer choices:*

(see index for correct answer)

- a. personal values
- b. similarity-attraction theory
- c. levels of analysis
- d. Recruitment

Guidance: level 1

:: Data analysis ::

In statistics, the _________ is a measure that is used to quantify the amount of variation or dispersion of a set of data values. A low _________ indicates that the data points tend to be close to the mean of the set, while a high _________ indicates that the data points are spread out over a wider range of values.

Exam Probability: **Low**

29. *Answer choices:*

(see index for correct answer)

- a. Standard deviation
- b. Multiple correspondence analysis
- c. Ariel Beresniak
- d. Inverse-variance weighting

Guidance: level 1

:: Management ::

__________ is an area of management concerned with designing and controlling the process of production and redesigning business operations in the production of goods or services. It involves the responsibility of ensuring that business operations are efficient in terms of using as few resources as needed and effective in terms of meeting customer requirements. __________ is primarily concerned with planning, organizing and supervising in the contexts of production, manufacturing or the provision of services.

Exam Probability: **High**

30. *Answer choices:*

(see index for correct answer)

- a. Design management
- b. Mobile sales enablement
- c. Operations management
- d. Plan

Guidance: level 1

:: Critical thinking ::

An __________ is a set of statements usually constructed to describe a set of facts which clarifies the causes, context, and consequences of those facts. This description of the facts et cetera may establish rules or laws, and may clarify the existing rules or laws in relation to any objects, or phenomena examined. The components of an __________ can be implicit, and interwoven with one another.

Exam Probability: **High**

31. *Answer choices:*

(see index for correct answer)

- a. Explanation
- b. Practical syllogism
- c. Evidence
- d. Topical logic

Guidance: level 1

:: Product design ::

__________ as a verb is to create a new product to be sold by a business to its customers. A very broad coefficient and effective generation and development of ideas through a process that leads to new products. Thus, it is a major aspect of new product development.

Exam Probability: **Low**

32. *Answer choices:*

(see index for correct answer)

- a. Studio Job
- b. Sara Little Turnbull
- c. Peter Opsvik

- d. Product design

Guidance: level 1

:: ::

The business environment is a marketing term and refers to factors and forces that affect a firm`s ability to build and maintain successful customer relationships. The business environment has been defined as "the totality of physical and social factors that are taken directly into consideration in the decision-making behaviour of individuals in the organisation."

Exam Probability: **High**

33. *Answer choices:*

(see index for correct answer)

- a. Environmental scanning
- b. Sarbanes-Oxley act of 2002
- c. co-culture
- d. hierarchical perspective

Guidance: level 1

:: ::

_________ is the practice of protecting the natural environment by individuals, organizations and governments. Its objectives are to conserve natural resources and the existing natural environment and, where possible, to repair damage and reverse trends.

Exam Probability: **High**

34. *Answer choices:*

(see index for correct answer)

- a. process perspective
- b. Environmental protection
- c. functional perspective
- d. hierarchical

Guidance: level 1

:: Statistical terminology ::

_________ is the magnitude or dimensions of a thing. _________ can be measured as length, width, height, diameter, perimeter, area, volume, or mass.

Exam Probability: **Low**

35. *Answer choices:*

(see index for correct answer)

- a. Chain linking
- b. Deviation
- c. Data binning
- d. Size

Guidance: level 1

:: Organizational behavior ::

__________ is the term now used more commonly in business management, particularly human resource management. __________ refers to the number of subordinates a supervisor has.

Exam Probability: **High**

36. *Answer choices:*

(see index for correct answer)

- a. Span of control
- b. Conformity
- c. Affective events theory
- d. Collaborative partnerships

Guidance: level 1

:: Human resource management ::

_________ means increasing the scope of a job through extending the range of its job duties and responsibilities generally within the same level and periphery. _________ involves combining various activities at the same level in the organization and adding them to the existing job. It is also called the horizontal expansion of job activities. This contradicts the principles of specialisation and the division of labour whereby work is divided into small units, each of which is performed repetitively by an individual worker and the responsibilities are always clear. Some motivational theories suggest that the boredom and alienation caused by the division of labour can actually cause efficiency to fall. Thus, _________ seeks to motivate workers through reversing the process of specialisation. A typical approach might be to replace assembly lines with modular work; instead of an employee repeating the same step on each product, they perform several tasks on a single item. In order for employees to be provided with _________ they will need to be retrained in new fields to understand how each field works.

Exam Probability: **High**

37. *Answer choices:*

(see index for correct answer)

- a. Skill mix
- b. Behavioral Competencies
- c. Talent supply chain management
- d. Management due diligence

Guidance: level 1

:: Majority–minority relations ::

__________ , also known as reservation in India and Nepal, positive discrimination / action in the United Kingdom, and employment equity in Canada and South Africa, is the policy of promoting the education and employment of members of groups that are known to have previously suffered from discrimination. Historically and internationally, support for __________ has sought to achieve goals such as bridging inequalities in employment and pay, increasing access to education, promoting diversity, and redressing apparent past wrongs, harms, or hindrances.

Exam Probability: **Low**

38. *Answer choices:*

(see index for correct answer)

- a. positive discrimination
- b. cultural Relativism
- c. Affirmative action

Guidance: level 1

:: Management accounting ::

_________ s are costs that change as the quantity of the good or service that a business produces changes. _________ s are the sum of marginal costs over all units produced. They can also be considered normal costs. Fixed costs and _________ s make up the two components of total cost. Direct costs are costs that can easily be associated with a particular cost object. However, not all _________ s are direct costs. For example, variable manufacturing overhead costs are _________ s that are indirect costs, not direct costs. _________ s are sometimes called unit-level costs as they vary with the number of units produced.

Exam Probability: **High**

39. *Answer choices:*

(see index for correct answer)

- a. Variable cost
- b. Job costing
- c. Inventory valuation
- d. Construction accounting

Guidance: level 1

:: ::

According to Torrington, a _________ is usually developed by conducting a job analysis, which includes examining the tasks and sequences of tasks necessary to perform the job. The analysis considers the areas of knowledge and skills needed for the job. A job usually includes several roles. According to Hall, the _________ might be broadened to form a person specification or may be known as "terms of reference". The person/job specification can be presented as a stand-alone document, but in practice it is usually included within the _________. A _________ is often used by employers in the recruitment process.

Exam Probability: **Low**

40. *Answer choices:*

(see index for correct answer)

- a. Job description
- b. personal values
- c. cultural
- d. imperative

Guidance: level 1

:: Business terms ::

Centralisation or _________ is the process by which the activities of an organization, particularly those regarding planning and decision-making, framing strategy and policies become concentrated within a particular geographical location group. This moves the important decision-making and planning powers within the center of the organisation.

Exam Probability: **High**

41. *Answer choices:*

(see index for correct answer)

- a. Owner Controlled Insurance Program
- b. granular
- c. customer base
- d. front office

Guidance: level 1

:: Hospitality management ::

A _________ is an establishment that provides paid lodging on a short-term basis. Facilities provided may range from a modest-quality mattress in a small room to large suites with bigger, higher-quality beds, a dresser, a refrigerator and other kitchen facilities, upholstered chairs, a flat screen television, and en-suite bathrooms. Small, lower-priced _________ s may offer only the most basic guest services and facilities. Larger, higher-priced _________ s may provide additional guest facilities such as a swimming pool, business centre , childcare, conference and event facilities, tennis or basketball courts, gymnasium, restaurants, day spa, and social function services. _________ rooms are usually numbered to allow guests to identify their room. Some boutique, high-end _________ s have custom decorated rooms. Some _________ s offer meals as part of a room and board arrangement. In the United Kingdom, a _________ is required by law to serve food and drinks to all guests within certain stated hours. In Japan, capsule _________ s provide a tiny room suitable only for sleeping and shared bathroom facilities.

Exam Probability: **Low**

42. *Answer choices:*

(see index for correct answer)

- a. Hotel manager
- b. Professional Development Program
- c. Swiss Hotel Schools Association
- d. Hotel

Guidance: level 1

:: ::

_________ is the means to see, hear, or become aware of something or someone through our fundamental senses. The term _________ derives from the Latin word perceptio, and is the organization, identification, and interpretation of sensory information in order to represent and understand the presented information, or the environment.

Exam Probability: **Low**

43. *Answer choices:*

(see index for correct answer)

- a. Perception
- b. information systems assessment

- c. open system
- d. functional perspective

Guidance: level 1

:: Labor rights ::

A ________ is a wrong or hardship suffered, real or supposed, which forms legitimate grounds of complaint. In the past, the word meant the infliction or cause of hardship.

Exam Probability: **Medium**

44. *Answer choices:*

(see index for correct answer)

- a. The Hyatt 100
- b. Swift raids
- c. China Labour Bulletin
- d. Kate Mullany House

Guidance: level 1

:: ::

__________ is the collection of mechanisms, processes and relations by which corporations are controlled and operated. Governance structures and principles identify the distribution of rights and responsibilities among different participants in the corporation and include the rules and procedures for making decisions in corporate affairs. __________ is necessary because of the possibility of conflicts of interests between stakeholders, primarily between shareholders and upper management or among shareholders.

Exam Probability: **High**

45. *Answer choices:*

(see index for correct answer)

- a. co-culture
- b. personal values
- c. Character
- d. functional perspective

Guidance: level 1

:: International trade ::

__________ involves the transfer of goods or services from one person or entity to another, often in exchange for money. A system or network that allows __________ is called a market.

Exam Probability: **High**

46. *Answer choices:*

(see index for correct answer)

- a. Intervention stocks
- b. Maquiladora
- c. Autarky
- d. Market access

Guidance: level 1

:: Life skills ::

__________ , emotional leadership , emotional quotient and __________ quotient , is the capability of individuals to recognize their own emotions and those of others, discern between different feelings and label them appropriately, use emotional information to guide thinking and behavior, and manage and/or adjust emotions to adapt to environments or achieve one`s goal.

Exam Probability: **High**

47. *Answer choices:*

(see index for correct answer)

- a. Emotional intelligence
- b. coping mechanism
- c. multiple intelligence
- d. Social intelligence

Guidance: level 1

:: Quality management ::

A _________ or quality control circle is a group of workers who do the same or similar work, who meet regularly to identify, analyze and solve work-related problems. Normally small in size, the group is usually led by a supervisor or manager and presents its solutions to management; where possible, workers implement the solutions themselves in order to improve the performance of the organization and motivate employees. _________ s were at their most popular during the 1980s, but continue to exist in the form of Kaizen groups and similar worker participation schemes.

Exam Probability: **Low**

48. *Answer choices:*

(see index for correct answer)

- a. Dana Ulery
- b. E-TQM College
- c. Quality circle
- d. Institute of Standards and Industrial Research of Iran

Guidance: level 1

:: Organizational theory ::

_________ is the process of groups of organisms working or acting together for common, mutual, or some underlying benefit, as opposed to working in competition for selfish benefit. Many animal and plant species cooperate both with other members of their own species and with members of other species .

Exam Probability: **Low**

49. *Answer choices:*

(see index for correct answer)

- a. Cooperation
- b. Team effectiveness
- c. Aston Group
- d. Staff augmentation

Guidance: level 1

:: Training ::

_________ is teaching, or developing in oneself or others, any skills and knowledge that relate to specific useful competencies. _________ has specific goals of improving one`s capability, capacity, productivity and performance. It forms the core of apprenticeships and provides the backbone of content at institutes of technology . In addition to the basic _________ required for a trade, occupation or profession, observers of the labor-market recognize as of 2008 the need to continue _________ beyond initial qualifications: to maintain, upgrade and update skills throughout working life. People within many professions and occupations may refer to this sort of _________ as professional development.

Exam Probability: **Low**

50. *Answer choices:*

(see index for correct answer)

- a. Instructor-led training
- b. Fartlek
- c. Discipline
- d. Training

Guidance: level 1

:: Offshoring ::

A __________ is the temporary suspension or permanent termination of employment of an employee or, more commonly, a group of employees for business reasons, such as personnel management or downsizing an organization. Originally, __________ referred exclusively to a temporary interruption in work, or employment but this has evolved to a permanent elimination of a position in both British and US English, requiring the addition of "temporary" to specify the original meaning of the word. A __________ is not to be confused with wrongful termination. Laid off workers or displaced workers are workers who have lost or left their jobs because their employer has closed or moved, there was insufficient work for them to do, or their position or shift was abolished . Downsizing in a company is defined to involve the reduction of employees in a workforce. Downsizing in companies became a popular practice in the 1980s and early 1990s as it was seen as a way to deliver better shareholder value as it helps to reduce the costs of employers . Indeed, recent research on downsizing in the U.S., UK, and Japan suggests that downsizing is being regarded by management as one of the preferred routes to help declining organizations, cutting unnecessary costs, and improve organizational performance. Usually a __________ occurs as a cost cutting measure.

Exam Probability: **Medium**

51. *Answer choices:*

(see index for correct answer)

- a. Global labor arbitrage
- b. Flag of convenience
- c. Layoff
- d. Nearshoring

Guidance: level 1

:: Human resource management ::

__________ is a family of procedures to identify the content of a job in terms of activities involved and attributes or job requirements needed to perform the activities. __________ provides information of organizations which helps to determine which employees are best fit for specific jobs. Through __________, the analyst needs to understand what the important tasks of the job are, how they are carried out, and the necessary human qualities needed to complete the job successfully.

Exam Probability: **Medium**

52. *Answer choices:*

(see index for correct answer)

- a. Action alert
- b. Sham peer review
- c. Management by objectives
- d. Job analysis

Guidance: level 1

:: Summary statistics ::

_________ is the number of occurrences of a repeating event per unit of time. It is also referred to as temporal _________ , which emphasizes the contrast to spatial _________ and angular _________ . The period is the duration of time of one cycle in a repeating event, so the period is the reciprocal of the _________ . For example: if a newborn baby's heart beats at a _________ of 120 times a minute, its period—the time interval between beats—is half a second . _________ is an important parameter used in science and engineering to specify the rate of oscillatory and vibratory phenomena, such as mechanical vibrations, audio signals , radio waves, and light.

Exam Probability: **Low**

53. *Answer choices:*

(see index for correct answer)

- a. Quantile
- b. Nonparametric skew
- c. Generalized entropy index
- d. Robin Hood index

Guidance: level 1

:: Outsourcing ::

_________ is the relocation of a business process from one country to another—typically an operational process, such as manufacturing, or supporting processes, such as accounting. Typically this refers to a company business, although state governments may also employ _________ . More recently, technical and administrative services have been offshored.

Exam Probability: **Medium**

54. *Answer choices:*

(see index for correct answer)

- a. Counsel On Call
- b. Offshoring
- c. Vested outsourcing
- d. Managed security service

Guidance: level 1

:: Belief ::

_________ is the study of general and fundamental questions about existence, knowledge, values, reason, mind, and language. Such questions are often posed as problems to be studied or resolved. The term was probably coined by Pythagoras . Philosophical methods include questioning, critical discussion, rational argument, and systematic presentation. Classic philosophical questions include: Is it possible to know anything and to prove it What is most real Philosophers also pose more practical and concrete questions such as: Is there a best way to live Is it better to be just or unjust Do humans have free will

Exam Probability: **Medium**

55. *Answer choices:*

(see index for correct answer)

- a. Life stance
- b. Ignorance
- c. Epistemic closure
- d. Philosophy

Guidance: level 1

:: Critical thinking ::

In psychology, __________ is regarded as the cognitive process resulting in the selection of a belief or a course of action among several alternative possibilities. Every __________ process produces a final choice, which may or may not prompt action.

Exam Probability: **Low**

56. *Answer choices:*

(see index for correct answer)

- a. Prudence
- b. Merseyside Skeptics Society
- c. Decision-making
- d. TregoED

Guidance: level 1

:: Management ::

A __________ is when two or more people come together to discuss one or more topics, often in a formal or business setting, but __________ s also occur in a variety of other environments. Many various types of __________ s exist.

Exam Probability: **Medium**

57. *Answer choices:*

(see index for correct answer)

- a. Total security management
- b. Meeting
- c. Records manager
- d. Change advisory board

Guidance: level 1

:: Personality tests ::

The Myers–Briggs Type Indicator is an introspective self-report questionnaire with the purpose of indicating differing psychological preferences in how people perceive the world around them and make decisions. . Though the test superficially resembles some psychological theories it is commonly classified as pseudoscience, especially as pertains to its supposed predictive abilities.

Exam Probability: **Medium**

58. *Answer choices:*

(see index for correct answer)

- a. Keirsey Temperament Sorter
- b. Myers-Briggs Type Indicator
- c. Myers-Briggs type
- d. personality quiz

Guidance: level 1

:: Product management ::

_________ s, also known as Shewhart charts or process-behavior charts, are a statistical process control tool used to determine if a manufacturing or business process is in a state of control.

Exam Probability: **Low**

59. *Answer choices:*

(see index for correct answer)

- a. Product information management
- b. Control chart
- c. Service life
- d. Service product management

Guidance: level 1

Business law

Corporate law (also known as business law) is the body of law governing the rights, relations, and conduct of persons, companies, organizations and businesses. It refers to the legal practice relating to, or the theory of corporations. Corporate law often describes the law relating to matters which derive directly from the life-cycle of a corporation. It thus encompasses the formation, funding, governance, and death of a corporation.

:: Real estate ::

_________, real estate, realty, or immovable property In English common law refers to landed properties belonging to some person. It include all structures, crops, buildings, machinery, wells, dams, ponds, mines, canals, and roads, among other things. The term is historic, arising from the now-discontinued form of action, which distinguish between _________ disputes and personal property disputes. Personal property was, and continues to refer to all properties that are not real properties.

Exam Probability: **Low**

1. *Answer choices:*

(see index for correct answer)

- a. Real property
- b. Immovable property
- c. Acre
- d. Cost approach

Guidance: level 1

:: Contract law ::

A _________ is a contract in which one party agrees to supply as much of a good or service as is required by the other party, and in exchange the other party expressly or implicitly promises that it will obtain its goods or services exclusively from the first party. For example, a grocery store might enter into a contract with the farmer who grows oranges under which the farmer would supply the grocery store with as many oranges as the store could sell. The farmer could sue for breach of contract if the store were thereafter to purchase oranges for this purpose from any other party. The converse of this situation is an output contract, in which one buyer agrees to purchase however much of a good or service the seller is able to produce.

Exam Probability: **Low**

2. *Answer choices:*

(see index for correct answer)

- a. Implied authority

- b. Requirements contract
- c. Morals clause
- d. Non-repudiation

Guidance: level 1

:: ::

A lawsuit is a proceeding by a party or parties against another in the civil court of law.The archaic term "suit in law" is found in only a small number of laws still in effect today.The term "lawsuit" is used in reference to a civil action brought in a court of law in which a plaintiff, a party who claims to have incurred loss as a result of a defendant`s actions, demands a legal or equitable remedy. The defendant is required to respond to the plaintiff`s complaint. If the plaintiff is successful, judgment is in the plaintiff`s favor, and a variety of court orders may be issued to enforce a right, award damages, or impose a temporary or permanent injunction to prevent an act or compel an act. A declaratory judgment may be issued to prevent future legal disputes.

Exam Probability: **Medium**

3. *Answer choices:*

(see index for correct answer)

- a. cultural
- b. Sarbanes-Oxley act of 2002
- c. functional perspective
- d. Litigation

Guidance: level 1

:: ::

_________ is a concept of English common law and is a necessity for simple contracts but not for special contracts . The concept has been adopted by other common law jurisdictions, including the US.

Exam Probability: **Low**

4. *Answer choices:*

(see index for correct answer)

- a. Consideration
- b. similarity-attraction theory
- c. interpersonal communication
- d. process perspective

Guidance: level 1

:: Commercial item transport and distribution ::

_________ s may be negotiable or non-negotiable. Negotiable _________ s allow transfer of ownership of that commodity without having to deliver the physical commodity. See Delivery order.

Exam Probability: **Medium**

5. *Answer choices:*

(see index for correct answer)

- a. SECU
- b. Standard Carrier Alpha Code
- c. Humanitarian Logistics
- d. Steam wagon

Guidance: level 1

:: Marketing ::

A _________ is an overall experience of a customer that distinguishes an organization or product from its rivals in the eyes of the customer. _________ s are used in business, marketing, and advertising. Name _________ s are sometimes distinguished from generic or store _________ s.

Exam Probability: **Medium**

6. *Answer choices:*

(see index for correct answer)

- a. Marketing warfare strategies
- b. Adobe Marketing Cloud
- c. Pricing strategies

- d. Brand

Guidance: level 1

:: ::

The __________ is the central philosophical concept in the deontological moral philosophy of Immanuel Kant. Introduced in Kant's 1785 Groundwork of the Metaphysics of Morals, it may be defined as a way of evaluating motivations for action.

Exam Probability: **Low**

7. *Answer choices:*

(see index for correct answer)

- a. Character
- b. open system
- c. Categorical imperative
- d. hierarchical perspective

Guidance: level 1

:: ::

A _________ , or trial by jury, is a lawful proceeding in which a jury makes a decision or findings of fact. It is distinguished from a bench trial in which a judge or panel of judges makes all decisions.

Exam Probability: **Low**

8. *Answer choices:*

(see index for correct answer)

- a. Sarbanes-Oxley act of 2002
- b. cultural
- c. Jury Trial
- d. personal values

Guidance: level 1

:: Decision theory ::

A _________ is a deliberate system of principles to guide decisions and achieve rational outcomes. A _________ is a statement of intent, and is implemented as a procedure or protocol. Policies are generally adopted by a governance body within an organization. Policies can assist in both subjective and objective decision making. Policies to assist in subjective decision making usually assist senior management with decisions that must be based on the relative merits of a number of factors, and as a result are often hard to test objectively, e.g. work-life balance _________ . In contrast policies to assist in objective decision making are usually operational in nature and can be objectively tested, e.g. password _________ .

Exam Probability: **High**

9. *Answer choices:*

(see index for correct answer)

- a. Fuzzy-trace theory
- b. Ellsberg paradox
- c. Policy
- d. Subjective expected utility

Guidance: level 1

:: Legal terms ::

_________, a form of alternative dispute resolution , is a way to resolve disputes outside the courts. The dispute will be decided by one or more persons , which renders the " _________ award". An _________ award is legally binding on both sides and enforceable in the courts.

Exam Probability: **High**

10. *Answer choices:*

(see index for correct answer)

- a. Arbitration
- b. Hung jury
- c. Informed refusal

- d. Mitigation

Guidance: level 1

:: ::

_________ is a process whereby a person assumes the parenting of another, usually a child, from that person`s biological or legal parent or parents. Legal _________s permanently transfers all rights and responsibilities, along with filiation, from the biological parent or parents.

Exam Probability: **Medium**

11. *Answer choices:*

(see index for correct answer)

- a. interpersonal communication
- b. personal values
- c. surface-level diversity
- d. Adoption

Guidance: level 1

:: Real property law ::

_________ is an area of criminal law or tort law broadly divided into three groups: _________ to the person, _________ to chattels and _________ to land.

Exam Probability: **Medium**

12. *Answer choices:*

(see index for correct answer)

- a. Nonpossessory interest in land
- b. Gaps and gores
- c. Buyer listing
- d. Quitclaim deed

Guidance: level 1

:: Contract law ::

__________ of Contract is a legal term. In contract law, it is the implied ability of an individual to make a legally binding contract on behalf of an organization, by way of uniform or interaction with the public on behalf of that organization. When a person is wearing a uniform or nametag bearing the logo or trademark of a business or organization; or if that person is functioning in an obviously authorized capacity on behalf of a business or organization, that person carries an __________ of Contract. __________ is authority that is not express or written into the contract, but which the agent is assumed to have in order to transact the business of insurance for the principal. __________ is incidental to express authority since not every single detail of an agent`s authority can be spelled out in the written contract.

Exam Probability: **Medium**

13. *Answer choices:*

(see index for correct answer)

- a. Material transfer agreement
- b. Pirate code
- c. Implied authority
- d. Recording contract

Guidance: level 1

:: Psychometrics ::

_________ is a dynamic, structured, interactive process where a neutral third party assists disputing parties in resolving conflict through the use of specialized communication and negotiation techniques. All participants in _________ are encouraged to actively participate in the process. _________ is a "party-centered" process in that it is focused primarily upon the needs, rights, and interests of the parties. The mediator uses a wide variety of techniques to guide the process in a constructive direction and to help the parties find their optimal solution. A mediator is facilitative in that she/he manages the interaction between parties and facilitates open communication. _________ is also evaluative in that the mediator analyzes issues and relevant norms , while refraining from providing prescriptive advice to the parties .

Exam Probability: **High**

14. *Answer choices:*

(see index for correct answer)

- a. Correction for attenuation
- b. Mediation
- c. Cognitive Process Profile
- d. Psychometric function

Guidance: level 1

:: Chemical industry ::

The _________ for the Protection of Literary and Artistic Works, usually known as the _________, is an international agreement governing copyright, which was first accepted in Berne, Switzerland, in 1886.

Exam Probability: **Low**

15. *Answer choices:*

(see index for correct answer)

- a. Regulation of chemicals
- b. Chemical leasing
- c. Berne Convention
- d. Chemical plant

Guidance: level 1

:: ::

_________ is the assignment of any responsibility or authority to another person to carry out specific activities. It is one of the core concepts of management leadership. However, the person who delegated the work remains accountable for the outcome of the delegated work. _________ empowers a subordinate to make decisions, i.e. it is a shifting of decision-making authority from one organizational level to a lower one. _________, if properly done, is not fabrication. The opposite of effective _________ is micromanagement, where a manager provides too much input, direction, and review of delegated work. In general, _________ is good and can save money and time, help in building skills, and motivate people. On the other hand, poor _________ might cause frustration and confusion to all the involved parties. Some agents, however, do not favour a _________ and consider the power of making a decision rather burdensome.

Exam Probability: **Low**

16. *Answer choices:*

(see index for correct answer)

- a. process perspective
- b. Sarbanes-Oxley act of 2002
- c. Delegation
- d. co-culture

Guidance: level 1

:: Business law ::

An __________ is an agreement in which a producer agrees to sell his or her entire production to the buyer, who in turn agrees to purchase the entire output. Example: an almond grower enters into an __________ with an almond packer: thus the producer has a "home" for output of nuts, and the packer of nuts is happy to try the particular product. The converse of this situation is a requirements contract, under which a seller agrees to supply the buyer with as much of a good or service as the buyer wants, in exchange for the buyer`s agreement not to buy that good or service elsewhere.

Exam Probability: **High**

17. *Answer choices:*

(see index for correct answer)

- a. Output contract
- b. Power harassment

- c. Voidable floating charge
- d. Doing business as

Guidance: level 1

:: ::

A _________ is a person or firm who arranges transactions between a buyer and a seller for a commission when the deal is executed. A _________ who also acts as a seller or as a buyer becomes a principal party to the deal. Neither role should be confused with that of an agent—one who acts on behalf of a principal party in a deal.

Exam Probability: **Low**

18. *Answer choices:*

(see index for correct answer)

- a. hierarchical perspective
- b. deep-level diversity
- c. information systems assessment
- d. co-culture

Guidance: level 1

:: Business law ::

In the United States, the United Kingdom, Australia, Canada and South Africa, _________ relates to the doctrines of the law of agency. It is relevant particularly in corporate law and constitutional law. _________ refers to a situation where a reasonable third party would understand that an agent had authority to act. This means a principal is bound by the agent's actions, even if the agent had no actual authority, whether express or implied. It raises an estoppel because the third party is given an assurance, which he relies on and would be inequitable for the principal to deny the authority given. _________ can legally be found, even if actual authority has not been given.

Exam Probability: **Low**

19. *Answer choices:*

(see index for correct answer)

- a. Apparent authority
- b. European Patent Convention
- c. WIPO Copyright Treaty
- d. Turnkey

Guidance: level 1

:: International trade ::

A _________ is a document issued by a carrier to acknowledge receipt of cargo for shipment. Although the term historically related only to carriage by sea, a _________ may today be used for any type of carriage of goods.

Exam Probability: **Low**

20. *Answer choices:*

(see index for correct answer)

- a. National Trade Estimate Report
- b. Bill of lading
- c. OPEC
- d. Parallel import

Guidance: level 1

:: ::

__________ is an abstract concept of management of complex systems according to a set of rules and trends. In systems theory, these types of rules exist in various fields of biology and society, but the term has slightly different meanings according to context. For example.

Exam Probability: **Medium**

21. *Answer choices:*

(see index for correct answer)

- a. Character
- b. cultural
- c. Regulation

- d. hierarchical

Guidance: level 1

:: Contract law ::

_________ , in human interactions, is a sincere intention to be fair, open, and honest, regardless of the outcome of the interaction. While some Latin phrases lose their literal meaning over centuries, this is not the case with bona fides; it is still widely used and interchangeable with its generally accepted modern-day English translation of _________ . It is an important concept within law and business. The opposed concepts are bad faith, mala fides and perfidy . In contemporary English, the usage of bona fides is synonymous with credentials and identity. The phrase is sometimes used in job advertisements, and should not be confused with the bona fide occupational qualifications or the employer`s _________ effort, as described below.

Exam Probability: **Medium**

22. *Answer choices:*

(see index for correct answer)

- a. Talent holding deal
- b. Invitation to treat
- c. Offeree
- d. Good faith

Guidance: level 1

:: Business law ::

A __________ is a group of people who jointly supervise the activities of an organization, which can be either a for-profit business, nonprofit organization, or a government agency. Such a board's powers, duties, and responsibilities are determined by government regulations and the organization's own constitution and bylaws. These authorities may specify the number of members of the board, how they are to be chosen, and how often they are to meet.

Exam Probability: **High**

23. *Answer choices:*

(see index for correct answer)

- a. Closed shop
- b. Advertising regulation
- c. Board of directors
- d. Retroactive overtime

Guidance: level 1

:: Project management ::

__________ is the right to exercise power, which can be formalized by a state and exercised by way of judges, appointed executives of government, or the ecclesiastical or priestly appointed representatives of a God or other deities.

Exam Probability: **High**

24. *Answer choices:*

(see index for correct answer)

- a. Axelos
- b. Authority
- c. TimeTac
- d. Project plan

Guidance: level 1

:: ::

A __________ is an individual or institution that legally owns one or more shares of stock in a public or private corporation. __________ s may be referred to as members of a corporation. Legally, a person is not a __________ in a corporation until their name and other details are entered in the corporation's register of __________ s or members.

Exam Probability: **High**

25. *Answer choices:*

(see index for correct answer)

- a. hierarchical
- b. information systems assessment

- c. corporate values
- d. imperative

Guidance: level 1

:: ::

__________ is the production of products for use or sale using labour and machines, tools, chemical and biological processing, or formulation. The term may refer to a range of human activity, from handicraft to high tech, but is most commonly applied to industrial design, in which raw materials are transformed into finished goods on a large scale. Such finished goods may be sold to other manufacturers for the production of other, more complex products, such as aircraft, household appliances, furniture, sports equipment or automobiles, or sold to wholesalers, who in turn sell them to retailers, who then sell them to end users and consumers.

Exam Probability: **Medium**

26. *Answer choices:*

(see index for correct answer)

- a. Manufacturing
- b. hierarchical
- c. interpersonal communication
- d. imperative

Guidance: level 1

:: Legal doctrines and principles ::

_________ , land acquisition , compulsory purchase , resumption , resumption/compulsory acquisition , or expropriation is the power of a state, provincial, or national government to take private property for public use. However, this power can be legislatively delegated by the state to municipalities, government subdivisions, or even to private persons or corporations, when they are authorized by the legislature to exercise the functions of public character.

Exam Probability: **Medium**

27. *Answer choices:*

(see index for correct answer)

- a. Mutual mistake
- b. Acquiescence
- c. Eminent domain
- d. negligence

Guidance: level 1

:: ::

_________ is a process under which executive or legislative actions are subject to review by the judiciary. A court with authority for _________ may invalidate laws, acts and governmental actions that are incompatible with a higher authority: an executive decision may be invalidated for being unlawful or a statute may be invalidated for violating the terms of a constitution. _________ is one of the checks and balances in the separation of powers: the power of the judiciary to supervise the legislative and executive branches when the latter exceed their authority. The doctrine varies between jurisdictions, so the procedure and scope of _________ may differ between and within countries.

Exam Probability: **Medium**

28. *Answer choices:*

(see index for correct answer)

- a. surface-level diversity
- b. Sarbanes-Oxley act of 2002
- c. similarity-attraction theory
- d. Judicial review

Guidance: level 1

:: ::

__________ is the act or practice of forbidding something by law; more particularly the term refers to the banning of the manufacture, storage , transportation, sale, possession, and consumption of alcoholic beverages. The word is also used to refer to a period of time during which such bans are enforced.

Exam Probability: **Low**

29. *Answer choices:*

(see index for correct answer)

- a. information systems assessment
- b. hierarchical perspective
- c. Sarbanes-Oxley act of 2002
- d. Prohibition

Guidance: level 1

:: Financial regulatory authorities of the United States ::

The __________ is the revenue service of the United States federal government. The government agency is a bureau of the Department of the Treasury, and is under the immediate direction of the Commissioner of Internal Revenue, who is appointed to a five-year term by the President of the United States. The IRS is responsible for collecting taxes and administering the Internal Revenue Code, the main body of federal statutory tax law of the United States. The duties of the IRS include providing tax assistance to taxpayers and pursuing and resolving instances of erroneous or fraudulent tax filings. The IRS has also overseen various benefits programs, and enforces portions of the Affordable Care Act.

Exam Probability: **Medium**

30. *Answer choices:*

(see index for correct answer)

- a. Federal Deposit Insurance Corporation
- b. Operation Choke Point
- c. Internal Revenue Service
- d. Farm Credit Administration

Guidance: level 1

:: Business ethics ::

_________ is a type of harassment technique that relates to a sexual nature and the unwelcome or inappropriate promise of rewards in exchange for sexual favors. _________ includes a range of actions from mild transgressions to sexual abuse or assault. Harassment can occur in many different social settings such as the workplace, the home, school, churches, etc. Harassers or victims may be of any gender.

Exam Probability: **Low**

31. *Answer choices:*

(see index for correct answer)

- a. Marketing ethics
- b. Sexual harassment
- c. Wheelmen
- d. McJob

Guidance: level 1

:: Business law ::

A _________ is a contractual arrangement calling for the lessee to pay the lessor for use of an asset. Property, buildings and vehicles are common assets that are _________d. Industrial or business equipment is also _________d.

Exam Probability: **Low**

32. *Answer choices:*

(see index for correct answer)

- a. Unfair Commercial Practices Directive
- b. Negative option billing
- c. Firm offer
- d. Lease

Guidance: level 1

:: ::

Business is the activity of making one`s living or making money by producing or buying and selling products . Simply put, it is "any activity or enterprise entered into for profit. It does not mean it is a company, a corporation, partnership, or have any such formal organization, but it can range from a street peddler to General Motors."

Exam Probability: **Low**

33. *Answer choices:*

(see index for correct answer)

- a. functional perspective
- b. Firm
- c. open system
- d. information systems assessment

Guidance: level 1

:: ::

The _________ is the highest court within the hierarchy of courts in many legal jurisdictions. Other descriptions for such courts include court of last resort, apex court, and high court of appeal. Broadly speaking, the decisions of a _________ are not subject to further review by any other court. _________ s typically function primarily as appellate courts, hearing appeals from decisions of lower trial courts, or from intermediate-level appellate courts.

Exam Probability: **High**

34. *Answer choices:*

(see index for correct answer)

- a. hierarchical
- b. similarity-attraction theory
- c. Character
- d. Supreme Court

Guidance: level 1

:: Contract law ::

_________ is a legal cause of action and a type of civil wrong, in which a binding agreement or bargained-for exchange is not honored by one or more of the parties to the contract by non-performance or interference with the other party`s performance. Breach occurs when a party to a contract fails to fulfill its obligation as described in the contract, or communicates an intent to fail the obligation or otherwise appears not to be able to perform its obligation under the contract. Where there is _________ , the resulting damages will have to be paid by the party breaching the contract to the aggrieved party.

Exam Probability: **High**

35. *Answer choices:*

(see index for correct answer)

- a. Principles of European Contract Law
- b. German contract law
- c. Seal
- d. Redhibition

Guidance: level 1

:: ::

_________ is the administration of an organization, whether it is a business, a not-for-profit organization, or government body. _________ includes the activities of setting the strategy of an organization and coordinating the efforts of its employees to accomplish its objectives through the application of available resources, such as financial, natural, technological, and human resources. The term " _________ " may also refer to those people who manage an organization.

Exam Probability: **High**

36. *Answer choices:*

(see index for correct answer)

- a. hierarchical
- b. similarity-attraction theory
- c. information systems assessment
- d. Management

Guidance: level 1

:: ::

A _________ is an aggregate of fundamental principles or established precedents that constitute the legal basis of a polity, organisation or other type of entity, and commonly determine how that entity is to be governed.

Exam Probability: **Low**

37. *Answer choices:*

(see index for correct answer)

- a. Constitution
- b. imperative
- c. co-culture
- d. functional perspective

Guidance: level 1

:: Judgment (law) ::

In law, a __________ is a judgment entered by a court for one party and against another party summarily, i.e., without a full trial. Such a judgment may be issued on the merits of an entire case, or on discrete issues in that case.

Exam Probability: **Low**

38. *Answer choices:*

(see index for correct answer)

- a. Entry of judgment
- b. judgment as a matter of law

Guidance: level 1

:: Stock market ::

_________ is freedom from, or resilience against, potential harm caused by others. Beneficiaries of _________ may be of persons and social groups, objects and institutions, ecosystems or any other entity or phenomenon vulnerable to unwanted change by its environment.

Exam Probability: **High**

39. *Answer choices:*

(see index for correct answer)

- a. The Congressional Effect
- b. Share price
- c. Piqqem
- d. Security

Guidance: level 1

:: ::

A _________ is a law passed by a legislative body in a common law system to set the maximum time after an event within which legal proceedings may be initiated.

Exam Probability: **Medium**

40. *Answer choices:*

(see index for correct answer)

- a. Character
- b. Statute of limitations
- c. Sarbanes-Oxley act of 2002
- d. corporate values

Guidance: level 1

:: American legal terms ::

The phrase "by _________ " is a legal term that indicates that a right or liability has been created for a party, irrespective of the intent of that party, because it is dictated by existing legal principles. For example, if a person dies without a will, his or her heirs are determined by _________ . Similarly, if a person marries or has a child after his or her will has been executed, the law writes this pretermitted spouse or pretermitted heir into the will if no provision for this situation was specifically included. Adverse possession, in which title to land passes because non-owners have occupied it for a certain period of time, is another important right that vests by _________ .

Exam Probability: **High**

41. *Answer choices:*

(see index for correct answer)

- a. Reasonable time

- b. Chilling effect

Guidance: level 1

:: ::

A __________ is an organization, usually a group of people or a company, authorized to act as a single entity and recognized as such in law. Early incorporated entities were established by charter . Most jurisdictions now allow the creation of new __________ s through registration.

Exam Probability: **Medium**

42. *Answer choices:*

(see index for correct answer)

- a. imperative
- b. corporate values
- c. Corporation
- d. Sarbanes-Oxley act of 2002

Guidance: level 1

:: Jurisdiction ::

In United States law, _________ jurisdiction is the subject-matter jurisdiction of United States federal courts to hear a civil case because the plaintiff has alleged a violation of the United States Constitution, federal law, or a treaty to which the United States is a party.

Exam Probability: **High**

43. *Answer choices:*

(see index for correct answer)

- a. Federal question
- b. Subject-matter jurisdiction
- c. Appellate jurisdiction
- d. exclusive jurisdiction

Guidance: level 1

:: Insurance terms ::

_________ is the assumption by a third party of another party's legal right to collect a debt or damages. It is a legal doctrine whereby one person is entitled to enforce the subsisting or revived rights of another for one's own benefit. A right of _________ typically arises by operation of law, but can also arise by statute or by agreement. _________ is an equitable remedy, having first developed in the English Court of Chancery. It is a familiar feature of common law systems. Analogous doctrines exist in civil law jurisdictions.

Exam Probability: **Medium**

44. *Answer choices:*

(see index for correct answer)

- a. Present value of new business premiums
- b. Split billing
- c. Finite Risk insurance
- d. Subrogation

Guidance: level 1

:: Contract law ::

Coercion is the practice of forcing another party to act in an involuntary manner by use of threats or force. It involves a set of various types of forceful actions that violate the free will of an individual to induce a desired response, for example: a bully demanding lunch money from a student or the student gets beaten. These actions may include extortion, blackmail, torture, threats to induce favors, or even sexual assault. In law, coercion is codified as a _________ crime. Such actions are used as leverage, to force the victim to act in a way contrary to their own interests. Coercion may involve the actual infliction of physical pain/injury or psychological harm in order to enhance the credibility of a threat. The threat of further harm may lead to the cooperation or obedience of the person being coerced.

Exam Probability: **Medium**

45. *Answer choices:*

(see index for correct answer)

- a. Talent holding deal
- b. Duress
- c. Essentialia negotii
- d. Non est factum

Guidance: level 1

:: ::

Employment is a relationship between two parties, usually based on a contract where work is paid for, where one party, which may be a corporation, for profit, not-for-profit organization, co-operative or other entity is the employer and the other is the employee. Employees work in return for payment, which may be in the form of an hourly wage, by piecework or an annual salary, depending on the type of work an employee does or which sector she or he is working in. Employees in some fields or sectors may receive gratuities, bonus payment or stock options. In some types of employment, employees may receive benefits in addition to payment. Benefits can include health insurance, housing, disability insurance or use of a gym. Employment is typically governed by employment laws, regulations or legal contracts.

Exam Probability: **Medium**

46. *Answer choices:*

(see index for correct answer)

- a. functional perspective

- b. personal values
- c. Personnel
- d. co-culture

Guidance: level 1

:: Sexual harassment in the United States ::

In law, a _________, reasonable man, or the man on the Clapham omnibus is a hypothetical person of legal fiction crafted by the courts and communicated through case law and jury instructions.

Exam Probability: **Medium**

47. *Answer choices:*

(see index for correct answer)

- a. Charol Shakeshaft
- b. Fitzgerald v. Barnstable School Committee
- c. Hostile Advances
- d. Reasonable person

Guidance: level 1

:: ::

__________ is the study and management of exchange relationships. __________ is the business process of creating relationships with and satisfying customers. With its focus on the customer, __________ is one of the premier components of business management.

Exam Probability: **High**

48. *Answer choices:*

(see index for correct answer)

- a. information systems assessment
- b. deep-level diversity
- c. Marketing
- d. personal values

Guidance: level 1

:: ::

__________ is a marketing communication that employs an openly sponsored, non-personal message to promote or sell a product, service or idea. Sponsors of __________ are typically businesses wishing to promote their products or services. __________ is differentiated from public relations in that an advertiser pays for and has control over the message. It differs from personal selling in that the message is non-personal, i.e., not directed to a particular individual. __________ is communicated through various mass media, including traditional media such as newspapers, magazines, television, radio, outdoor __________ or direct mail; and new media such as search results, blogs, social media, websites or text messages. The actual presentation of the message in a medium is referred to as an advertisement, or "ad" or advert for short.

Exam Probability: **Medium**

49. *Answer choices:*

(see index for correct answer)

- a. hierarchical perspective
- b. levels of analysis
- c. Character
- d. process perspective

Guidance: level 1

:: ::

A __________ is a formal written enactment of a legislative authority that governs the legal entities of a city, state, or country by way of consent. Typically, __________s command or prohibit something, or declare policy. __________s are rules made by legislative bodies; they are distinguished from case law or precedent, which is decided by courts, and regulations issued by government agencies.

Exam Probability: **Low**

50. *Answer choices:*

(see index for correct answer)

- a. cultural
- b. personal values
- c. open system
- d. Statute

Guidance: level 1

:: Legal procedure ::

__________, adjective law, or rules of court comprises the rules by which a court hears and determines what happens in civil, lawsuit, criminal or administrative proceedings. The rules are designed to ensure a fair and consistent application of due process or fundamental justice to all cases that come before a court.

Exam Probability: **High**

51. *Answer choices:*

(see index for correct answer)

- a. civil procedure
- b. Closing argument
- c. appellate
- d. Procedural law

Guidance: level 1

:: ::

_________ is "property consisting of land and the buildings on it, along with its natural resources such as crops, minerals or water; immovable property of this nature; an interest vested in this an item of real property, buildings or housing in general. Also: the business of _________ ; the profession of buying, selling, or renting land, buildings, or housing." It is a legal term used in jurisdictions whose legal system is derived from English common law, such as India, England, Wales, Northern Ireland, United States, Canada, Pakistan, Australia, and New Zealand.

Exam Probability: **Low**

52. *Answer choices:*

(see index for correct answer)

- a. imperative
- b. personal values

- c. Sarbanes-Oxley act of 2002
- d. open system

Guidance: level 1

:: Contract law ::

_________ is the act of recall or annulment. It is the cancelling of an act, the recalling of a grant or privilege, or the making void of some deed previously existing.

Exam Probability: **Medium**

53. *Answer choices:*

(see index for correct answer)

- a. Risk of loss
- b. Revocation
- c. Warranty
- d. Efficient breach

Guidance: level 1

:: Business law ::

A __________ is a business entity created by two or more parties, generally characterized by shared ownership, shared returns and risks, and shared governance. Companies typically pursue __________ s for one of four reasons: to access a new market, particularly emerging markets; to gain scale efficiencies by combining assets and operations; to share risk for major investments or projects; or to access skills and capabilities.

Exam Probability: **Low**

54. *Answer choices:*

(see index for correct answer)

- a. Limited liability company
- b. Rules of origin
- c. Joint venture
- d. Contract A

Guidance: level 1

:: Law ::

__________ is a body of law which defines the role, powers, and structure of different entities within a state, namely, the executive, the parliament or legislature, and the judiciary; as well as the basic rights of citizens and, in federal countries such as the United States and Canada, the relationship between the central government and state, provincial, or territorial governments.

Exam Probability: **High**

55. *Answer choices:*

(see index for correct answer)

- a. Constitutional law
- b. Legal case

Guidance: level 1

:: Contract law ::

In common law jurisdictions, an _________ is a contract law term for certain assurances that are presumed to be made in the sale of products or real property, due to the circumstances of the sale. These assurances are characterized as warranties irrespective of whether the seller has expressly promised them orally or in writing. They include an _________ of fitness for a particular purpose, an _________ of merchantability for products, _________ of workmanlike quality for services, and an _________ of habitability for a home.

Exam Probability: **Medium**

56. *Answer choices:*

(see index for correct answer)

- a. Contingent contracts
- b. Implied warranty

- c. Reciprocal obligation
- d. Parol evidence rule

Guidance: level 1

:: Criminal law ::

__________ is the body of law that relates to crime. It proscribes conduct perceived as threatening, harmful, or otherwise endangering to the property, health, safety, and moral welfare of people inclusive of one`s self. Most __________ is established by statute, which is to say that the laws are enacted by a legislature. __________ includes the punishment and rehabilitation of people who violate such laws. __________ varies according to jurisdiction, and differs from civil law, where emphasis is more on dispute resolution and victim compensation, rather than on punishment or rehabilitation. Criminal procedure is a formalized official activity that authenticates the fact of commission of a crime and authorizes punitive or rehabilitative treatment of the offender.

Exam Probability: **Medium**

57. *Answer choices:*

(see index for correct answer)

- a. mitigating factor
- b. Mala in se
- c. Self-incrimination
- d. Criminal law

Guidance: level 1

:: Real estate valuation ::

_________ or OMV is the price at which an asset would trade in a competitive auction setting. _________ is often used interchangeably with open _________ , fair value or fair _________ , although these terms have distinct definitions in different standards, and may or may not differ in some circumstances.

Exam Probability: **High**

58. *Answer choices:*

(see index for correct answer)

- a. Days on market
- b. Market value
- c. E.surv
- d. cap rate

Guidance: level 1

:: ::

An __________ is a written sworn statement of fact voluntarily made by an affiant or deponent under an oath or affirmation administered by a person authorized to do so by law. Such statement is witnessed as to the authenticity of the affiant`s signature by a taker of oaths, such as a notary public or commissioner of oaths. An __________ is a type of verified statement or showing, or in other words, it contains a verification, meaning it is under oath or penalty of perjury, and this serves as evidence to its veracity and is required for court proceedings.

Exam Probability: **High**

59. *Answer choices:*

(see index for correct answer)

- a. functional perspective
- b. Sarbanes-Oxley act of 2002
- c. Affidavit
- d. empathy

Guidance: level 1

Finance

Finance is a field that is concerned with the allocation (investment) of assets and liabilities over space and time, often under conditions of risk or uncertainty. Finance can also be defined as the science of money management. Participants in the market aim to price assets based on their risk level, fundamental value, and their expected rate of return. Finance can be split into three sub-categories: public finance, corporate finance and personal finance.

:: Global systemically important banks ::

The _________ Corporation is an American multinational investment bank and financial services company based in Charlotte, North Carolina with central hubs in New York City, London, Hong Kong, Minneapolis, and Toronto. _________ was formed through NationsBank`s acquisition of BankAmerica in 1998. It is the second largest banking institution in the United States, after JP Morgan Chase. As a part of the Big Four, it services approximately 10.73% of all American bank deposits, in direct competition with Citigroup, Wells Fargo, and JPMorgan Chase. Its primary financial services revolve around commercial banking, wealth management, and investment banking.

Exam Probability: **High**

1. *Answer choices:*

(see index for correct answer)

- a. The Bank of New York Mellon
- b. Sumitomo Mitsui Banking Corporation
- c. Barclays
- d. Bank of America

Guidance: level 1

:: Debt ::

A __________ is a party that has a claim on the services of a second party. It is a person or institution to whom money is owed. The first party, in general, has provided some property or service to the second party under the assumption that the second party will return an equivalent property and service. The second party is frequently called a debtor or borrower. The first party is called the __________, which is the lender of property, service, or money.

Exam Probability: **Low**

2. *Answer choices:*

(see index for correct answer)

- a. External financing
- b. External debt
- c. Financial assistance
- d. Creditor

Guidance: level 1

:: Inventory ::

__________ is the amount of inventory a company has in stock at the end of its fiscal year. It is closely related with __________ cost, which is the amount of money spent to get these goods in stock. It should be calculated at the lower of cost or market.

Exam Probability: **Low**

3. *Answer choices:*

(see index for correct answer)

- a. Perpetual inventory
- b. Item-level tagging
- c. Ending inventory
- d. Specific identification

Guidance: level 1

:: Financial ratios ::

_________ is a measure of how revenue growth translates into growth in operating income. It is a measure of leverage, and of how risky, or volatile, a company`s operating income is.

Exam Probability: **Low**

4. *Answer choices:*

(see index for correct answer)

- a. Capital adequacy ratio
- b. Financial ratio
- c. Operating leverage
- d. Total revenue share

Guidance: level 1

:: Generally Accepted Accounting Principles ::

The term _________ is most often used to describe a practice or document that is provided as a courtesy or satisfies minimum requirements, conforms to a norm or doctrine, tends to be performed perfunctorily or is considered a formality.

Exam Probability: **Low**

5. *Answer choices:*

(see index for correct answer)

- a. Goodwill
- b. deferred revenue
- c. Earnings before interest, taxes, depreciation, and amortization
- d. Gross profit

Guidance: level 1

:: Derivatives (finance) ::

_________ is any bodily activity that enhances or maintains physical fitness and overall health and wellness. It is performed for various reasons, to aid growth and improve strength, preventing aging, developing muscles and the cardiovascular system, honing athletic skills, weight loss or maintenance, improving health and also for enjoyment. Many individuals choose to _________ outdoors where they can congregate in groups, socialize, and enhance well-being.

Exam Probability: **Medium**

6. *Answer choices:*

(see index for correct answer)

- a. Intrinsic value
- b. Exercise
- c. Iron butterfly
- d. Equity swap

Guidance: level 1

:: Business economics ::

A _________ is a term used primarily in cost accounting to describe something to which costs are assigned. Common examples of _________ s are: product lines, geographic territories, customers, departments or anything else for which management would like to quantify cost.

Exam Probability: **High**

7. *Answer choices:*

(see index for correct answer)

- a. Gross operating surplus
- b. Round-tripping
- c. Cost object
- d. Trade sale

Guidance: level 1

:: Options (finance) ::

A _________ , often simply labeled a "call", is a financial contract between two parties, the buyer and the seller of this type of option. The buyer of the _________ has the right, but not the obligation, to buy an agreed quantity of a particular commodity or financial instrument from the seller of the option at a certain time for a certain price . The seller is obligated to sell the commodity or financial instrument to the buyer if the buyer so decides. The buyer pays a fee for this right. The term "call" comes from the fact that the owner has the right to "call the stock away" from the seller.

Exam Probability: **Medium**

8. *Answer choices:*

(see index for correct answer)

- a. Naked put
- b. Call option

- c. Naked call
- d. Option symbol

Guidance: level 1

:: Generally Accepted Accounting Principles ::

_________ , or non-current liabilities, are liabilities that are due beyond a year or the normal operation period of the company. The normal operation period is the amount of time it takes for a company to turn inventory into cash. On a classified balance sheet, liabilities are separated between current and _________ to help users assess the company`s financial standing in short-term and long-term periods. _________ give users more information about the long-term prosperity of the company, while current liabilities inform the user of debt that the company owes in the current period. On a balance sheet, accounts are listed in order of liquidity, so _________ come after current liabilities. In addition, the specific long-term liability accounts are listed on the balance sheet in order of liquidity. Therefore, an account due within eighteen months would be listed before an account due within twenty-four months. Examples of _________ are bonds payable, long-term loans, capital leases, pension liabilities, post-retirement healthcare liabilities, deferred compensation, deferred revenues, deferred income taxes, and derivative liabilities.

Exam Probability: **High**

9. *Answer choices:*

(see index for correct answer)

- a. deferred revenue
- b. Expense

- c. Liability
- d. Long-term liabilities

Guidance: level 1

:: Commerce ::

A _______ , is a document acknowledging that a person has received money or property in payment following a sale or other transfer of goods or provision of a service. All _______ s must have the date of purchase on them. If the recipient of the payment is legally required to collect sales tax or VAT from the customer, the amount would be added to the _______ and the collection would be deemed to have been on behalf of the relevant tax authority. In many countries, a retailer is required to include the sales tax or VAT in the displayed price of goods sold, from which the tax amount would be calculated at point of sale and remitted to the tax authorities in due course. Similarly, amounts may be deducted from amounts payable, as in the case of wage withholding taxes. On the other hand, tips or other gratuities given by a customer, for example in a restaurant, would not form part of the payment amount or appear on the _______ .

Exam Probability: **High**

10. *Answer choices:*

(see index for correct answer)

- a. Receipt
- b. GT Nexus
- c. Mail order
- d. Return merchandise authorization

Guidance: level 1

:: Generally Accepted Accounting Principles ::

In accrual accounting, the revenue recognition principle states that expenses should be recorded during the period in which they are incurred, regardless of when the transfer of cash occurs. Conversely, cash basis accounting calls for the recognition of an expense when the cash is paid, regardless of when the expense was actually incurred.

Exam Probability: **High**

11. *Answer choices:*

(see index for correct answer)

- a. Generally accepted accounting principles
- b. Matching principle
- c. Operating income before depreciation and amortization
- d. Provision

Guidance: level 1

:: Accounting terminology ::

_________ or capital expense is the money a company spends to buy, maintain, or improve its fixed assets, such as buildings, vehicles, equipment, or land. It is considered a _________ when the asset is newly purchased or when money is used towards extending the useful life of an existing asset, such as repairing the roof.

Exam Probability: **Low**

12. *Answer choices:*

(see index for correct answer)

- a. profit and loss statement
- b. Double-entry accounting
- c. Capital expenditure
- d. Share premium

Guidance: level 1

:: Finance ::

A _________ , publicly-traded company, publicly-held company, publicly-listed company, or public limited company is a corporation whose ownership is dispersed among the general public in many shares of stock which are freely traded on a stock exchange or in over-the-counter markets. In some jurisdictions, public companies over a certain size must be listed on an exchange. A _________ can be listed or unlisted .

Exam Probability: **High**

13. *Answer choices:*

(see index for correct answer)

- a. Public company
- b. Signature line of credit
- c. Amortization schedule
- d. Leveraged recapitalization

Guidance: level 1

:: Generally Accepted Accounting Principles ::

In accounting, _________ is the income that a business have from its normal business activities, usually from the sale of goods and services to customers. _________ is also referred to as sales or turnover.Some companies receive _________ from interest, royalties, or other fees. _________ may refer to business income in general, or it may refer to the amount, in a monetary unit, earned during a period of time, as in "Last year, Company X had _________ of $42 million". Profits or net income generally imply total _________ minus total expenses in a given period. In accounting, in the balance statement it is a subsection of the Equity section and _________ increases equity, it is often referred to as the "top line" due to its position on the income statement at the very top. This is to be contrasted with the "bottom line" which denotes net income .

Exam Probability: **High**

14. *Answer choices:*

(see index for correct answer)

- a. Revenue recognition
- b. French generally accepted accounting principles
- c. Deprival value
- d. Closing entries

Guidance: level 1

:: Financial accounting ::

In accounting, _________ is the value of an asset according to its balance sheet account balance. For assets, the value is based on the original cost of the asset less any depreciation, amortization or impairment costs made against the asset. Traditionally, a company`s _________ is its total assets minus intangible assets and liabilities. However, in practice, depending on the source of the calculation, _________ may variably include goodwill, intangible assets, or both. The value inherent in its workforce, part of the intellectual capital of a company, is always ignored. When intangible assets and goodwill are explicitly excluded, the metric is often specified to be "tangible _________ ".

Exam Probability: **High**

15. *Answer choices:*

(see index for correct answer)

- a. Finance charge
- b. Working capital
- c. Book value
- d. Mark-to-market accounting

Guidance: level 1

:: Finance ::

_________, in finance and accounting, means stated value or face value. From this come the expressions at par, over par and under par.

Exam Probability: **Low**

16. *Answer choices:*

(see index for correct answer)

- a. Par value
- b. Convention of conservatism
- c. Debt rescheduling
- d. CBDC NORTIP

Guidance: level 1

:: Commerce ::

A _________, manufacturing plant or a production plant is an industrial site, usually consisting of buildings and machinery, or more commonly a complex having several buildings, where workers manufacture goods or operate machines processing one product into another.

Exam Probability: **Low**

17. *Answer choices:*

(see index for correct answer)

- a. Drawback
- b. White Elephant Sale
- c. Bidding
- d. Factory

Guidance: level 1

:: Accounting journals and ledgers ::

The subledger, or __________ , provides details behind entries in the general ledger used in accounting. The subledger shows detail for part of the accounting records such as property and equipment, prepaid expenses, etc. The detail would include such items as date the item was purchased or expense incurred, a description of the item, the original balance, and the net book value. The total of the subledger would match the line item amount on the general ledger. This corresponding line item in the general ledger is referred to as the controlling account. The __________ balance is compared with its controlling account balance as part of the process of preparing a trial balance.

Exam Probability: **High**

18. *Answer choices:*

(see index for correct answer)

- a. Check register
- b. General journal
- c. Subsidiary ledger
- d. Subledger

Guidance: level 1

:: Data analysis ::

In statistics, the _________ is a measure that is used to quantify the amount of variation or dispersion of a set of data values. A low _________ indicates that the data points tend to be close to the mean of the set, while a high _________ indicates that the data points are spread out over a wider range of values.

Exam Probability: **Medium**

19. *Answer choices:*

(see index for correct answer)

- a. Crosstab
- b. Variance-stabilizing transformation
- c. Health care analytics
- d. Explained variation

Guidance: level 1

:: Finance ::

_________ is a field that is concerned with the allocation of assets and liabilities over space and time, often under conditions of risk or uncertainty. _________ can also be defined as the art of money management. Participants in the market aim to price assets based on their risk level, fundamental value, and their expected rate of return. _________ can be split into three sub-categories: public _________, corporate _________ and personal _________.

Exam Probability: **Medium**

20. *Answer choices:*

(see index for correct answer)

- a. Stock buyback
- b. Debt buyer
- c. Decoupled debit card
- d. Orix USA

Guidance: level 1

:: Payments ::

A _________ is the trade of value from one party to another for goods, or services, or to fulfill a legal obligation.

Exam Probability: **Medium**

21. *Answer choices:*

(see index for correct answer)

- a. Tuition payments
- b. Payment
- c. Thirty pieces of silver
- d. Market transition payments

Guidance: level 1

:: ::

_________ or accountancy is the measurement, processing, and communication of financial information about economic entities such as businesses and corporations. The modern field was established by the Italian mathematician Luca Pacioli in 1494. _________, which has been called the "language of business", measures the results of an organization`s economic activities and conveys this information to a variety of users, including investors, creditors, management, and regulators. Practitioners of _________ are known as accountants. The terms " _________ " and "financial reporting" are often used as synonyms.

Exam Probability: **High**

22. *Answer choices:*

(see index for correct answer)

- a. hierarchical
- b. functional perspective
- c. imperative
- d. Accounting

Guidance: level 1

:: Manufacturing ::

__________ s are goods that have completed the manufacturing process but have not yet been sold or distributed to the end user.

Exam Probability: **Low**

23. *Answer choices:*

(see index for correct answer)

- a. PackML
- b. Surface integrity
- c. Finished good
- d. fixed position

Guidance: level 1

:: Accounting terminology ::

_________ are liabilities that reflect expenses that have not yet been paid or logged under accounts payable during an accounting period; in other words, a company`s obligation to pay for goods and services that have been provided for which invoices have not yet been received. Examples would include accrued wages payable, accrued sales tax payable, and accrued rent payable.

Exam Probability: **Low**

24. *Answer choices:*

(see index for correct answer)

- a. Impairment cost
- b. General ledger
- c. revenue recognition principle
- d. Accounts receivable

Guidance: level 1

:: ::

_________ refers to a business or organization attempting to acquire goods or services to accomplish its goals. Although there are several organizations that attempt to set standards in the _________ process, processes can vary greatly between organizations. Typically the word " _________ " is not used interchangeably with the word "procurement", since procurement typically includes expediting, supplier quality, and transportation and logistics in addition to _________ .

Exam Probability: **High**

25. *Answer choices:*

(see index for correct answer)

- a. personal values
- b. similarity-attraction theory
- c. Sarbanes-Oxley act of 2002
- d. Purchasing

Guidance: level 1

:: Costs ::

In economics, __________ is the total economic cost of production and is made up of variable cost, which varies according to the quantity of a good produced and includes inputs such as labour and raw materials, plus fixed cost, which is independent of the quantity of a good produced and includes inputs that cannot be varied in the short term: fixed costs such as buildings and machinery, including sunk costs if any. Since cost is measured per unit of time, it is a flow variable.

Exam Probability: **Medium**

26. *Answer choices:*

(see index for correct answer)

- a. Search cost

- b. Total cost of acquisition
- c. Total cost
- d. Economic cost

Guidance: level 1

:: Generally Accepted Accounting Principles ::

A __________ or reacquired stock is stock which is bought back by the issuing company, reducing the amount of outstanding stock on the open market .

Exam Probability: **Medium**

27. *Answer choices:*

(see index for correct answer)

- a. French generally accepted accounting principles
- b. Engagement letter
- c. Deferred income
- d. Treasury stock

Guidance: level 1

:: Generally Accepted Accounting Principles ::

In accounting and finance, earnings before interest and taxes is a measure of a firm`s profit that includes all incomes and expenses except interest expenses and income tax expenses.

Exam Probability: **Low**

28. *Answer choices:*

(see index for correct answer)

- a. Cost principle
- b. Cost pool
- c. Consolidation
- d. Operating income before depreciation and amortization

Guidance: level 1

:: Generally Accepted Accounting Principles ::

In business and accounting, _________ is an entity`s income minus cost of goods sold, expenses and taxes for an accounting period. It is computed as the residual of all revenues and gains over all expenses and losses for the period, and has also been defined as the net increase in shareholders` equity that results from a company`s operations. In the context of the presentation of financial statements, the IFRS Foundation defines _________ as synonymous with profit and loss. The difference between revenue and the cost of making a product or providing a service, before deducting overheads, payroll, taxation, and interest payments. This is different from operating income .

Exam Probability: **Medium**

29. *Answer choices:*

(see index for correct answer)

- a. Petty cash
- b. Gross sales
- c. Indian Accounting Standards
- d. Net income

Guidance: level 1

:: Marketing ::

__________ or stock is the goods and materials that a business holds for the ultimate goal of resale .

Exam Probability: **Low**

30. *Answer choices:*

(see index for correct answer)

- a. Free Comic Book Day
- b. Inventory
- c. Online ethnography
- d. Bass diffusion model

Guidance: level 1

:: Financial ratios ::

The _________ or dividend-price ratio of a share is the dividend per share, divided by the price per share. It is also a company`s total annual dividend payments divided by its market capitalization, assuming the number of shares is constant. It is often expressed as a percentage.

Exam Probability: **Low**

31. *Answer choices:*

(see index for correct answer)

- a. Theoretical ex-rights price
- b. Treynor ratio
- c. Debtor days
- d. Dividend yield

Guidance: level 1

:: Accounting source documents ::

A __________ or account statement is a summary of financial transactions which have occurred over a given period on a bank account held by a person or business with a financial institution.

Exam Probability: **Medium**

32. *Answer choices:*

(see index for correct answer)

- a. Air waybill
- b. Remittance advice
- c. Invoice
- d. Bank statement

Guidance: level 1

:: Accounting terminology ::

__________ is a legally enforceable claim for payment held by a business for goods supplied and/or services rendered that customers/clients have ordered but not paid for. These are generally in the form of invoices raised by a business and delivered to the customer for payment within an agreed time frame. __________ is shown in a balance sheet as an asset. It is one of a series of accounting transactions dealing with the billing of a customer for goods and services that the customer has ordered. These may be distinguished from notes receivable, which are debts created through formal legal instruments called promissory notes.

Exam Probability: **Low**

33. *Answer choices:*

(see index for correct answer)

- a. Accounts receivable
- b. profit and loss statement
- c. outstanding balance
- d. Fund accounting

Guidance: level 1

:: Accounting systems ::

In bookkeeping, a _________ statement is a process that explains the difference on a specified date between the bank balance shown in an organization`s bank statement, as supplied by the bank and the corresponding amount shown in the organization`s own accounting records.

Exam Probability: **Medium**

34. *Answer choices:*

(see index for correct answer)

- a. Unified ledger accounting
- b. Bookkeeping association
- c. Debits and credits

- d. Accounting reform

Guidance: level 1

:: Financial accounting ::

_________ in accounting is the process of treating investments in associate companies. Equity accounting is usually applied where an investor entity holds 20–50% of the voting stock of the associate company. The investor records such investments as an asset on its balance sheet. The investor`s proportional share of the associate company`s net income increases the investment , and proportional payments of dividends decrease it. In the investor's income statement, the proportional share of the investor's net income or net loss is reported as a single-line item.

Exam Probability: **High**

35. *Answer choices:*

(see index for correct answer)

- a. Equity method
- b. Carry
- c. Capital account
- d. Asset swap

Guidance: level 1

:: ::

In the field of analysis of algorithms in computer science, the _________ is a method of amortized analysis based on accounting. The _________ often gives a more intuitive account of the amortized cost of an operation than either aggregate analysis or the potential method. Note, however, that this does not guarantee such analysis will be immediately obvious; often, choosing the correct parameters for the _________ requires as much knowledge of the problem and the complexity bounds one is attempting to prove as the other two methods.

Exam Probability: **Medium**

36. *Answer choices:*

(see index for correct answer)

- a. process perspective
- b. Accounting method
- c. Sarbanes-Oxley act of 2002
- d. personal values

Guidance: level 1

:: Mathematical finance ::

In economics and finance, _________ , also known as present discounted value, is the value of an expected income stream determined as of the date of valuation. The _________ is always less than or equal to the future value because money has interest-earning potential, a characteristic referred to as the time value of money, except during times of negative interest rates, when the _________ will be more than the future value. Time value can be described with the simplified phrase, "A dollar today is worth more than a dollar tomorrow". Here, `worth more` means that its value is greater. A dollar today is worth more than a dollar tomorrow because the dollar can be invested and earn a day`s worth of interest, making the total accumulate to a value more than a dollar by tomorrow. Interest can be compared to rent. Just as rent is paid to a landlord by a tenant without the ownership of the asset being transferred, interest is paid to a lender by a borrower who gains access to the money for a time before paying it back. By letting the borrower have access to the money, the lender has sacrificed the exchange value of this money, and is compensated for it in the form of interest. The initial amount of the borrowed funds is less than the total amount of money paid to the lender.

Exam Probability: **Medium**

37. *Answer choices:*

(see index for correct answer)

- a. Stochastic calculus
- b. Trinomial tree
- c. Implied volatility
- d. Present value

Guidance: level 1

:: Generally Accepted Accounting Principles ::

In accounting, _________ , gross margin, sales profit, or credit sales is the difference between revenue and the cost of making a product or providing a service, before deducting overheads, payroll, taxation, and interest payments. This is different from operating profit . Gross margin is the term normally used in the U.S., while _________ is the more common usage in the UK and Australia.

Exam Probability: **Low**

38. *Answer choices:*

(see index for correct answer)

- a. Chinese accounting standards
- b. Generally accepted accounting principles
- c. Revenue
- d. Gross profit

Guidance: level 1

:: Money market instruments ::

_________ , in the global financial market, is an unsecured promissory note with a fixed maturity of not more than 270 days.

Exam Probability: **Medium**

39. *Answer choices:*

(see index for correct answer)

- a. Commercial paper in India
- b. Banker's acceptance

Guidance: level 1

:: Accounting ::

__________ is a process of providing relief to shared service organization`s cost centers that provide a product or service. In turn, the associated expense is assigned to internal clients` cost centers that consume the products and services. For example, the CIO may provide all IT services within the company and assign the costs back to the business units that consume each offering.

Exam Probability: **Low**

40. *Answer choices:*

(see index for correct answer)

- a. Accountant General
- b. Part exchange
- c. Special journals
- d. Cost allocation

Guidance: level 1

:: Social security ::

_________ is "any government system that provides monetary assistance to people with an inadequate or no income." In the United States, this is usually called welfare or a social safety net, especially when talking about Canada and European countries.

Exam Probability: **Medium**

41. *Answer choices:*

(see index for correct answer)

- a. Social Security Agency
- b. Intergenerational struggle
- c. South African Social Security Agency
- d. Social security

Guidance: level 1

:: Income taxes ::

An _________ is a tax imposed on individuals or entities that varies with respective income or profits . _________ generally is computed as the product of a tax rate times taxable income. Taxation rates may vary by type or characteristics of the taxpayer.

Exam Probability: **Low**

42. *Answer choices:*

(see index for correct answer)

- a. Income tax
- b. Income taxes in Canada
- c. Rouanet Law
- d. Income tax in Spain

Guidance: level 1

:: Management accounting ::

" _________ s are the structural determinants of the cost of an activity, reflecting any linkages or interrelationships that affect it". Therefore we could assume that the _________ s determine the cost behavior within the activities, reflecting the links that these have with other activities and relationships that affect them.

Exam Probability: **Low**

43. *Answer choices:*

(see index for correct answer)

- a. Target income sales
- b. Throughput accounting
- c. Process costing
- d. Chartered Institute of Management Accountants

Guidance: level 1

:: Accounting journals and ledgers ::

A _________ , in accounting, is the logging of a transaction in an accounting journal that shows a company`s debit and credit balances. The _________ can consist of several recordings, each of which is either a debit or a credit. The total of the debits must equal the total of the credits or the _________ is considered unbalanced. Journal entries can record unique items or recurring items such as depreciation or bond amortization. In accounting software, journal entries are usually entered using a separate module from accounts payable, which typically has its own subledger, that indirectly affects the general ledger. As a result, journal entries directly change the account balances on the general ledger. A properly documented _________ consists of the correct date, amount that will be debited, amount that will be credited, description of transaction, and unique reference number .

Exam Probability: **Low**

44. *Answer choices:*

(see index for correct answer)

- a. Subledger
- b. General journal
- c. Sales journal
- d. Subsidiary ledger

Guidance: level 1

:: Accounting terminology ::

Total ________ is a method of Accounting cost which entails the full cost of manufacturing or providing a service. TAC includes not just the costs of materials and labour, but also of all manufacturing overheads . The cost of each cost center can be direct or indirect. The direct cost can be easily identified with individual cost centers. Whereas indirect cost cannot be easily identified with the cost center. The distribution of overhead among the departments is called apportionment.

Exam Probability: **High**

45. *Answer choices:*

(see index for correct answer)

- a. Accrual
- b. Absorption costing
- c. Statement of financial position
- d. Double-entry accounting

Guidance: level 1

:: ::

The _________ of a function of a real variable measures the sensitivity to change of the function value with respect to a change in its argument. _________ s are a fundamental tool of calculus. For example, the _________ of the position of a moving object with respect to time is the object`s velocity: this measures how quickly the position of the object changes when time advances.

Exam Probability: **High**

46. *Answer choices:*

(see index for correct answer)

- a. interpersonal communication
- b. surface-level diversity
- c. deep-level diversity
- d. corporate values

Guidance: level 1

:: Generally Accepted Accounting Principles ::

A _________ is a reduction of the recognized value of something. In accounting, this is a recognition of the reduced or zero value of an asset. In income tax statements, this is a reduction of taxable income, as a recognition of certain expenses required to produce the income.

Exam Probability: **Low**

47. *Answer choices:*

(see index for correct answer)

- a. Write-off
- b. Financial position of the United States
- c. Goodwill
- d. Gross sales

Guidance: level 1

:: ::

An __________ is an area of the production, distribution, or trade, and consumption of goods and services by different agents. Understood in its broadest sense, `The __________ is defined as a social domain that emphasize the practices, discourses, and material expressions associated with the production, use, and management of resources`. Economic agents can be individuals, businesses, organizations, or governments. Economic transactions occur when two parties agree to the value or price of the transacted good or service, commonly expressed in a certain currency. However, monetary transactions only account for a small part of the economic domain.

Exam Probability: **Medium**

48. *Answer choices:*

(see index for correct answer)

- a. Economy
- b. process perspective

- c. empathy
- d. imperative

Guidance: level 1

:: Free accounting software ::

A _________ is the principal book or computer file for recording and totaling economic transactions measured in terms of a monetary unit of account by account type, with debits and credits in separate columns and a beginning monetary balance and ending monetary balance for each account.

Exam Probability: **Low**

49. *Answer choices:*

(see index for correct answer)

- a. Ledger
- b. Grisbi
- c. Frontaccounting
- d. JFin

Guidance: level 1

:: Financial economics ::

A __________ is defined to include property of any kind held by an assessee, whether connected with their business or profession or not connected with their business or profession. It includes all kinds of property, movable or immovable, tangible or intangible, fixed or circulating. Thus, land and building, plant and machinery, motorcar, furniture, jewellery, route permits, goodwill, tenancy rights, patents, trademarks, shares, debentures, securities, units, mutual funds, zero-coupon bonds etc. are __________ s.

Exam Probability: **Medium**

50. *Answer choices:*

(see index for correct answer)

- a. Customer value
- b. Capital asset
- c. Asset specificity
- d. Information coefficient

Guidance: level 1

:: Management accounting ::

In finance, the __________ or net present worth applies to a series of cash flows occurring at different times. The present value of a cash flow depends on the interval of time between now and the cash flow. It also depends on the discount rate. NPV accounts for the time value of money. It provides a method for evaluating and comparing capital projects or financial products with cash flows spread over time, as in loans, investments, payouts from insurance contracts plus many other applications.

Exam Probability: **Low**

51. *Answer choices:*

(see index for correct answer)

- a. Direct material usage variance
- b. Certified Management Accountants of Canada
- c. Total benefits of ownership
- d. Extended cost

Guidance: level 1

:: ::

_________ Corporation was an American energy, commodities, and services company based in Houston, Texas. It was founded in 1985 as a merger between Houston Natural Gas and InterNorth, both relatively small regional companies. Before its bankruptcy on December 3, 2001, _________ employed approximately 29,000 staff and was a major electricity, natural gas, communications and pulp and paper company, with claimed revenues of nearly $101 billion during 2000. Fortune named _________ "America`s Most Innovative Company" for six consecutive years.

Exam Probability: **Low**

52. *Answer choices:*

(see index for correct answer)

- a. deep-level diversity
- b. functional perspective
- c. Character
- d. Enron

Guidance: level 1

:: Expense ::

_________ relates to the cost of borrowing money. It is the price that a lender charges a borrower for the use of the lender`s money. On the income statement, _________ can represent the cost of borrowing money from banks, bond investors, and other sources. _________ is different from operating expense and CAPEX, for it relates to the capital structure of a company, and it is usually tax-deductible.

Exam Probability: **Medium**

53. *Answer choices:*

(see index for correct answer)

- a. Operating expense
- b. Interest expense
- c. expenditure
- d. Freight expense

Guidance: level 1

:: Financial ratios ::

The ________ is a financial ratio indicating the relative proportion of shareholders` equity and debt used to finance a company`s assets. Closely related to leveraging, the ratio is also known as risk, gearing or leverage. The two components are often taken from the firm`s balance sheet or statement of financial position , but the ratio may also be calculated using market values for both, if the company`s debt and equity are publicly traded, or using a combination of book value for debt and market value for equity financially.

Exam Probability: **Low**

54. *Answer choices:*

(see index for correct answer)

- a. Average propensity to save
- b. Debt-to-capital ratio
- c. Texas ratio
- d. Asset turnover

Guidance: level 1

:: ::

A _________ is the period used by governments for accounting and budget purposes, which varies between countries. It is also used for financial reporting by business and other organizations. Laws in many jurisdictions require company financial reports to be prepared and published on an annual basis, but generally do not require the reporting period to align with the calendar year . Taxation laws generally require accounting records to be maintained and taxes calculated on an annual basis, which usually corresponds to the _________ used for government purposes. The calculation of tax on an annual basis is especially relevant for direct taxation, such as income tax. Many annual government fees—such as Council rates, licence fees, etc.—are also levied on a _________ basis, while others are charged on an anniversary basis.

Exam Probability: **Low**

55. *Answer choices:*

(see index for correct answer)

- a. interpersonal communication
- b. Fiscal year
- c. Character
- d. hierarchical

Guidance: level 1

:: Financial ratios ::

A _________ or accounting ratio is a relative magnitude of two selected numerical values taken from an enterprise`s financial statements. Often used in accounting, there are many standard ratios used to try to evaluate the overall financial condition of a corporation or other organization. _________ s may be used by managers within a firm, by current and potential shareholders of a firm, and by a firm`s creditors. Financial analysts use _________ s to compare the strengths and weaknesses in various companies. If shares in a company are traded in a financial market, the market price of the shares is used in certain _________ s.

Exam Probability: **Low**

56. *Answer choices:*

(see index for correct answer)

- a. Return on tangible equity
- b. Net profit margin
- c. Implied multiple
- d. CROCI

Guidance: level 1

:: ::

In marketing, a _________ is a ticket or document that can be redeemed for a financial discount or rebate when purchasing a product.

Exam Probability: **High**

57. *Answer choices:*

(see index for correct answer)

- a. open system
- b. corporate values
- c. hierarchical perspective
- d. levels of analysis

Guidance: level 1

:: ::

__________ is the production of products for use or sale using labour and machines, tools, chemical and biological processing, or formulation. The term may refer to a range of human activity, from handicraft to high tech, but is most commonly applied to industrial design, in which raw materials are transformed into finished goods on a large scale. Such finished goods may be sold to other manufacturers for the production of other, more complex products, such as aircraft, household appliances, furniture, sports equipment or automobiles, or sold to wholesalers, who in turn sell them to retailers, who then sell them to end users and consumers.

Exam Probability: **Low**

58. *Answer choices:*

(see index for correct answer)

- a. Manufacturing
- b. deep-level diversity

- c. hierarchical perspective
- d. similarity-attraction theory

Guidance: level 1

:: Decision theory ::

A _________ is a deliberate system of principles to guide decisions and achieve rational outcomes. A _________ is a statement of intent, and is implemented as a procedure or protocol. Policies are generally adopted by a governance body within an organization. Policies can assist in both subjective and objective decision making. Policies to assist in subjective decision making usually assist senior management with decisions that must be based on the relative merits of a number of factors, and as a result are often hard to test objectively, e.g. work-life balance _________ . In contrast policies to assist in objective decision making are usually operational in nature and can be objectively tested, e.g. password _________ .

Exam Probability: **Low**

59. *Answer choices:*

(see index for correct answer)

- a. Decision engineering
- b. Decisional balance sheet
- c. Trade study
- d. Policy

Guidance: level 1

Human resource management

Human resource (HR) management is the strategic approach to the effective management of organization workers so that they help the business gain a competitive advantage. It is designed to maximize employee performance in service of an employer's strategic objectives. HR is primarily concerned with the management of people within organizations, focusing on policies and on systems. HR departments are responsible for overseeing employee-benefits design, employee recruitment, training and development, performance appraisal, and rewarding (e.g., managing pay and benefit systems). HR also concerns itself with organizational change and industrial relations, that is, the balancing of organizational practices with requirements arising from collective bargaining and from governmental laws.

:: Problem solving ::

A __________ is a unit or formation established to work on a single defined task or activity. Originally introduced by the United States Navy, the term has now caught on for general usage and is a standard part of NATO terminology. Many non-military organizations now create " __________ s" or task groups for temporary activities that might have once been performed by ad hoc committees.

Exam Probability: **High**

1. *Answer choices:*

(see index for correct answer)

- a. Brainstorming
- b. Task force
- c. Problem finding
- d. Candle problem

Guidance: level 1

:: ::

A __________ is the ability to carry out a task with determined results often within a given amount of time, energy, or both. __________ s can often be divided into domain-general and domain-specific __________ s. For example, in the domain of work, some general __________ s would include time management, teamwork and leadership, self-motivation and others, whereas domain-specific __________ s would be used only for a certain job. __________ usually requires certain environmental stimuli and situations to assess the level of __________ being shown and used.

Exam Probability: **Medium**

2. *Answer choices:*

(see index for correct answer)

- a. deep-level diversity
- b. co-culture
- c. similarity-attraction theory
- d. Skill

Guidance: level 1

:: Labor rights ::

A _________ is a wrong or hardship suffered, real or supposed, which forms legitimate grounds of complaint. In the past, the word meant the infliction or cause of hardship.

Exam Probability: **High**

3. *Answer choices:*

(see index for correct answer)

- a. Swift raids
- b. Labor rights
- c. China Labor Watch
- d. China Labour Bulletin

Guidance: level 1

:: Employment compensation ::

A __________ is a type of employee benefit plan offered in the United States pursuant to Section 125 of the Internal Revenue Code. Its name comes from the earliest such plans that allowed employees to choose between different types of benefits, similar to the ability of a customer to choose among available items in a cafeteria. Qualified __________ s are excluded from gross income. To qualify, a __________ must allow employees to choose from two or more benefits consisting of cash or qualified benefit plans. The Internal Revenue Code explicitly excludes deferred compensation plans from qualifying as a __________ subject to a gross income exemption. Section 125 also provides two exceptions.

Exam Probability: **High**

4. *Answer choices:*

(see index for correct answer)

- a. Federal Salary Council
- b. Protection of Wages Convention, 1949
- c. Employee stock ownership plan
- d. Health Reimbursement Account

Guidance: level 1

:: Management ::

In the field of management, _________ involves the formulation and implementation of the major goals and initiatives taken by an organization`s top management on behalf of owners, based on consideration of resources and an assessment of the internal and external environments in which the organization operates.

Exam Probability: **Low**

5. *Answer choices:*

(see index for correct answer)

- a. Social business model
- b. Corporate foresight
- c. Project management
- d. Strategic management

Guidance: level 1

:: Validity (statistics) ::

In psychometrics, criterion or concrete validity is the extent to which a measure is related to an outcome. __________ is often divided into concurrent and predictive validity. Concurrent validity refers to a comparison between the measure in question and an outcome assessed at the same time. In Standards for Educational & Psychological Tests, it states, "concurrent validity reflects only the status quo at a particular time." Predictive validity, on the other hand, compares the measure in question with an outcome assessed at a later time. Although concurrent and predictive validity are similar, it is cautioned to keep the terms and findings separated. "Concurrent validity should not be used as a substitute for predictive validity without an appropriate supporting rationale."

Exam Probability: **Medium**

6. *Answer choices:*

(see index for correct answer)

- a. Convergent validity
- b. Statistical conclusion
- c. Concurrent validity
- d. External validity

Guidance: level 1

:: ::

_________ involves the development of an action plan designed to motivate and guide a person or group toward a goal. _________ can be guided by goal-setting criteria such as SMART criteria. _________ is a major component of personal-development and management literature.

Exam Probability: **High**

7. *Answer choices:*

(see index for correct answer)

- a. Goal setting
- b. cultural
- c. levels of analysis
- d. open system

Guidance: level 1

:: Personal finance ::

_________ is an arrangement in which a portion of an employee`s income is paid out at a later date after which the income was earned. Examples of _________ include pensions, retirement plans, and employee stock options. The primary benefit of most _________ is the deferral of tax to the date at which the employee receives the income.

Exam Probability: **High**

8. *Answer choices:*

(see index for correct answer)

- a. Escrow
- b. Deferred compensation
- c. West One Bridging Index
- d. Saving

Guidance: level 1

:: ::

The causes of _________ are heavily debated. Classical economics, new classical economics, and the Austrian School of economics argued that market mechanisms are reliable means of resolving _________. These theories argue against interventions imposed on the labor market from the outside, such as unionization, bureaucratic work rules, minimum wage laws, taxes, and other regulations that they claim discourage the hiring of workers. Keynesian economics emphasizes the cyclical nature of _________ and recommends government interventions in the economy that it claims will reduce _________ during recessions. This theory focuses on recurrent shocks that suddenly reduce aggregate demand for goods and services and thus reduce demand for workers. Keynesian models recommend government interventions designed to increase demand for workers; these can include financial stimuli, publicly funded job creation, and expansionist monetary policies. Its namesake economist, John Maynard Keynes, believed that the root cause of _________ is the desire of investors to receive more money rather than produce more products, which is not possible without public bodies producing new money. A third group of theories emphasize the need for a stable supply of capital and investment to maintain full employment. On this view, government should guarantee full employment through fiscal policy, monetary policy and trade policy as stated, for example, in the US Employment Act of 1946, by counteracting private sector or trade investment volatility, and reducing inequality.

Exam Probability: **High**

9. *Answer choices:*

(see index for correct answer)

- a. open system
- b. co-culture
- c. interpersonal communication
- d. Unemployment

Guidance: level 1

:: Validity (statistics) ::

In psychometrics, _________ refers to the extent to which a measure represents all facets of a given construct. For example, a depression scale may lack _________ if it only assesses the affective dimension of depression but fails to take into account the behavioral dimension. An element of subjectivity exists in relation to determining _________ , which requires a degree of agreement about what a particular personality trait such as extraversion represents. A disagreement about a personality trait will prevent the gain of a high _________ .

Exam Probability: **High**

10. *Answer choices:*

(see index for correct answer)

- a. Test validity
- b. Content validity
- c. Convergent validity
- d. Internal validity

Guidance: level 1

:: Financial accounting ::

__________ is the intangible value of a business, covering its people , the value relating to its relationships , and everything that is left when the employees go home , of which intellectual property is but one component. It is the sum of everything everybody in a company knows that gives it a competitive edge. The term is used in academia in an attempt to account for the value of intangible assets not listed explicitly on a company`s balance sheets. On a national level __________ refers to national intangible capital, NIC.A second meaning that is used in academia and was adopted in large corporations is focused on the recycling of knowledge via knowledge management and __________ management . Creating, shaping and updating the stock of __________ requires the formulation of a strategic vision, which blends together all three dimensions of __________ within the organisational context through exploration, exploitation, measurement, and disclosure. __________ is used in the context of assessing the wealth of organizations. A metric for the value of __________ is the amount by which the enterprise value of a firm exceeds the value of its tangible assets. Directly visible on corporate books is capital embodied in its physical assets and financial capital; however all three make up the value of an enterprise. Measuring the real value and the total performance of __________`s components is a critical part of running a company in the knowledge economy and Information Age. Understanding the __________ in an enterprise allows leveraging of its intellectual assets. For a corporation, the result will optimize its stock price.

Exam Probability: **Low**

11. *Answer choices:*

(see index for correct answer)

- a. Deferred financing cost
- b. Certified Public Accountants Association
- c. Book value
- d. SEC filing

Guidance: level 1

:: Problem solving ::

In other words, __________ is a situation where a group of people meet to generate new ideas and solutions around a specific domain of interest by removing inhibitions. People are able to think more freely and they suggest as many spontaneous new ideas as possible. All the ideas are noted down and those ideas are not criticized and after __________ session the ideas are evaluated.The term was popularized by Alex Faickney Osborn in the 1953 book Applied Imagination.

Exam Probability: **High**

12. *Answer choices:*

(see index for correct answer)

- a. Eight Disciplines Problem Solving
- b. Collective Induction
- c. Disney method
- d. Self-organising heuristic

Guidance: level 1

:: Employment compensation ::

__________, merit increase or pay for performance, is performance-related pay, most frequently in the context of educational reform or government civil service reform . It provides bonuses for workers who perform their jobs effectively, according to easily measurable criteria. In the United States, policy makers are divided on whether __________ should be offered to public school teachers, and other public employees, as is commonly the case in the United Kingdom.

Exam Probability: **High**

13. *Answer choices:*

(see index for correct answer)

- a. Interactive accommodation process
- b. Stock appreciation right
- c. Merit pay
- d. Total Reward

Guidance: level 1

:: Human resource management ::

__________ is the strategic approach to the effective management of people in an organization so that they help the business to gain a competitive advantage. It is designed to maximize employee performance in service of an employer`s strategic objectives. HR is primarily concerned with the management of people within organizations, focusing on policies and on systems. HR departments are responsible for overseeing employee-benefits design, employee recruitment, training and development, performance appraisal, and Reward management . HR also concerns itself with organizational change and industrial relations, that is, the balancing of organizational practices with requirements arising from collective bargaining and from governmental laws.

Exam Probability: **Medium**

14. *Answer choices:*

(see index for correct answer)

- a. Service record
- b. Continuing professional development
- c. Human resource management
- d. The war for talent

Guidance: level 1

:: Labour law ::

A __________ is a legal contract that is meant to limit the liability of an employer whose employees are romantically involved. An employer may choose to require a __________ when a romantic relationship within the company becomes known, in order to indemnify the company in case the employees` romantic relationship fails, primarily so that one party can`t bring a sexual harassment lawsuit against the company. To that end, the __________ states that the relationship is consensual, and both parties of the relationship must sign it. The __________ may also stipulate rules for acceptable romantic behavior in the workplace.

Exam Probability: **High**

15. *Answer choices:*

(see index for correct answer)

- a. Individual capacity
- b. Love contract
- c. Principles of Labor Legislation
- d. Unfair dismissal

Guidance: level 1

:: Stochastic processes ::

_________ in its modern meaning is a "new idea, creative thoughts, new imaginations in form of device or method". _________ is often also viewed as the application of better solutions that meet new requirements, unarticulated needs, or existing market needs. Such _________ takes place through the provision of more-effective products, processes, services, technologies, or business models that are made available to markets, governments and society. An _________ is something original and more effective and, as a consequence, new, that "breaks into" the market or society. _________ is related to, but not the same as, invention, as _________ is more apt to involve the practical implementation of an invention to make a meaningful impact in the market or society, and not all _________s require an invention. _________ often manifests itself via the engineering process, when the problem being solved is of a technical or scientific nature. The opposite of _________ is exnovation.

Exam Probability: **Medium**

16. *Answer choices:*

(see index for correct answer)

- a. Brownian tree
- b. Innovation
- c. Master equation
- d. G/M/1 queue

Guidance: level 1

:: Labor ::

_________ s are workers whose main capital is knowledge. Examples include programmers, physicians, pharmacists, architects, engineers, scientists, design thinkers, public accountants, lawyers, and academics, and any other white-collar workers, whose line of work requires the one to "think for a living".

Exam Probability: **Low**

17. *Answer choices:*

(see index for correct answer)

- a. Company man
- b. Labor intensity
- c. Manual labour
- d. Knowledge worker

Guidance: level 1

:: Sexual harassment in the United States ::

In law, a _________ , reasonable man, or the man on the Clapham omnibus is a hypothetical person of legal fiction crafted by the courts and communicated through case law and jury instructions.

Exam Probability: **Low**

18. *Answer choices:*

(see index for correct answer)

- a. Reasonable person
- b. Charol Shakeshaft
- c. Alexander v. Yale
- d. Sexual harassment in education in the United States

Guidance: level 1

:: Organizational theory ::

Decentralisation is the process by which the activities of an organization, particularly those regarding planning and decision making, are distributed or delegated away from a central, authoritative location or group. Concepts of _________ have been applied to group dynamics and management science in private businesses and organizations, political science, law and public administration, economics, money and technology.

Exam Probability: **High**

19. *Answer choices:*

(see index for correct answer)

- a. Employee research
- b. Organigraph
- c. Decentralization
- d. Bureaucratic inertia

Guidance: level 1

:: Organizational behavior ::

Greenberg introduced the concept of _________ with regard to how an employee judges the behaviour of the organization and the employee`s resulting attitude and behaviour. .

Exam Probability: **Low**

20. *Answer choices:*

(see index for correct answer)

- a. Organizational justice
- b. Behavioral systems analysis
- c. Organizational citizenship behavior
- d. Nut Island effect

Guidance: level 1

:: Human resource management ::

__________ are the people who make up the workforce of an organization, business sector, or economy. "Human capital" is sometimes used synonymously with " __________ ", although human capital typically refers to a narrower effect . Likewise, other terms sometimes used include manpower, talent, labor, personnel, or simply people.

Exam Probability: **High**

21. *Answer choices:*

(see index for correct answer)

- a. Management development
- b. Mergers and acquisitions
- c. Organizational chart
- d. Human resources

Guidance: level 1

:: Employee relations ::

The __________ can be used to bring together employment and job-related information which employees need to know. It typically has three types of content.

Exam Probability: **Low**

22. *Answer choices:*

(see index for correct answer)

- a. Fringe benefit
- b. Employee handbook
- c. Employee motivation
- d. Employee surveys

Guidance: level 1

:: Occupations ::

An _________ is a person who has a position of authority in a hierarchical organization. The term derives from the late Latin from officiarius, meaning "official".

Exam Probability: **High**

23. *Answer choices:*

(see index for correct answer)

- a. Officer
- b. Village head
- c. Sarpanch
- d. Senior lecturer

Guidance: level 1

:: Financial terminology ::

__________ is the cost of maintaining a certain standard of living. Changes in the __________ over time are often operationalized in a cost-of-living index. __________ calculations are also used to compare the cost of maintaining a certain standard of living in different geographic areas. Differences in __________ between locations can also be measured in terms of purchasing power parity rates.

Exam Probability: **Medium**

24. *Answer choices:*

(see index for correct answer)

- a. Cost price
- b. Inverse floater
- c. Delivery point
- d. Earnings test

Guidance: level 1

:: Recruitment ::

_________ is a tool companies and organizations use as a way to communicate the good and the bad characteristics of the job during the hiring process of new employees, or as a tool to reestablish job specificity for existing employees. _________ s should provide the individuals with a well-rounded description that details what obligations the individual can expect to perform while working for that specific company. Descriptions may include, but are not limited to, work environment, expectations, and Company policies .

Exam Probability: **High**

25. *Answer choices:*

(see index for correct answer)

- a. Realistic job preview
- b. Acquisourcing
- c. Jeopardy! audition process
- d. Recruitment process insourcing

Guidance: level 1

:: Unemployment by country ::

Unemployment benefits are payments made by back authorized bodies to unemployed people. In the United States, benefits are funded by a compulsory governmental insurance system, not taxes on individual citizens. Depending on the jurisdiction and the status of the person, those sums may be small, covering only basic needs, or may compensate the lost time proportionally to the previous earned salary.

Exam Probability: **Medium**

26. *Answer choices:*

(see index for correct answer)

- a. Unemployment in Spain
- b. Unemployment in Poland
- c. Unemployment insurance

Guidance: level 1

:: Income ::

In business and accounting, net income is an entity`s income minus cost of goods sold, expenses and taxes for an accounting period. It is computed as the residual of all revenues and gains over all expenses and losses for the period, and has also been defined as the net increase in shareholders` equity that results from a company`s operations. In the context of the presentation of financial statements, the IFRS Foundation defines net income as synonymous with profit and loss. The difference between revenue and the cost of making a product or providing a service, before deducting overheads, payroll, taxation, and interest payments. This is different from operating income .

Exam Probability: **Medium**

27. *Answer choices:*

(see index for correct answer)

- a. Family income

- b. Bottom line
- c. Net national income
- d. Income earner

Guidance: level 1

:: ::

__________ are interactive computer-mediated technologies that facilitate the creation and sharing of information, ideas, career interests and other forms of expression via virtual communities and networks. The variety of stand-alone and built-in __________ services currently available introduces challenges of definition; however, there are some common features.

Exam Probability: **Medium**

28. *Answer choices:*

(see index for correct answer)

- a. information systems assessment
- b. Social media
- c. open system
- d. functional perspective

Guidance: level 1

:: Unemployment ::

The __________ is the negative relationship between the levels of unemployment and wages that arises when these variables are expressed in local terms. According to David Blanchflower and Andrew Oswald , the __________ summarizes the fact that "A worker who is employed in an area of high unemployment earns less than an identical individual who works in a region with low joblessness."

Exam Probability: **Low**

29. *Answer choices:*

(see index for correct answer)

- a. Waithood
- b. Wage curve
- c. Functional finance
- d. Involuntary unemployment

Guidance: level 1

:: Human resource management ::

An _________ is a software application that enables the electronic handling of recruitment needs. An ATS can be implemented or accessed online on an enterprise or small business level, depending on the needs of the company and there is also free and open source ATS software available. An ATS is very similar to customer relationship management systems, but are designed for recruitment tracking purposes. In many cases they filter applications automatically based on given criteria such as keywords, skills, former employers, years of experience and schools attended. This has caused many to adapt resume optimization techniques similar to those used in search engine optimization when creating and formatting their résumé.

Exam Probability: **Low**

30. *Answer choices:*

(see index for correct answer)

- a. Applicant tracking system
- b. Cross-functional team
- c. Emotional labor
- d. Flextime

Guidance: level 1

:: Behavior ::

_________ refers to behavior-change procedures that were employed during the 1970s and early 1980s. Based on methodological behaviorism, overt behavior was modified with presumed consequences, including artificial positive and negative reinforcement contingencies to increase desirable behavior, or administering positive and negative punishment and/or extinction to reduce problematic behavior. For the treatment of phobias, habituation and punishment were the basic principles used in flooding, a subcategory of desensitization.

Exam Probability: **Medium**

31. *Answer choices:*

(see index for correct answer)

- a. theory of reasoned action
- b. Behavior modification

Guidance: level 1

:: Learning methods ::

_________ is an approach to problem solving. It involves taking action and reflecting upon the results. This helps improve the problem-solving process as well as simplify the solutions developed by the team.

Exam Probability: **High**

32. *Answer choices:*

(see index for correct answer)

- a. double loop learning
- b. Collaborative learning
- c. Double-loop learning
- d. Audience response system

Guidance: level 1

:: Job interview ::

A __________ is a job interview in which the applicant is presented with a challenging business scenario that he/she must investigate and propose a solution to. __________ s are designed to test the candidate`s analytical skills and "soft" skills within a realistic business context. The case is often a business situation or a business case that the interviewer has worked on in real life.

Exam Probability: **Medium**

33. *Answer choices:*

(see index for correct answer)

- a. Case interview
- b. Mock interview
- c. Programming interview
- d. SOARA

Guidance: level 1

:: Labor rights ::

The _________ is the concept that people have a human _________ , or engage in productive employment, and may not be prevented from doing so. The _________ is enshrined in the Universal Declaration of Human Rights and recognized in international human rights law through its inclusion in the International Covenant on Economic, Social and Cultural Rights, where the _________ emphasizes economic, social and cultural development.

Exam Probability: **Low**

34. *Answer choices:*

(see index for correct answer)

- a. The Hyatt 100
- b. Swift raids
- c. Grievance
- d. Right to work

Guidance: level 1

:: Power (social and political) ::

In a notable study of power conducted by social psychologists John R. P. French and Bertram Raven in 1959, power is divided into five separate and distinct forms. In 1965 Raven revised this model to include a sixth form by separating the informational power base as distinct from the _________ base.

Exam Probability: **Medium**

35. *Answer choices:*

(see index for correct answer)

- a. Hard power
- b. need for power
- c. Expert power

Guidance: level 1

:: ::

_________ is an experience a person may have when one moves to a cultural environment which is different from one`s own; it is also the personal disorientation a person may feel when experiencing an unfamiliar way of life due to immigration or a visit to a new country, a move between social environments, or simply transition to another type of life. One of the most common causes of _________ involves individuals in a foreign environment. _________ can be described as consisting of at least one of four distinct phases: honeymoon, negotiation, adjustment, and adaptation.

Exam Probability: **Low**

36. *Answer choices:*

(see index for correct answer)

- a. interpersonal communication
- b. Culture shock
- c. hierarchical
- d. hierarchical perspective

Guidance: level 1

:: Business law ::

A _________ is an arrangement where parties, known as partners, agree to cooperate to advance their mutual interests. The partners in a _________ may be individuals, businesses, interest-based organizations, schools, governments or combinations. Organizations may partner to increase the likelihood of each achieving their mission and to amplify their reach. A _________ may result in issuing and holding equity or may be only governed by a contract.

Exam Probability: **Low**

37. *Answer choices:*

(see index for correct answer)

- a. Consumer privacy
- b. Partnership
- c. Lessor
- d. Arbitration award

Guidance: level 1

:: Financial statements ::

In financial accounting, a _________ or statement of financial position or statement of financial condition is a summary of the financial balances of an individual or organization, whether it be a sole proprietorship, a business partnership, a corporation, private limited company or other organization such as Government or not-for-profit entity. Assets, liabilities and ownership equity are listed as of a specific date, such as the end of its financial year. A _________ is often described as a "snapshot of a company`s financial condition". Of the four basic financial statements, the _________ is the only statement which applies to a single point in time of a business` calendar year.

Exam Probability: **Medium**

38. *Answer choices:*

(see index for correct answer)

- a. quarterly report
- b. Clean surplus accounting
- c. Balance sheet
- d. Quarterly finance report

Guidance: level 1

:: Employment compensation ::

A __________ , also known as a flexible spending arrangement, is one of a number of tax-advantaged financial accounts, resulting in payroll tax savings. Before the Patient Protection and Affordable Care Act, one significant disadvantage to using an FSA was that funds not used by the end of the plan year were forfeited to the employer, known as the "use it or lose it" rule. Under the terms of the Affordable Care Act, a plan may permit an employee to carry over up to $500 into the following year without losing the funds.

Exam Probability: **High**

39. *Answer choices:*

(see index for correct answer)

- a. Employee benefit
- b. executive stock option
- c. Lilly Ledbetter Fair Pay Act of 2009
- d. Flexible spending account

Guidance: level 1

:: International trade ::

_________ or globalisation is the process of interaction and integration among people, companies, and governments worldwide. As a complex and multifaceted phenomenon, _________ is considered by some as a form of capitalist expansion which entails the integration of local and national economies into a global, unregulated market economy. _________ has grown due to advances in transportation and communication technology. With the increased global interactions comes the growth of international trade, ideas, and culture. _________ is primarily an economic process of interaction and integration that`s associated with social and cultural aspects. However, conflicts and diplomacy are also large parts of the history of _________, and modern _________.

Exam Probability: **Medium**

40. *Answer choices:*

(see index for correct answer)

- a. Globalization
- b. Mutual recognition agreement
- c. Section 201
- d. Invisible balance

Guidance: level 1

:: Business ethics ::

__________ is a type of harassment technique that relates to a sexual nature and the unwelcome or inappropriate promise of rewards in exchange for sexual favors. __________ includes a range of actions from mild transgressions to sexual abuse or assault. Harassment can occur in many different social settings such as the workplace, the home, school, churches, etc. Harassers or victims may be of any gender.

Exam Probability: **High**

41. *Answer choices:*

(see index for correct answer)

- a. Earnings quality
- b. Sexual harassment
- c. Unfree labour
- d. Pension spiking

Guidance: level 1

:: Labour relations ::

A bargaining __________ occurs when the two sides negotiating an agreement are unable to reach an agreement and become deadlocked. An __________ is almost invariably mutually harmful, either as a result of direct action which may be taken such as a strike in employment negotiation or sanctions/military action in international relations, or simply due to the resulting delay in negotiating a mutually beneficial agreement. The word __________ may also refer to any situation in which no progress can be made. __________s provide opportunities for problem solving to provide an insight that leads to progress.

Exam Probability: **Low**

42. *Answer choices:*

(see index for correct answer)

- a. Review Body
- b. Broad left
- c. Impasse
- d. Negotiated cartelism

Guidance: level 1

:: ::

The _________ or labour force is the labour pool in employment. It is generally used to describe those working for a single company or industry, but can also apply to a geographic region like a city, state, or country. Within a company, its value can be labelled as its " _________ in Place". The _________ of a country includes both the employed and the unemployed. The labour force participation rate, LFPR , is the ratio between the labour force and the overall size of their cohort . The term generally excludes the employers or management, and can imply those involved in manual labour. It may also mean all those who are available for work.

Exam Probability: **Low**

43. *Answer choices:*

(see index for correct answer)

- a. similarity-attraction theory
- b. Character
- c. Workforce
- d. levels of analysis

Guidance: level 1

:: Organizational behavior ::

__________ is the act of matching attitudes, beliefs, and behaviors to group norms or politics. Norms are implicit, specific rules, shared by a group of individuals, that guide their interactions with others. People often choose to conform to society rather than to pursue personal desires because it is often easier to follow the path others have made already, rather than creating a new one. This tendency to conform occurs in small groups and/or society as a whole, and may result from subtle unconscious influences , or direct and overt social pressure. __________ can occur in the presence of others, or when an individual is alone. For example, people tend to follow social norms when eating or watching television, even when alone.

Exam Probability: **Medium**

44. *Answer choices:*

(see index for correct answer)

- a. Organizational retaliatory behavior
- b. Conformity
- c. Organizational Expedience
- d. Behavioral systems analysis

Guidance: level 1

:: Working time ::

The shift plan, rota or roster is the central component of a shift schedule in shift work. The schedule includes considerations of shift overlap, shift change times and alignment with the clock, vacation, training, shift differentials, holidays, etc. The shift plan determines the sequence of work and free days within a shift system.

Exam Probability: **Medium**

45. *Answer choices:*

(see index for correct answer)

- a. Presenteeism
- b. Forty-Hour Week Convention, 1935
- c. Graveyard shift
- d. Bunting v. Oregon

Guidance: level 1

:: Industrial relations ::

_________ or employee satisfaction is a measure of workers` contentedness with their job, whether or not they like the job or individual aspects or facets of jobs, such as nature of work or supervision. _________ can be measured in cognitive , affective , and behavioral components. Researchers have also noted that _________ measures vary in the extent to which they measure feelings about the job . or cognitions about the job .

Exam Probability: **Low**

46. *Answer choices:*

(see index for correct answer)

- a. Workforce Investment Board
- b. Industrial violence
- c. Injury prevention
- d. European Journal of Industrial Relations

Guidance: level 1

:: Labor ::

_________ refers to the process of grouping activities into departments. Division of labour creates specialists who need coordination. This coordination is facilitated by grouping specialists together in departments.

Exam Probability: **Medium**

47. *Answer choices:*

(see index for correct answer)

- a. Departmentalization
- b. Affective labor
- c. Labor pool
- d. Motorman

Guidance: level 1

:: Trade unions in the United States ::

_________ is a labor union in the United States and Canada with roughly 300,000 active members. The union`s members work predominantly in the hotel, food service, laundry, warehouse, and casino gaming industries. The union was formed in 2004 by the merger of Union of Needletrades, Industrial, and Textile Employees and Hotel Employees and Restaurant Employees Union .

Exam Probability: **High**

48. *Answer choices:*

(see index for correct answer)

- a. League of Independent Workers of the San Joaquin Valley
- b. UNITE HERE
- c. The Animation Guild, I.A.T.S.E. Local 839
- d. Working for America Institute

Guidance: level 1

:: ::

An __________ is a process where candidates are examined to determine their suitability for specific types of employment, especially management or military command. The candidates` personality and aptitudes are determined by techniques including interviews, group exercises, presentations, examinations and psychometric testing.

Exam Probability: **Low**

49. *Answer choices:*

(see index for correct answer)

- a. surface-level diversity
- b. Assessment center
- c. hierarchical
- d. empathy

Guidance: level 1

:: Employment compensation ::

Compensation and benefits is a sub-discipline of human resources, focused on employee compensation and benefits policy-making. While compensation and benefits are tangible, there are intangible rewards such as recognition, work-life and development. Combined, these are referred to as _________ s . The term "compensation and benefits" refers to the discipline as well as the rewards themselves.

Exam Probability: **Low**

50. *Answer choices:*

(see index for correct answer)

- a. Uninsured employer
- b. Sliding wage scale
- c. Employee stock option
- d. Thirteenth salary

Guidance: level 1

:: ::

A _________ , covering letter, motivation letter, motivational letter or a letter of motivation is a letter of introduction attached to, or accompanying another document such as a résumé or curriculum vitae.

Exam Probability: **High**

51. *Answer choices:*

(see index for correct answer)

- a. personal values
- b. Cover letter
- c. process perspective
- d. imperative

Guidance: level 1

:: Employee relations ::

_________ ownership, or employee share ownership, is an ownership interest in a company held by the company`s workforce. The ownership interest may be facilitated by the company as part of employees` remuneration or incentive compensation for work performed, or the company itself may be employee owned.

Exam Probability: **Low**

52. *Answer choices:*

(see index for correct answer)

- a. Employee stock
- b. Employee motivation
- c. employee stock ownership
- d. Employee morale

Guidance: level 1

:: Employment compensation ::

_________ s is a method for companies to give their management or employees a bonus if the company performs well financially. Such a method is called a `plan`. SARs resemble employee stock options in that the holder/employee benefits from an increase in stock price. They differ from options in that the holder/employee does not have to purchase anything to receive the proceeds. They are not required to pay the exercise price, but just receive the amount of the increase in cash or stock.

Exam Probability: **High**

53. *Answer choices:*

(see index for correct answer)

- a. Wages for housework
- b. Equal Pay Act 1970
- c. Stock appreciation right
- d. Pay scale

Guidance: level 1

:: Employment compensation ::

An ________ is an employee benefit program that assists employees with personal problems and/or work-related problems that may impact their job performance, health, mental and emotional well-being. EAPs generally offer free and confidential assessments, short-term counseling, referrals, and follow-up services for employees and their household members. EAP counselors also work in a consultative role with managers and supervisors to address employee and organizational challenges and needs. Many corporations, academic institution and/or government agencies are active in helping organizations prevent and cope with workplace violence, trauma, and other emergency response situations. There is a variety of support programs offered for employees. Even though EAPs are mainly aimed at work-related problems, there are a variety of programs that can assist with problems outside of the workplace. EAPs have grown over the years, and are more desirable economically and socially.

Exam Probability: **Medium**

54. *Answer choices:*

(see index for correct answer)

- a. Streamlining Claims Processing for Federal Contractor Employees Act
- b. Workers Compensation Act 1987
- c. Employee assistance program
- d. Employees%27 Compensation Appeals Board

Guidance: level 1

:: Human resource management ::

A __________ is an outsourcing firm which provides services to small and medium sized businesses . Typically, the PEO offering may include human resource consulting, safety and risk mitigation services, payroll processing, employer payroll tax filing, workers` compensation insurance, health benefits, employers` practice and liability insurance , retirement vehicles , regulatory compliance assistance, workforce management technology, and training and development. The PEO enters into a contractual co-employment agreement with its clientele. Through co-employment, the PEO becomes the employer of record for tax purposes through filing payroll taxes under its own tax identification numbers.

Exam Probability: **Low**

55. *Answer choices:*

(see index for correct answer)

- a. Job enlargement
- b. Open plan
- c. Job knowledge
- d. Up or out

Guidance: level 1

:: Industrial agreements ::

A _________, in labor relations, is a group of employees with a clear and identifiable community of interests who are represented by a single labor union in collective bargaining and other dealings with management. Examples would be non-management professors, law enforcement professionals, blue-collar workers, clerical and administrative employees, etc. Geographic location as well as the number of facilities included in _________ s can be at issue during representation cases.

Exam Probability: **High**

56. *Answer choices:*

(see index for correct answer)

- a. Federal Labor Relations Act
- b. Bargaining unit
- c. McCrone Agreement
- d. Court of Arbitration

Guidance: level 1

:: Minimum wage ::

A _________ is the lowest remuneration that employers can legally pay their workers—the price floor below which workers may not sell their labor. Most countries had introduced _________ legislation by the end of the 20th century.

Exam Probability: **High**

57. *Answer choices:*

(see index for correct answer)

- a. National Anti-Sweating League
- b. Minimum wage in Taiwan
- c. Minimum Wage Fairness Act
- d. Minimum wage

Guidance: level 1

:: Termination of employment ::

The _________ of 1988 is a US labor law which protects employees, their families, and communities by requiring most employers with 100 or more employees to provide 60 calendar-day advance notification of plant closings and mass layoffs of employees, as defined in the Act. In 2001, there were about 2,000 mass layoffs and plant closures which were subject to WARN advance notice requirements and which affected about 660,000 employees.

Exam Probability: **High**

58. *Answer choices:*

(see index for correct answer)

- a. The Disposable American
- b. Luis Gabriel Aguilera
- c. Pink slip
- d. Termination of Employment Convention, 1982

Guidance: level 1

:: Human resource management ::

_________ is the corporate management term for the act of reorganizing the legal, ownership, operational, or other structures of a company for the purpose of making it more profitable, or better organized for its present needs. Other reasons for _________ include a change of ownership or ownership structure, demerger, or a response to a crisis or major change in the business such as bankruptcy, repositioning, or buyout. _________ may also be described as corporate _________, debt _________ and financial _________.

Exam Probability: **High**

59. *Answer choices:*

(see index for correct answer)

- a. Perceived organizational support
- b. Hemsley Fraser
- c. Employee retention
- d. Vendor management system

Guidance: level 1

Information systems

Information systems (IS) are formal, sociotechnical, organizational systems designed to collect, process, store, and distribute information. In a sociotechnical perspective Information Systems are composed by four components: technology, process, people and organizational structure.

:: Information systems ::

__________ are formal, sociotechnical, organizational systems designed to collect, process, store, and distribute information. In a sociotechnical perspective, __________ are composed by four components: task, people, structure , and technology.

Exam Probability: **Medium**

1. *Answer choices:*

(see index for correct answer)

- a. Information systems
- b. ISCRAM
- c. CreditorWatch
- d. Control flow diagram

Guidance: level 1

:: Business models ::

__________ , or The Computer Utility, is a service provisioning model in which a service provider makes computing resources and infrastructure management available to the customer as needed, and charges them for specific usage rather than a flat rate. Like other types of on-demand computing , the utility model seeks to maximize the efficient use of resources and/or minimize associated costs. Utility is the packaging of system resources, such as computation, storage and services, as a metered service. This model has the advantage of a low or no initial cost to acquire computer resources; instead, resources are essentially rented.

Exam Probability: **High**

2. *Answer choices:*

(see index for correct answer)

- a. Home business
- b. Utility computing
- c. Freemium
- d. One stop shop

Guidance: level 1

:: Human–computer interaction ::

_________ is the ease of use and learnability of a human-made object such as a tool or device. In software engineering, _________ is the degree to which a software can be used by specified consumers to achieve quantified objectives with effectiveness, efficiency, and satisfaction in a quantified context of use.

Exam Probability: **High**

3. *Answer choices:*

(see index for correct answer)

- a. Wikirating
- b. Cognitive ergonomics
- c. Wizard of Oz experiment
- d. Usability

Guidance: level 1

:: Transaction processing ::

In _________ , information systems typically facilitate and manage transaction-oriented applications.

Exam Probability: **Low**

4. *Answer choices:*

(see index for correct answer)

- a. Change vector
- b. Transactions per second
- c. Online transaction processing
- d. WS-Transaction

Guidance: level 1

:: Credit cards ::

The _________ Company, also known as Amex, is an American multinational financial services corporation headquartered in Three World Financial Center in New York City. The company was founded in 1850 and is one of the 30 components of the Dow Jones Industrial Average. The company is best known for its charge card, credit card, and traveler`s cheque businesses.

Exam Probability: **Low**

5. *Answer choices:*

(see index for correct answer)

- a. Credit Saison
- b. OnePulse
- c. Accolades Card
- d. Universal Air Travel Plan

Guidance: level 1

:: ::

A __________ is a research instrument consisting of a series of questions for the purpose of gathering information from respondents. The __________ was invented by the Statistical Society of London in 1838.

Exam Probability: **High**

6. *Answer choices:*

(see index for correct answer)

- a. cultural
- b. imperative
- c. co-culture
- d. Questionnaire

Guidance: level 1

:: SQL ::

SQL is a domain-specific language used in programming and designed for managing data held in a relational database management system , or for stream processing in a relational data stream management system . It is particularly useful in handling structured data where there are relations between different entities/variables of the data. SQL offers two main advantages over older read/write APIs like ISAM or VSAM. First, it introduced the concept of accessing many records with one single command; and second, it eliminates the need to specify how to reach a record, e.g. with or without an index.

Exam Probability: **Medium**

7. *Answer choices:*

(see index for correct answer)

- a. SQL/XML
- b. Hint
- c. SQL/Schemata
- d. Structured type

Guidance: level 1

:: ::

Collaborative software or _________ is application software designed to help people involved in a common task to achieve their goals. One of the earliest definitions of collaborative software is "intentional group processes plus software to support them".

Exam Probability: **Low**

8. *Answer choices:*

(see index for correct answer)

- a. levels of analysis
- b. co-culture
- c. Groupware
- d. information systems assessment

Guidance: level 1

:: Enterprise modelling ::

_________ are large-scale application software packages that support business processes, information flows, reporting, and data analytics in complex organizations. While ES are generally packaged enterprise application software systems they can also be bespoke, custom developed systems created to support a specific organization`s needs.

Exam Probability: **Low**

9. *Answer choices:*

(see index for correct answer)

- a. Enterprise systems
- b. IDEF0
- c. Application Portability Profile
- d. Open-system environment reference model

Guidance: level 1

:: Cloud storage ::

_________ was an online backup service for both Windows and macOS users. Linux support was made available in Q3, 2014. In 2007 _________ was acquired by EMC, and in 2013 _________ was included in the EMC Backup Recovery Systems division's product list.On September 7, 2016, Dell Inc. acquired EMC Corporation to form Dell Technologies, restructuring the original Dell Inc. as a subsidiary of Dell Technologies.. On March 19, 2018 Carbonite acquired _________ from Dell for $148.5 million in cash and in 2019 shut down the service, incorporating _________'s clients into its own online backup service programs.

Exam Probability: **High**

10. *Answer choices:*

(see index for correct answer)

- a. LIBOX
- b. Mozy

- c. Video spokesperson
- d. GreenButton

Guidance: level 1

:: Data transmission ::

In telecommunications and computing, _________ is the number of bits that are conveyed or processed per unit of time.

Exam Probability: **High**

11. *Answer choices:*

(see index for correct answer)

- a. Wiegand interface
- b. Parallel communication
- c. Bit rate
- d. Buffer underrun

Guidance: level 1

:: Data management ::

_________ means protecting digital data, such as those in a database, from destructive forces and from the unwanted actions of unauthorized users, such as a cyberattack or a data breach.

Exam Probability: **Medium**

12. *Answer choices:*

(see index for correct answer)

- a. Nested transaction
- b. Data management
- c. Data security
- d. Enterprise bus matrix

Guidance: level 1

:: Business models ::

_________, a portmanteau of the words "free" and "premium", is a pricing strategy by which a product or service is provided free of charge, but money is charged for additional features, services, or virtual or physical goods. The business model has been in use by the software industry since the 1980s as a licensing scheme. A subset of this model used by the video game industry is called free-to-play.

Exam Probability: **Medium**

13. *Answer choices:*

(see index for correct answer)

- a. Lawyers on Demand
- b. Artel
- c. Co-operative economics
- d. Brainsworking

Guidance: level 1

:: Information technology organisations ::

The Internet Corporation for Assigned Names and Numbers is a nonprofit organization responsible for coordinating the maintenance and procedures of several databases related to the namespaces and numerical spaces of the Internet, ensuring the network`s stable and secure operation. _________ performs the actual technical maintenance work of the Central Internet Address pools and DNS root zone registries pursuant to the Internet Assigned Numbers Authority function contract. The contract regarding the IANA stewardship functions between _________ and the National Telecommunications and Information Administration of the United States Department of Commerce ended on October 1, 2016, formally transitioning the functions to the global multistakeholder community.

Exam Probability: **Low**

14. *Answer choices:*

(see index for correct answer)

- a. ICANN
- b. Federation Against Copyright Theft
- c. Information Technology Association of America
- d. BytesForAll

Guidance: level 1

:: Sensitivity analysis ::

__________ is the study of how the uncertainty in the output of a mathematical model or system can be divided and allocated to different sources of uncertainty in its inputs. A related practice is uncertainty analysis, which has a greater focus on uncertainty quantification and propagation of uncertainty; ideally, uncertainty and __________ should be run in tandem.

Exam Probability: **Medium**

15. *Answer choices:*

(see index for correct answer)

- a. Fourier amplitude sensitivity testing
- b. Sensitivity analysis
- c. Elementary effects method
- d. Variance-based sensitivity analysis

Guidance: level 1

:: Reputation management ::

_________ refers to the influencing and controlling of an individual`s or group`s reputation. Originally a public relations term, the growth of the internet and social media, along with _________ companies, have made search results a core part of an individual`s or group`s reputation. Online _________ , sometimes abbreviated as ORM, focuses on the management of product and service search website results. Ethical grey areas include mug shot removal sites, astroturfing customer review sites, censoring negative complaints, and using search engine optimization tactics to influence results.

Exam Probability: **Low**

16. *Answer choices:*

(see index for correct answer)

- a. Trust metric
- b. Meta-moderation system
- c. Reputation management
- d. Yasni

Guidance: level 1

:: ::

A __________ is a system designed to capture, store, manipulate, analyze, manage, and present spatial or geographic data. GIS applications are tools that allow users to create interactive queries , analyze spatial information, edit data in maps, and present the results of all these operations. GIS sometimes refers to geographic information science , the science underlying geographic concepts, applications, and systems.

Exam Probability: **Low**

17. *Answer choices:*

(see index for correct answer)

- a. functional perspective
- b. Geographic information system
- c. surface-level diversity
- d. information systems assessment

Guidance: level 1

:: ::

__________ is software designed to perform a group of coordinated functions, tasks, or activities for the benefit of the user. Examples of an application include a word processor, a spreadsheet, an accounting application, a web browser, an email client,a media player, a file viewer, an aeronautical flight simulator, a console game or a photo editor. The collective noun __________ refers to all applications collectively. This contrasts with system software, which is mainly involved with running the computer.

Exam Probability: **Low**

18. *Answer choices:*

(see index for correct answer)

- a. corporate values
- b. Application software
- c. interpersonal communication
- d. co-culture

Guidance: level 1

:: ::

A __________ is an abstract model that organizes elements of data and standardizes how they relate to one another and to properties of the real world entities. For instance, a __________ may specify that the data element representing a car be composed of a number of other elements which, in turn, represent the color and size of the car and define its owner.

Exam Probability: **Low**

19. *Answer choices:*

(see index for correct answer)

- a. Data model
- b. cultural

- c. Character
- d. deep-level diversity

Guidance: level 1

:: Marketing ::

__________ , in marketing, manufacturing, call centres and management, is the use of flexible computer-aided manufacturing systems to produce custom output. Such systems combine the low unit costs of mass production processes with the flexibility of individual customization.

Exam Probability: **High**

20. *Answer choices:*

(see index for correct answer)

- a. Matomy Media
- b. Mass customization
- c. Personalized marketing
- d. Promise marketing

Guidance: level 1

:: Information technology management ::

_________ concerns a cycle of organizational activity: the acquisition of information from one or more sources, the custodianship and the distribution of that information to those who need it, and its ultimate disposition through archiving or deletion.

Exam Probability: **Low**

21. *Answer choices:*

(see index for correct answer)

- a. IT risk management
- b. Infra Corporation
- c. Information management
- d. Enterprise information management

Guidance: level 1

:: Data management ::

_________ is "data [information] that provides information about other data". Many distinct types of _________ exist, among these descriptive _________, structural _________, administrative _________, reference _________ and statistical _________.

Exam Probability: **Medium**

22. *Answer choices:*

(see index for correct answer)

- a. Data proliferation
- b. Clustered file system
- c. Metadata
- d. Bitmap index

Guidance: level 1

:: E-commerce ::

_________ is a method of e-commerce where shoppers` friends become involved in the shopping experience. _________ attempts to use technology to mimic the social interactions found in physical malls and stores. With the rise of mobile devices, _________ is now extending beyond the online world and into the offline world of shopping.

Exam Probability: **Low**

23. *Answer choices:*

(see index for correct answer)

- a. Mobify
- b. Social shopping
- c. Shopping directory
- d. Government-to-employees

Guidance: level 1

:: ::

The __________ is a unit of digital information that most commonly consists of eight bits, representing a binary number. Historically, the __________ was the number of bits used to encode a single character of text in a computer and for this reason it is the smallest addressable unit of memory in many computer architectures.

Exam Probability: **Medium**

24. *Answer choices:*

(see index for correct answer)

- a. Character
- b. deep-level diversity
- c. process perspective
- d. functional perspective

Guidance: level 1

:: Computer data ::

In computer science, _________ is the ability to access an arbitrary element of a sequence in equal time or any datum from a population of addressable elements roughly as easily and efficiently as any other, no matter how many elements may be in the set. It is typically contrasted to sequential access.

Exam Probability: **Medium**

25. *Answer choices:*

(see index for correct answer)

- a. Data efficiency
- b. Seed loading
- c. WinHex
- d. JBOB

Guidance: level 1

:: Telecommunication theory ::

In reliability theory and reliability engineering, the term _________ has the following meanings.

Exam Probability: **Medium**

26. *Answer choices:*

(see index for correct answer)

- a. Transactive communication
- b. Phase perturbation
- c. Availability
- d. Critical frequency

Guidance: level 1

:: Computing input devices ::

In computing, an __________ is a piece of computer hardware equipment used to provide data and control signals to an information processing system such as a computer or information appliance. Examples of __________ s include keyboards, mouse, scanners, digital cameras and joysticks. Audio __________ s may be used for purposes including speech recognition. Many companies are utilizing speech recognition to help assist users to use their device.

Exam Probability: **High**

27. *Answer choices:*

(see index for correct answer)

- a. Input device
- b. Ofoto
- c. CueCat
- d. Light pen

Guidance: level 1

:: Information technology management ::

__________ s or pop-ups are forms of online advertising on the World Wide Web. A pop-up is a graphical user interface display area, usually a small window, that suddenly appears in the foreground of the visual interface. The pop-up window containing an advertisement is usually generated by JavaScript that uses cross-site scripting , sometimes with a secondary payload that uses Adobe Flash. They can also be generated by other vulnerabilities/security holes in browser security.

Exam Probability: **Low**

28. *Answer choices:*

(see index for correct answer)

- a. People Capability Maturity Model
- b. Early-arriving fact
- c. Business-to-business
- d. Knowledge management software

Guidance: level 1

:: Commerce websites ::

__________ is an American classified advertisements website with sections devoted to jobs, housing, for sale, items wanted, services, community service, gigs, résumés, and discussion forums.

Exam Probability: **Low**

29. *Answer choices:*

(see index for correct answer)

- a. DE Photo
- b. Craigslist
- c. Mobile17
- d. 1-800-Flowers

Guidance: level 1

:: Marketing ::

__________ is a business model in which consumers create value and businesses consume that value. For example, when a consumer writes reviews or when a consumer gives a useful idea for new product development then that consumer is creating value for the business if the business adopts the input. In the C2B model, a reverse auction or demand collection model, enables buyers to name or demand their own price, which is often binding, for a specific good or service. Inside of a consumer to business market the roles involved in the transaction must be established and the consumer must offer something of value to the business.

Exam Probability: **Medium**

30. *Answer choices:*

(see index for correct answer)

- a. Immersion marketing
- b. Interactive collateral management
- c. Commodity chain
- d. Consumer-to-business

Guidance: level 1

:: Data management ::

_________ s or data _________ s are computer languages used to make queries in databases and information systems.

Exam Probability: **Medium**

31. *Answer choices:*

(see index for correct answer)

- a. Virtual data room
- b. Junction table
- c. XLDB
- d. Query language

Guidance: level 1

:: Stochastic processes ::

_________ in its modern meaning is a "new idea, creative thoughts, new imaginations in form of device or method". _________ is often also viewed as the application of better solutions that meet new requirements, unarticulated needs, or existing market needs. Such _________ takes place through the provision of more-effective products, processes, services, technologies, or business models that are made available to markets, governments and society. An _________ is something original and more effective and, as a consequence, new, that "breaks into" the market or society. _________ is related to, but not the same as, invention, as _________ is more apt to involve the practical implementation of an invention to make a meaningful impact in the market or society, and not all _________ s require an invention. _________ often manifests itself via the engineering process, when the problem being solved is of a technical or scientific nature. The opposite of _________ is exnovation.

Exam Probability: **Low**

32. *Answer choices:*

(see index for correct answer)

- a. Markov model
- b. M/D/c queue
- c. Innovation
- d. Continuous stochastic process

Guidance: level 1

:: Automatic identification and data capture ::

__________ uses electromagnetic fields to automatically identify and track tags attached to objects. The tags contain electronically stored information. Passive tags collect energy from a nearby RFID reader`s interrogating radio waves. Active tags have a local power source and may operate hundreds of meters from the RFID reader. Unlike a barcode, the tag need not be within the line of sight of the reader, so it may be embedded in the tracked object. RFID is one method of automatic identification and data capture .

Exam Probability: **High**

33. *Answer choices:*

(see index for correct answer)

- a. Molecular computational identification
- b. Direct TPMS
- c. Radio-frequency identification
- d. Automatic number plate recognition

Guidance: level 1

:: Information systems ::

__________ s are information systems that are developed in response to corporate business initiative. They are intended to give competitive advantage to the organization. They may deliver a product or service that is at a lower cost, that is differentiated, that focuses on a particular market segment, or is innovative.

Exam Probability: **Low**

34. *Answer choices:*

(see index for correct answer)

- a. Virtual USA
- b. STARLIMS
- c. TOPS
- d. Internavi

Guidance: level 1

:: ::

A __________ or data centre is a building, dedicated space within a building, or a group of buildings used to house computer systems and associated components, such as telecommunications and storage systems.

Exam Probability: **Low**

35. *Answer choices:*

(see index for correct answer)

- a. deep-level diversity
- b. hierarchical
- c. Data center
- d. functional perspective

Guidance: level 1

:: Management ::

__________ is the identification of an organization`s assets , followed by the development, documentation, and implementation of policies and procedures for protecting these assets.

Exam Probability: **Low**

36. *Answer choices:*

(see index for correct answer)

- a. Overtime rate
- b. Enterprise decision management
- c. Security management
- d. Pareto analysis

Guidance: level 1

:: Customer relationship management software ::

_________ Software Corporation is a Global Business Software company based in Austin, TX and was founded in 1972. Its products are aimed at the manufacturing, distribution, retail and services industries.

Exam Probability: **Medium**

37. *Answer choices:*

(see index for correct answer)

- a. Introhive
- b. Epicor
- c. 24SevenOffice
- d. Kayako

Guidance: level 1

:: Virtual economies ::

_________ Inc. is an American social game developer running social video game services founded in April 2007 and headquartered in San Francisco, California, United States. The company primarily focuses on mobile and social networking platforms. _________ states its mission as "connecting the world through games."

Exam Probability: **Low**

38. *Answer choices:*

(see index for correct answer)

- a. Shattered World
- b. Zynga
- c. TirNua
- d. Monopoly money

Guidance: level 1

:: Network analyzers ::

A __________ , meaning "meat eater" , is an organism that derives its energy and nutrient requirements from a diet consisting mainly or exclusively of animal tissue, whether through predation or scavenging. Animals that depend solely on animal flesh for their nutrient requirements are called obligate __________ s while those that also consume non-animal food are called facultative __________ s. Omnivores also consume both animal and non-animal food, and, apart from the more general definition, there is no clearly defined ratio of plant to animal material that would distinguish a facultative __________ from an omnivore. A __________ at the top of the food chain, not preyed upon by other animals, is termed an apex predator.

Exam Probability: **Medium**

39. *Answer choices:*

(see index for correct answer)

- a. PathPing

- b. Carnivore
- c. AirSnort
- d. Weplab

Guidance: level 1

:: E-commerce ::

Customer to customer markets provide an innovative way to allow customers to interact with each other. Traditional markets require business to customer relationships, in which a customer goes to the business in order to purchase a product or service. In customer to customer markets, the business facilitates an environment where customers can sell goods or services to each other. Other types of markets include business to business and business to customer .

Exam Probability: **Low**

40. *Answer choices:*

(see index for correct answer)

- a. Typhoid adware
- b. Notice and take down
- c. Consumer-to-consumer
- d. Buyhatke

Guidance: level 1

:: Web security exploits ::

A _________ is a baked or cooked food that is small, flat and sweet. It usually contains flour, sugar and some type of oil or fat. It may include other ingredients such as raisins, oats, chocolate chips, nuts, etc.

Exam Probability: **High**

41. *Answer choices:*

(see index for correct answer)

- a. PLA Unit 61398
- b. Reflected DOM Injection
- c. Cookie
- d. Browser exploit

Guidance: level 1

:: Survey methodology ::

A _________ is the procedure of systematically acquiring and recording information about the members of a given population. The term is used mostly in connection with national population and housing _________ es; other common _________ es include agriculture, business, and traffic _________ es. The United Nations defines the essential features of population and housing _________ es as "individual enumeration, universality within a defined territory, simultaneity and defined periodicity", and recommends that population _________ es be taken at least every 10 years. United Nations recommendations also cover _________ topics to be collected, official definitions, classifications and other useful information to co-ordinate international practice.

Exam Probability: **Medium**

42. *Answer choices:*

(see index for correct answer)

- a. Sampling
- b. Survey research
- c. Census
- d. American Association for Public Opinion Research

Guidance: level 1

:: E-commerce ::

The phrase _________ was originally coined in 1997 by Kevin Duffey at the launch of the Global _________ Forum, to mean "the delivery of electronic commerce capabilities directly into the consumer's hand, anywhere, via wireless technology." Many choose to think of _________ as meaning "a retail outlet in your customer's pocket."

Exam Probability: **High**

43. *Answer choices:*

(see index for correct answer)

- a. Online food ordering
- b. Government-to-employees
- c. Mobile commerce
- d. Digital wallet

Guidance: level 1

:: Internet advertising ::

_________ , according to the United States federal law known as the Anti _________ Consumer Protection Act, is registering, trafficking in, or using an Internet domain name with bad faith intent to profit from the goodwill of a trademark belonging to someone else. The cybersquatter then offers to sell the domain to the person or company who owns a trademark contained within the name at an inflated price.

Exam Probability: **Medium**

44. *Answer choices:*

(see index for correct answer)

- a. Deep linking
- b. CyberThrill
- c. Filterset.G
- d. LeadBolt

Guidance: level 1

:: Google services ::

__________ is a web mapping service developed by Google. It offers satellite imagery, aerial photography, street maps, 360° panoramic views of streets , real-time traffic conditions, and route planning for traveling by foot, car, bicycle and air , or public transportation.

Exam Probability: **Low**

45. *Answer choices:*

(see index for correct answer)

- a. Gizmo5
- b. Google WiFi
- c. Google Mobile Services
- d. A Google A Day

Guidance: level 1

:: Data ::

In computer main memory, auxiliary storage and computer buses, _________ is the existence of data that is additional to the actual data and permits correction of errors in stored or transmitted data. The additional data can simply be a complete copy of the actual data, or only select pieces of data that allow detection of errors and reconstruction of lost or damaged data up to a certain level.

Exam Probability: **High**

46. *Answer choices:*

(see index for correct answer)

- a. Statistics
- b. Data Transmission
- c. Sonar
- d. Data citation

Guidance: level 1

:: Data analysis ::

__________ , also referred to as text data mining, roughly equivalent to text analytics, is the process of deriving high-quality information from text. High-quality information is typically derived through the devising of patterns and trends through means such as statistical pattern learning. __________ usually involves the process of structuring the input text , deriving patterns within the structured data, and finally evaluation and interpretation of the output. `High quality` in __________ usually refers to some combination of relevance, novelty, and interest. Typical __________ tasks include text categorization, text clustering, concept/entity extraction, production of granular taxonomies, sentiment analysis, document summarization, and entity relation modeling .

Exam Probability: **Medium**

47. *Answer choices:*

(see index for correct answer)

- a. Multiple correspondence analysis
- b. Outlier
- c. Double mass analysis
- d. Text mining

Guidance: level 1

:: Database management systems ::

A __________ is a type of data model that determines the logical structure of a database and fundamentally determines in which manner data can be stored, organized and manipulated. The most popular example of a __________ is the relational model, which uses a table-based format.

Exam Probability: **High**

48. *Answer choices:*

(see index for correct answer)

- a. In-memory database
- b. Life cycle of a relational database
- c. Database model
- d. Federated database system

Guidance: level 1

:: Economic globalization ::

__________ is an agreement in which one company hires another company to be responsible for a planned or existing activity that is or could be done internally,and sometimes involves transferring employees and assets from one firm to another.

Exam Probability: **High**

49. *Answer choices:*

(see index for correct answer)

- a. reshoring
- b. Outsourcing

Guidance: level 1

:: Internet marketing ::

__________ is the process of increasing the quality and quantity of website traffic, increasing visibility of a website or a web page to users of a web search engine.SEO refers to the improvement of unpaid results , and excludes the purchase of paid placement.

Exam Probability: **Medium**

50. *Answer choices:*

(see index for correct answer)

- a. Personalized retargeting
- b. Search engine marketing
- c. Impression
- d. Search engine optimization

Guidance: level 1

:: Data management ::

__________ is a set of processes and technologies that supports the collection, managing, and publishing of information in any form or medium. When stored and accessed via computers, this information may be more specifically referred to as digital content, or simply as content.

Exam Probability: **Medium**

51. *Answer choices:*

(see index for correct answer)

- a. Learning object metadata
- b. Content management
- c. Data Transformation Services
- d. Ontology merging

Guidance: level 1

:: Big data ::

__________ is the discovery, interpretation, and communication of meaningful patterns in data; and the process of applying those patterns towards effective decision making. In other words, __________ can be understood as the connective tissue between data and effective decision making, within an organization. Especially valuable in areas rich with recorded information, __________ relies on the simultaneous application of statistics, computer programming and operations research to quantify performance.

Exam Probability: **Low**

52. *Answer choices:*

(see index for correct answer)

- a. ECL
- b. Analytics
- c. Sessionization
- d. Datameer

Guidance: level 1

:: ::

A _________ is a computer network that interconnects computers within a limited area such as a residence, school, laboratory, university campus or office building. By contrast, a wide area network not only covers a larger geographic distance, but also generally involves leased telecommunication circuits.

Exam Probability: **Medium**

53. *Answer choices:*

(see index for correct answer)

- a. hierarchical perspective
- b. open system

- c. empathy
- d. levels of analysis

Guidance: level 1

:: Data security ::

In information technology, a _________ , or data _________ , or the process of backing up, refers to the copying into an archive file of computer data that is already in secondary storage—so that it may be used to restore the original after a data loss event. The verb form is "back up" , whereas the noun and adjective form is " _________ ".

Exam Probability: **Medium**

54. *Answer choices:*

(see index for correct answer)

- a. Backup
- b. Multi-party authorization
- c. Certified Information Systems Security Professional
- d. Extended Access Control

Guidance: level 1

:: Market structure and pricing ::

_________ is a term denoting that a product includes permission to use its source code, design documents, or content. It most commonly refers to the open-source model, in which open-source software or other products are released under an open-source license as part of the open-source-software movement. Use of the term originated with software, but has expanded beyond the software sector to cover other open content and forms of open collaboration.

Exam Probability: **High**

55. *Answer choices:*

(see index for correct answer)

- a. Open-source economics
- b. Market structure
- c. Liberalization
- d. Installed base

Guidance: level 1

:: E-commerce ::

_________ , and its now-deprecated predecessor, Secure Sockets Layer , are cryptographic protocols designed to provide communications security over a computer network. Several versions of the protocols find widespread use in applications such as web browsing, email, instant messaging, and voice over IP . Websites can use TLS to secure all communications between their servers and web browsers.

Exam Probability: **Low**

56. *Answer choices:*

(see index for correct answer)

- a. The Cluetrain Manifesto
- b. E-commerce
- c. Transport Layer Security
- d. Mobimoneybox

Guidance: level 1

:: Types of marketing ::

In microeconomics and management, __________ is an arrangement in which the supply chain of a company is owned by that company. Usually each member of the supply chain produces a different product or service, and the products combine to satisfy a common need. It is contrasted with horizontal integration, wherein a company produces several items which are related to one another. __________ has also described management styles that bring large portions of the supply chain not only under a common ownership, but also into one corporation .

Exam Probability: **Low**

57. *Answer choices:*

(see index for correct answer)

- a. Multi-domestic strategy

- b. Vertical integration
- c. Evangelism marketing
- d. Figure of merit

Guidance: level 1

:: Mereology ::

_________ , in the abstract, is what belongs to or with something, whether as an attribute or as a component of said thing. In the context of this article, it is one or more components , whether physical or incorporeal, of a person`s estate; or so belonging to, as in being owned by, a person or jointly a group of people or a legal entity like a corporation or even a society. Depending on the nature of the _________ , an owner of _________ has the right to consume, alter, share, redefine, rent, mortgage, pawn, sell, exchange, transfer, give away or destroy it, or to exclude others from doing these things, as well as to perhaps abandon it; whereas regardless of the nature of the _________ , the owner thereof has the right to properly use it , or at the very least exclusively keep it.

Exam Probability: **High**

58. *Answer choices:*

(see index for correct answer)

- a. Mereology
- b. Simple
- c. Non-wellfounded mereology
- d. Mereotopology

Guidance: level 1

:: Fault tolerance ::

__________ is the property that enables a system to continue operating properly in the event of the failure of some of its components. If its operating quality decreases at all, the decrease is proportional to the severity of the failure, as compared to a naively designed system, in which even a small failure can cause total breakdown. __________ is particularly sought after in high-availability or life-critical systems. The ability of maintaining functionality when portions of a system break down is referred to as graceful degradation.

Exam Probability: **Low**

59. *Answer choices:*

(see index for correct answer)

- a. Dual modular redundancy
- b. Operational availability
- c. Fault-tolerant computer system
- d. Hot spare

Guidance: level 1

Marketing

Marketing is the study and management of exchange relationships. Marketing is the business process of creating relationships with and satisfying customers. With its focus on the customer, marketing is one of the premier components of business management.

Marketing is defined by the American Marketing Association as "the activity, set of institutions, and processes for creating, communicating, delivering, and exchanging offerings that have value for customers, clients, partners, and society at large."

:: Monopoly (economics) ::

A __________ exists when a specific person or enterprise is the only supplier of a particular commodity. This contrasts with a monopsony which relates to a single entity`s control of a market to purchase a good or service, and with oligopoly which consists of a few sellers dominating a market. Monopolies are thus characterized by a lack of economic competition to produce the good or service, a lack of viable substitute goods, and the possibility of a high __________ price well above the seller`s marginal cost that leads to a high __________ profit. The verb monopolise or monopolize refers to the process by which a company gains the ability to raise prices or exclude competitors. In economics, a __________ is a single seller. In law, a __________ is a business entity that has significant market power, that is, the power to charge overly high prices. Although monopolies may be big businesses, size is not a characteristic of a __________. A small business may still have the power to raise prices in a small industry .

Exam Probability: **Medium**

1. *Answer choices:*

(see index for correct answer)

- a. Chamberlinian monopolistic competition
- b. Wartime Law on Industrial Property
- c. Cost per procedure
- d. Monopoly

Guidance: level 1

:: Credit cards ::

The __________ Company, also known as Amex, is an American multinational financial services corporation headquartered in Three World Financial Center in New York City. The company was founded in 1850 and is one of the 30 components of the Dow Jones Industrial Average. The company is best known for its charge card, credit card, and traveler`s cheque businesses.

Exam Probability: **Medium**

2. *Answer choices:*

(see index for correct answer)

- a. NexG PrePaid
- b. Payoneer
- c. American Express
- d. Diners Club International

Guidance: level 1

:: Management ::

__________ is the organizational discipline which focuses on the practical application of marketing orientation, techniques and methods inside enterprises and organizations and on the management of a firm`s marketing resources and activities.

Exam Probability: **Medium**

3. *Answer choices:*

(see index for correct answer)

- a. Core competency
- b. One in, one out policy
- c. Evidence-based management
- d. Event management

Guidance: level 1

:: Marketing analytics ::

__________ is a long-term, forward-looking approach to planning with the fundamental goal of achieving a sustainable competitive advantage. Strategic planning involves an analysis of the company`s strategic initial situation prior to the formulation, evaluation and selection of market-oriented competitive position that contributes to the company`s goals and marketing objectives.

Exam Probability: **High**

4. *Answer choices:*

(see index for correct answer)

- a. Return on marketing investment
- b. Advertising adstock
- c. Marketing performance measurement and management
- d. Marketing strategy

Guidance: level 1

:: ::

Business is the activity of making one`s living or making money by producing or buying and selling products . Simply put, it is "any activity or enterprise entered into for profit. It does not mean it is a company, a corporation, partnership, or have any such formal organization, but it can range from a street peddler to General Motors."

Exam Probability: **Low**

5. *Answer choices:*

(see index for correct answer)

- a. Sarbanes-Oxley act of 2002
- b. information systems assessment
- c. deep-level diversity
- d. interpersonal communication

Guidance: level 1

:: Consumer theory ::

A _________ is a technical term in psychology, economics and philosophy usually used in relation to choosing between alternatives. For example, someone prefers A over B if they would rather choose A than B.

Exam Probability: **High**

6. *Answer choices:*

(see index for correct answer)

- a. Snob effect
- b. Preference
- c. Income effect
- d. Elasticity of substitution

Guidance: level 1

:: Management ::

A _________ describes the rationale of how an organization creates, delivers, and captures value, in economic, social, cultural or other contexts. The process of _________ construction and modification is also called _________ innovation and forms a part of business strategy.

Exam Probability: **High**

7. *Answer choices:*

(see index for correct answer)

- a. Business model
- b. Resource breakdown structure
- c. Change advisory board
- d. Production flow analysis

Guidance: level 1

:: Information technology ::

__________ is the use of computers to store, retrieve, transmit, and manipulate data, or information, often in the context of a business or other enterprise. IT is considered to be a subset of information and communications technology . An __________ system is generally an information system, a communications system or, more specifically speaking, a computer system – including all hardware, software and peripheral equipment – operated by a limited group of users.

Exam Probability: **Medium**

8. *Answer choices:*

(see index for correct answer)

- a. Infocommunications
- b. Information Technology Generalist
- c. ISO/IEC JTC 1/SC 23
- d. Information technology

Guidance: level 1

:: ::

_________ involves decision making. It can include judging the merits of multiple options and selecting one or more of them. One can make a _________ between imagined options or between real options followed by the corresponding action. For example, a traveler might choose a route for a journey based on the preference of arriving at a given destination as soon as possible. The preferred route can then follow from information such as the length of each of the possible routes, traffic conditions, etc. The arrival at a _________ can include more complex motivators such as cognition, instinct, and feeling.

Exam Probability: **Medium**

9. *Answer choices:*

(see index for correct answer)

- a. surface-level diversity
- b. co-culture
- c. Sarbanes-Oxley act of 2002
- d. Choice

Guidance: level 1

:: Market research ::

_________ is an organized effort to gather information about target markets or customers. It is a very important component of business strategy. The term is commonly interchanged with marketing research; however, expert practitioners may wish to draw a distinction, in that marketing research is concerned specifically about marketing processes, while _________ is concerned specifically with markets.

Exam Probability: **Medium**

10. *Answer choices:*

(see index for correct answer)

- a. Product forecasting
- b. Travel survey
- c. Market research
- d. Marketing research

Guidance: level 1

:: Business planning ::

_________ is an organization's process of defining its strategy, or direction, and making decisions on allocating its resources to pursue this strategy. It may also extend to control mechanisms for guiding the implementation of the strategy. _________ became prominent in corporations during the 1960s and remains an important aspect of strategic management. It is executed by strategic planners or strategists, who involve many parties and research sources in their analysis of the organization and its relationship to the environment in which it competes.

Exam Probability: **Medium**

11. *Answer choices:*

(see index for correct answer)

- a. Exit planning
- b. Gap analysis
- c. Community Futures
- d. Strategic planning

Guidance: level 1

:: National accounts ::

__________ is a monetary measure of the market value of all the final goods and services produced in a period of time, often annually. GDP per capita does not, however, reflect differences in the cost of living and the inflation rates of the countries; therefore using a basis of GDP per capita at purchasing power parity is arguably more useful when comparing differences in living standards between nations.

Exam Probability: **High**

12. *Answer choices:*

(see index for correct answer)

- a. Fixed capital
- b. National Income

- c. Gross domestic product

Guidance: level 1

:: ::

_________ is the means to see, hear, or become aware of something or someone through our fundamental senses. The term _________ derives from the Latin word perceptio, and is the organization, identification, and interpretation of sensory information in order to represent and understand the presented information, or the environment.

Exam Probability: **Medium**

13. *Answer choices:*

(see index for correct answer)

- a. open system
- b. co-culture
- c. empathy
- d. surface-level diversity

Guidance: level 1

:: ::

_________ is a process whereby a person assumes the parenting of another, usually a child, from that person`s biological or legal parent or parents. Legal _________ s permanently transfers all rights and responsibilities, along with filiation, from the biological parent or parents.

Exam Probability: **Low**

14. *Answer choices:*

(see index for correct answer)

- a. levels of analysis
- b. similarity-attraction theory
- c. deep-level diversity
- d. hierarchical perspective

Guidance: level 1

:: Marketing ::

_________ is a pricing strategy where the price of a product is initially set low to rapidly reach a wide fraction of the market and initiate word of mouth. The strategy works on the expectation that customers will switch to the new brand because of the lower price. _________ is most commonly associated with marketing objectives of enlarging market share and exploiting economies of scale or experience.

Exam Probability: **High**

15. *Answer choices:*

(see index for correct answer)

- a. Aftersales
- b. Penetration pricing
- c. Promo
- d. Generic brand

Guidance: level 1

:: Business ::

The seller, or the provider of the goods or services, completes a sale in response to an acquisition, appropriation, requisition or a direct interaction with the buyer at the point of sale. There is a passing of title of the item, and the settlement of a price, in which agreement is reached on a price for which transfer of ownership of the item will occur. The seller, not the purchaser typically executes the sale and it may be completed prior to the obligation of payment. In the case of indirect interaction, a person who sells goods or service on behalf of the owner is known as a salesman or saleswoman or salesperson, but this often refers to someone _________ goods in a store/shop, in which case other terms are also common, including salesclerk, shop assistant, and retail clerk.

Exam Probability: **Low**

16. *Answer choices:*

(see index for correct answer)

- a. Les Vergers du Mekong
- b. GoCardless
- c. Selling
- d. Shriram Properties

Guidance: level 1

:: ::

A __________ is an organization, usually a group of people or a company, authorized to act as a single entity and recognized as such in law. Early incorporated entities were established by charter . Most jurisdictions now allow the creation of new __________ s through registration.

Exam Probability: **High**

17. *Answer choices:*

(see index for correct answer)

- a. interpersonal communication
- b. Sarbanes-Oxley act of 2002
- c. Corporation
- d. deep-level diversity

Guidance: level 1

:: Promotion and marketing communications ::

_________ is one of the elements of the promotional mix. . _________ uses both media and non-media marketing communications for a pre-determined, limited time to increase consumer demand, stimulate market demand or improve product availability. Examples include contests, coupons, freebies, loss leaders, point of purchase displays, premiums, prizes, product samples, and rebates.

Exam Probability: **High**

18. *Answer choices:*

(see index for correct answer)

- a. Trade literature
- b. Sales promotion
- c. Shop fitting
- d. Market Contact Audit

Guidance: level 1

:: Marketing ::

_________ is a market strategy in which a firm decides to ignore market segment differences and appeal the whole market with one offer or one strategy, which supports the idea of broadcasting a message that will reach the largest number of people possible. Traditionally _________ has focused on radio, television and newspapers as the media used to reach this broad audience. By reaching the largest audience possible, exposure to the product is maximized, and in theory this would directly correlate with a larger number of sales or buys into the product.

Exam Probability: **Medium**

19. *Answer choices:*

(see index for correct answer)

- a. Editorial calendar
- b. Mass marketing
- c. Corporate capabilities package
- d. Chaotics

Guidance: level 1

:: ::

In law, a _________ is a coming together of parties to a dispute, to present information in a tribunal, a formal setting with the authority to adjudicate claims or disputes. One form of tribunal is a court. The tribunal, which may occur before a judge, jury, or other designated trier of fact, aims to achieve a resolution to their dispute.

Exam Probability: **Medium**

20. *Answer choices:*

(see index for correct answer)

- a. Character
- b. Trial
- c. information systems assessment
- d. hierarchical perspective

Guidance: level 1

:: Marketing ::

_________ is the marketing of products that are presumed to be environmentally safe. It incorporates a broad range of activities, including product modification, changes to the production process, sustainable packaging, as well as modifying advertising. Yet defining _________ is not a simple task where several meanings intersect and contradict each other; an example of this will be the existence of varying social, environmental and retail definitions attached to this term. Other similar terms used are environmental marketing and ecological marketing.

Exam Probability: **High**

21. *Answer choices:*

(see index for correct answer)

- a. Marketing communications planning framework
- b. Green marketing
- c. Prommercial
- d. Multicultural marketing

Guidance: level 1

:: Management ::

A __________ is a promise of value to be delivered, communicated, and acknowledged. It is also a belief from the customer about how value will be delivered, experienced and acquired.

Exam Probability: **High**

22. *Answer choices:*

(see index for correct answer)

- a. Topple rate
- b. Opera management
- c. Management fad
- d. Community-based management

Guidance: level 1

:: Supply chain management terms ::

In business and finance, _________ is a system of organizations, people, activities, information, and resources involved inmoving a product or service from supplier to customer. _________ activities involve the transformation of natural resources, raw materials, and components into a finished product that is delivered to the end customer. In sophisticated _________ systems, used products may re-enter the _________ at any point where residual value is recyclable. _________ s link value chains.

Exam Probability: **Low**

23. *Answer choices:*

(see index for correct answer)

- a. Work in process
- b. inventory management
- c. Supply chain
- d. Direct shipment

Guidance: level 1

:: Trade associations ::

A ________ , also known as an industry trade group, business association, sector association or industry body, is an organization founded and funded by businesses that operate in a specific industry. An industry ________ participates in public relations activities such as advertising, education, political donations, lobbying and publishing, but its focus is collaboration between companies. Associations may offer other services, such as producing conferences, networking or charitable events or offering classes or educational materials. Many associations are non-profit organizations governed by bylaws and directed by officers who are also members.

Exam Probability: **High**

24. *Answer choices:*

(see index for correct answer)

- a. Investment Adviser Association
- b. Association for Information and Image Management
- c. Federation of Irish Fishermen
- d. Association for International Broadcasting

Guidance: level 1

:: Production and manufacturing ::

__________ consists of organization-wide efforts to "install and make permanent climate where employees continuously improve their ability to provide on demand products and services that customers will find of particular value." "Total" emphasizes that departments in addition to production are obligated to improve their operations; "management" emphasizes that executives are obligated to actively manage quality through funding, training, staffing, and goal setting. While there is no widely agreed-upon approach, TQM efforts typically draw heavily on the previously developed tools and techniques of quality control. TQM enjoyed widespread attention during the late 1980s and early 1990s before being overshadowed by ISO 9000, Lean manufacturing, and Six Sigma.

Exam Probability: **Medium**

25. *Answer choices:*

(see index for correct answer)

- a. ISO/TS 16949
- b. Total Quality Management
- c. LPA512
- d. Product layout

Guidance: level 1

:: Progressive Era in the United States ::

The Clayton Antitrust Act of 1914 , was a part of United States antitrust law with the goal of adding further substance to the U.S. antitrust law regime; the __________ sought to prevent anticompetitive practices in their incipiency. That regime started with the Sherman Antitrust Act of 1890, the first Federal law outlawing practices considered harmful to consumers . The __________ specified particular prohibited conduct, the three-level enforcement scheme, the exemptions, and the remedial measures.

Exam Probability: **Low**

26. *Answer choices:*

(see index for correct answer)

- a. pragmatism
- b. Clayton Act
- c. Mann Act

Guidance: level 1

:: ::

__________ is the practice of deliberately managing the spread of information between an individual or an organization and the public. __________ may include an organization or individual gaining exposure to their audiences using topics of public interest and news items that do not require direct payment. This differentiates it from advertising as a form of marketing communications. __________ is the idea of creating coverage for clients for free, rather than marketing or advertising. But now, advertising is also a part of greater PR Activities.An example of good __________ would be generating an article featuring a client, rather than paying for the client to be advertised next to the article. The aim of __________ is to inform the public, prospective customers, investors, partners, employees, and other stakeholders and ultimately persuade them to maintain a positive or favorable view about the organization, its leadership, products, or political decisions. __________ professionals typically work for PR and marketing firms, businesses and companies, government, and public officials as PIOs and nongovernmental organizations, and nonprofit organizations. Jobs central to __________ include account coordinator, account executive, account supervisor, and media relations manager.

Exam Probability: **High**

27. *Answer choices:*

(see index for correct answer)

- a. process perspective
- b. open system
- c. deep-level diversity
- d. Public relations

Guidance: level 1

:: Marketing ::

__________, in marketing, manufacturing, call centres and management, is the use of flexible computer-aided manufacturing systems to produce custom output. Such systems combine the low unit costs of mass production processes with the flexibility of individual customization.

Exam Probability: **Medium**

28. *Answer choices:*

(see index for correct answer)

- a. Ayelet Gneezy
- b. Partnerized inventory management
- c. Behance
- d. Industrial marketing

Guidance: level 1

:: Marketing ::

__________ uses different marketing channels and tools in combination: Marketing communication channels focus on any way a business communicates a message to its desired market, or the market in general. A marketing communication tool can be anything from: advertising, personal selling, direct marketing, sponsorship, communication, and promotion to public relations.

Exam Probability: **High**

29. *Answer choices:*

(see index for correct answer)

- a. Target market
- b. Marketing communications
- c. Marketspace
- d. Industrial marketing

Guidance: level 1

:: ::

A __________ or sample __________ is a single measure of some attribute of a sample . It is calculated by applying a function to the values of the items of the sample, which are known together as a set of data.

Exam Probability: **Low**

30. *Answer choices:*

(see index for correct answer)

- a. open system
- b. process perspective
- c. Statistic
- d. empathy

Guidance: level 1

:: Retailing ::

A _________ is a retail establishment offering a wide range of consumer goods in different product categories known as "departments". In modern major cities, the _________ made a dramatic appearance in the middle of the 19th century, and permanently reshaped shopping habits, and the definition of service and luxury. Similar developments were under way in London , in Paris and in New York .

Exam Probability: **Low**

31. *Answer choices:*

(see index for correct answer)

- a. Department store
- b. St. Vincent de Paul Thrift Store
- c. Enoteca
- d. Zeeman

Guidance: level 1

:: Consumer behaviour ::

_________ refers to the ability of a company or product to retain its customers over some specified period. High _________ means customers of the product or business tend to return to, continue to buy or in some other way not defect to another product or business, or to non-use entirely. Selling organizations generally attempt to reduce customer defections. _________ starts with the first contact an organization has with a customer and continues throughout the entire lifetime of a relationship and successful retention efforts take this entire lifecycle into account. A company`s ability to attract and retain new customers is related not only to its product or services, but also to the way it services its existing customers, the value the customers actually generate as a result of utilizing the solutions, and the reputation it creates within and across the marketplace.

Exam Probability: **High**

32. *Answer choices:*

(see index for correct answer)

- a. Consumer confusion
- b. Customer retention
- c. Itamar Simonson
- d. Geodemography

Guidance: level 1

:: Costs ::

In economics, _________ is the total economic cost of production and is made up of variable cost, which varies according to the quantity of a good produced and includes inputs such as labour and raw materials, plus fixed cost, which is independent of the quantity of a good produced and includes inputs that cannot be varied in the short term: fixed costs such as buildings and machinery, including sunk costs if any. Since cost is measured per unit of time, it is a flow variable.

Exam Probability: **Low**

33. *Answer choices:*

(see index for correct answer)

- a. Cost per paper
- b. Economic cost
- c. Direct labor cost
- d. Total cost

Guidance: level 1

:: Market research ::

__________ is "the process or set of processes that links the producers, customers, and end users to the marketer through information used to identify and define marketing opportunities and problems; generate, refine, and evaluate marketing actions; monitor marketing performance; and improve understanding of marketing as a process. __________ specifies the information required to address these issues, designs the method for collecting information, manages and implements the data collection process, analyzes the results, and communicates the findings and their implications."

Exam Probability: **High**

34. *Answer choices:*

(see index for correct answer)

- a. Innovation game
- b. Gerson Lehrman Group
- c. DIY research
- d. Marketing research

Guidance: level 1

:: Management ::

__________ is the process of thinking about the activities required to achieve a desired goal. It is the first and foremost activity to achieve desired results. It involves the creation and maintenance of a plan, such as psychological aspects that require conceptual skills. There are even a couple of tests to measure someone's capability of __________ well. As such, __________ is a fundamental property of intelligent behavior. An important further meaning, often just called "__________" is the legal context of permitted building developments.

Exam Probability: **Low**

35. *Answer choices:*

(see index for correct answer)

- a. Reverse innovation
- b. Real property administrator
- c. Planning
- d. One in, one out policy

Guidance: level 1

:: Packaging ::

In work place, __________ or job __________ means good ranking with the hypothesized conception of requirements of a role. There are two types of job __________ s: contextual and task. Task __________ is related to cognitive ability while contextual __________ is dependent upon personality. Task __________ are behavioral roles that are recognized in job descriptions and by remuneration systems, they are directly related to organizational __________, whereas, contextual __________ are value based and additional behavioral roles that are not recognized in job descriptions and covered by compensation; they are extra roles that are indirectly related to organizational __________. Citizenship __________ like contextual __________ means a set of individual activity/contribution that supports the organizational culture.

Exam Probability: **Low**

36. *Answer choices:*

(see index for correct answer)

- a. Cyperus tegetiformis
- b. Muselet
- c. Record sleeve
- d. Performance

Guidance: level 1

:: E-commerce ::

__________ is the activity of buying or selling of products on online services or over the Internet. Electronic commerce draws on technologies such as mobile commerce, electronic funds transfer, supply chain management, Internet marketing, online transaction processing, electronic data interchange , inventory management systems, and automated data collection systems.

Exam Probability: **Medium**

37. *Answer choices:*

(see index for correct answer)

- a. Buyhatke
- b. Plantify
- c. Online savings account
- d. E-commerce

Guidance: level 1

:: Public relations ::

__________ is the public visibility or awareness for any product, service or company. It may also refer to the movement of information from its source to the general public, often but not always via the media. The subjects of __________ include people , goods and services, organizations, and works of art or entertainment.

Exam Probability: **Medium**

38. *Answer choices:*

(see index for correct answer)

- a. Corporate Representatives for Ethical Wikipedia Engagement
- b. Publicity
- c. Public affairs
- d. LaunchSquad

Guidance: level 1

:: ::

An _________ is a systematic and independent examination of books, accounts, statutory records, documents and vouchers of an organization to ascertain how far the financial statements as well as non-financial disclosures present a true and fair view of the concern. It also attempts to ensure that the books of accounts are properly maintained by the concern as required by law. _________ ing has become such a ubiquitous phenomenon in the corporate and the public sector that academics started identifying an " _________ Society". The _________ or perceives and recognises the propositions before them for examination, obtains evidence, evaluates the same and formulates an opinion on the basis of his judgement which is communicated through their _________ ing report.

Exam Probability: **High**

39. *Answer choices:*

(see index for correct answer)

- a. hierarchical perspective
- b. open system
- c. interpersonal communication
- d. Audit

Guidance: level 1

:: ::

__________ is the process whereby a business sets the price at which it will sell its products and services, and may be part of the business`s marketing plan. In setting prices, the business will take into account the price at which it could acquire the goods, the manufacturing cost, the market place, competition, market condition, brand, and quality of product.

Exam Probability: **Medium**

40. *Answer choices:*

(see index for correct answer)

- a. Pricing
- b. empathy
- c. interpersonal communication
- d. Sarbanes-Oxley act of 2002

Guidance: level 1

:: Marketing ::

_________ is multi-channel online marketing technique focused at reaching a specific audience on their smartphones, tablets, or any other related devices through websites, E-mail, SMS and MMS, social media, or mobile applications. _________ can provide customers with time and location sensitive, personalized information that promotes goods, services and ideas. In a more theoretical manner, academic Andreas Kaplan defines _________ as "any marketing activity conducted through a ubiquitous network to which consumers are constantly connected using a personal mobile device".

Exam Probability: **Low**

41. *Answer choices:*

(see index for correct answer)

- a. Market segmentation index
- b. push and pull
- c. History of marketing
- d. Mobile marketing

Guidance: level 1

:: ::

_________ is a concept of English common law and is a necessity for simple contracts but not for special contracts . The concept has been adopted by other common law jurisdictions, including the US.

Exam Probability: **Low**

42. *Answer choices:*

(see index for correct answer)

- a. Consideration
- b. levels of analysis
- c. open system
- d. surface-level diversity

Guidance: level 1

:: Product management ::

__________ or brand stretching is a marketing strategy in which a firm marketing a product with a well-developed image uses the same brand name in a different product category. The new product is called a spin-off. Organizations use this strategy to increase and leverage brand equity . An example of a __________ is Jello-gelatin creating Jello pudding pops. It increases awareness of the brand name and increases profitability from offerings in more than one product category.

Exam Probability: **High**

43. *Answer choices:*

(see index for correct answer)

- a. Brand extension

- b. Product management
- c. Service product management
- d. Product manager

Guidance: level 1

:: Contract law ::

A _________ is a legally-binding agreement which recognises and governs the rights and duties of the parties to the agreement. A _________ is legally enforceable because it meets the requirements and approval of the law. An agreement typically involves the exchange of goods, services, money, or promises of any of those. In the event of breach of _________, the law awards the injured party access to legal remedies such as damages and cancellation.

Exam Probability: **Low**

44. *Answer choices:*

(see index for correct answer)

- a. Unjust enrichment
- b. Contract
- c. Proprietary estoppel
- d. Collateral contract

Guidance: level 1

:: Industrial design ::

In physics and mathematics, the _________ of a mathematical space is informally defined as the minimum number of coordinates needed to specify any point within it. Thus a line has a _________ of one because only one coordinate is needed to specify a point on it for example, the point at 5 on a number line. A surface such as a plane or the surface of a cylinder or sphere has a _________ of two because two coordinates are needed to specify a point on it for example, both a latitude and longitude are required to locate a point on the surface of a sphere. The inside of a cube, a cylinder or a sphere is three- _________ al because three coordinates are needed to locate a point within these spaces.

Exam Probability: **Low**

45. *Answer choices:*

(see index for correct answer)

- a. Design and Technology
- b. Design for manufacturability
- c. Stefan Radev
- d. I.D.

Guidance: level 1

:: Management accounting ::

In economics, _________ s, indirect costs or overheads are business expenses that are not dependent on the level of goods or services produced by the business. They tend to be time-related, such as interest or rents being paid per month, and are often referred to as overhead costs. This is in contrast to variable costs, which are volume-related and unknown at the beginning of the accounting year. For a simple example, such as a bakery, the monthly rent for the baking facilities, and the monthly payments for the security system and basic phone line are _________ s, as they do not change according to how much bread the bakery produces and sells. On the other hand, the wage costs of the bakery are variable, as the bakery will have to hire more workers if the production of bread increases. Economists reckon _________ as a entry barrier for new entrepreneurs.

Exam Probability: **High**

46. *Answer choices:*

(see index for correct answer)

- a. Process costing
- b. Fixed cost
- c. activity based costing
- d. Entity-level controls

Guidance: level 1

:: ::

In __________ relations and communication science, __________ s are groups of individual people, and the __________ is the totality of such groupings. This is a different concept to the sociological concept of the Öffentlichkeit or __________ sphere. The concept of a __________ has also been defined in political science, psychology, marketing, and advertising. In __________ relations and communication science, it is one of the more ambiguous concepts in the field. Although it has definitions in the theory of the field that have been formulated from the early 20th century onwards, it has suffered in more recent years from being blurred, as a result of conflation of the idea of a __________ with the notions of audience, market segment, community, constituency, and stakeholder.

Exam Probability: **Medium**

47. *Answer choices:*

(see index for correct answer)

- a. process perspective
- b. Sarbanes-Oxley act of 2002
- c. co-culture
- d. Public

Guidance: level 1

:: International trade ::

_________ or globalisation is the process of interaction and integration among people, companies, and governments worldwide. As a complex and multifaceted phenomenon, _________ is considered by some as a form of capitalist expansion which entails the integration of local and national economies into a global, unregulated market economy. _________ has grown due to advances in transportation and communication technology. With the increased global interactions comes the growth of international trade, ideas, and culture. _________ is primarily an economic process of interaction and integration that`s associated with social and cultural aspects. However, conflicts and diplomacy are also large parts of the history of _________, and modern _________.

Exam Probability: **Medium**

48. *Answer choices:*

(see index for correct answer)

- a. Consular invoice
- b. Globalization
- c. Asian Clearing Union
- d. Economic nationalism

Guidance: level 1

:: Product management ::

A __________ is a professional role which is responsible for the development of products for an organization, known as the practice of product management. __________s own the business strategy behind a product , specify its functional requirements and generally manage the launch of features. They coordinate work done by many other functions and are ultimately responsible for the business success of the product.

Exam Probability: **High**

49. *Answer choices:*

(see index for correct answer)

- a. Trademark look
- b. Electronic registration mark
- c. Requirement prioritization
- d. Product manager

Guidance: level 1

:: ::

In business and engineering, new __________ covers the complete process of bringing a new product to market. A central aspect of NPD is product design, along with various business considerations. New __________ is described broadly as the transformation of a market opportunity into a product available for sale. The product can be tangible or intangible , though sometimes services and other processes are distinguished from "products." NPD requires an understanding of customer needs and wants, the competitive environment, and the nature of the market.Cost, time and quality are the main variables that drive customer needs. Aiming at these three variables, innovative companies develop continuous practices and strategies to better satisfy customer requirements and to increase their own market share by a regular development of new products. There are many uncertainties and challenges which companies must face throughout the process. The use of best practices and the elimination of barriers to communication are the main concerns for the management of the NPD .

Exam Probability: **High**

50. *Answer choices:*

(see index for correct answer)

- a. hierarchical
- b. Product development
- c. information systems assessment
- d. imperative

Guidance: level 1

:: Marketing ::

A _________ is the quantity of payment or compensation given by one party to another in return for one unit of goods or services.. A _________ is influenced by both production costs and demand for the product. A _________ may be determined by a monopolist or may be imposed on the firm by market conditions.

Exam Probability: **High**

51. *Answer choices:*

(see index for correct answer)

- a. Paddock girl
- b. Impulse purchase
- c. Earned media
- d. Health marketing

Guidance: level 1

:: ::

Advertising is a marketing communication that employs an openly sponsored, non-personal message to promote or sell a product, service or idea. Sponsors of advertising are typically businesses wishing to promote their products or services. Advertising is differentiated from public relations in that an advertiser pays for and has control over the message. It differs from personal selling in that the message is non-personal, i.e., not directed to a particular individual.Advertising is communicated through various mass media, including traditional media such as newspapers, magazines, television, radio, outdoor advertising or direct mail; and new media such as search results, blogs, social media, websites or text messages. The actual presentation of the message in a medium is referred to as an _________, or "ad" or advert for short.

Exam Probability: **Medium**

52. *Answer choices:*

(see index for correct answer)

- a. functional perspective
- b. cultural
- c. Sarbanes-Oxley act of 2002
- d. Advertisement

Guidance: level 1

:: Evaluation methods ::

In natural and social sciences, and sometimes in other fields, _________ is the systematic empirical investigation of observable phenomena via statistical, mathematical, or computational techniques. The objective of _________ is to develop and employ mathematical models, theories, and hypotheses pertaining to phenomena. The process of measurement is central to _________ because it provides the fundamental connection between empirical observation and mathematical expression of quantitative relationships.

Exam Probability: **Low**

53. *Answer choices:*

(see index for correct answer)

- a. Position weight matrix
- b. Pick chart
- c. Rubric
- d. Quantitative research

Guidance: level 1

:: ::

In financial markets, a share is a unit used as mutual funds, limited partnerships, and real estate investment trusts. The owner of _________ in the corporation/company is a shareholder of the corporation. A share is an indivisible unit of capital, expressing the ownership relationship between the company and the shareholder. The denominated value of a share is its face value, and the total of the face value of issued _________ represent the capital of a company, which may not reflect the market value of those _________ .

Exam Probability: **High**

54. *Answer choices:*

(see index for correct answer)

- a. levels of analysis
- b. functional perspective
- c. similarity-attraction theory
- d. Shares

Guidance: level 1

:: Product development ::

In business and engineering, _________ covers the complete process of bringing a new product to market. A central aspect of NPD is product design, along with various business considerations. _________ is described broadly as the transformation of a market opportunity into a product available for sale. The product can be tangible or intangible , though sometimes services and other processes are distinguished from "products." NPD requires an understanding of customer needs and wants, the competitive environment, and the nature of the market.Cost, time and quality are the main variables that drive customer needs. Aiming at these three variables, innovative companies develop continuous practices and strategies to better satisfy customer requirements and to increase their own market share by a regular development of new products. There are many uncertainties and challenges which companies must face throughout the process. The use of best practices and the elimination of barriers to communication are the main concerns for the management of the NPD .

Exam Probability: **Medium**

55. *Answer choices:*

(see index for correct answer)

- a. Product concept
- b. New product development
- c. Y Media Labs
- d. Virtual product development

Guidance: level 1

:: Strategic alliances ::

A _________ is an agreement between two or more parties to pursue a set of agreed upon objectives needed while remaining independent organizations. A _________ will usually fall short of a legal partnership entity, agency, or corporate affiliate relationship. Typically, two companies form a _________ when each possesses one or more business assets or have expertise that will help the other by enhancing their businesses. _________s can develop in outsourcing relationships where the parties desire to achieve long-term win-win benefits and innovation based on mutually desired outcomes.

Exam Probability: **Low**

56. *Answer choices:*

(see index for correct answer)

- a. Strategic alliance
- b. Cross-licensing
- c. Defensive termination
- d. Management contract

Guidance: level 1

:: Data collection ::

A _________ is an utterance which typically functions as a request for information. _________ s can thus be understood as a kind of illocutionary act in the field of pragmatics or as special kinds of propositions in frameworks of formal semantics such as alternative semantics or inquisitive semantics. The information requested is expected to be provided in the form of an answer. _________ s are often conflated with interrogatives, which are the grammatical forms typically used to achieve them. Rhetorical _________ s, for example, are interrogative in form but may not be considered true _________ s as they are not expected to be answered. Conversely, non-interrogative grammatical structures may be considered _________ s as in the case of the imperative sentence "tell me your name".

Exam Probability: **Medium**

57. *Answer choices:*

(see index for correct answer)

- a. Datalogix
- b. Question
- c. Natural experiment
- d. Web mining

Guidance: level 1

:: Health promotion ::

_________, as defined by the World _________ Organization , is "a state of complete physical, mental and social well-being and not merely the absence of disease or infirmity." This definition has been subject to controversy, as it may have limited value for implementation. _________ may be defined as the ability to adapt and manage physical, mental and social challenges throughout life.

Exam Probability: **Low**

58. *Answer choices:*

(see index for correct answer)

- a. Eberhard Wenzel
- b. Lalonde report
- c. Health care reform
- d. Health

Guidance: level 1

:: ::

_________ is a term frequently used in marketing. It is a measure of how products and services supplied by a company meet or surpass customer expectation. _________ is defined as "the number of customers, or percentage of total customers, whose reported experience with a firm, its products, or its services exceeds specified satisfaction goals."

Exam Probability: **Medium**

59. *Answer choices:*

(see index for correct answer)

- a. hierarchical perspective
- b. cultural
- c. similarity-attraction theory
- d. process perspective

Guidance: level 1

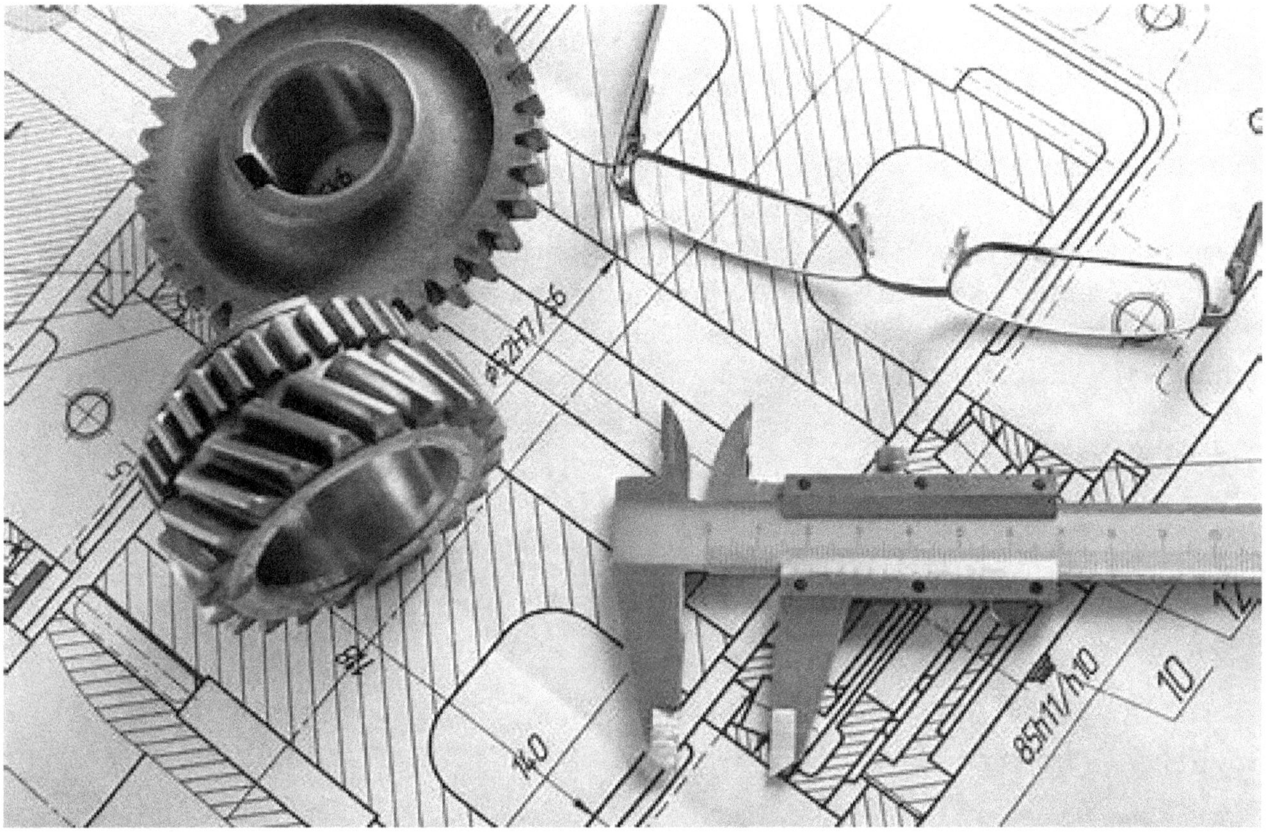

Manufacturing

Manufacturing is the production of merchandise for use or sale using labor and machines, tools, chemical and biological processing, or formulation. The term may refer to a range of human activity, from handicraft to high tech, but is most commonly applied to industrial design , in which raw materials are transformed into finished goods on a large scale. Such finished goods may be sold to other manufacturers for the production of other, more complex products, such as aircraft, household appliances, furniture, sports equipment or automobiles, or sold to wholesalers, who in turn sell them to retailers, who then sell them to end users and consumers.

:: Mereology ::

__________, in the abstract, is what belongs to or with something, whether as an attribute or as a component of said thing. In the context of this article, it is one or more components , whether physical or incorporeal, of a person`s estate; or so belonging to, as in being owned by, a person or jointly a group of people or a legal entity like a corporation or even a society. Depending on the nature of the __________, an owner of __________ has the right to consume, alter, share, redefine, rent, mortgage, pawn, sell, exchange, transfer, give away or destroy it, or to exclude others from doing these things, as well as to perhaps abandon it; whereas regardless of the nature of the __________, the owner thereof has the right to properly use it , or at the very least exclusively keep it.

Exam Probability: **Medium**

1. *Answer choices:*

(see index for correct answer)

- a. Mereology
- b. Meronomy
- c. Mereological nihilism
- d. Non-wellfounded mereology

Guidance: level 1

:: Project management ::

Rolling-wave planning is the process of project planning in waves as the project proceeds and later details become clearer; similar to the techniques used in agile software development approaches like Scrum..

Exam Probability: **Medium**

2. *Answer choices:*

(see index for correct answer)

- a. Jeff Sutherland
- b. Logical framework approach
- c. Rolling Wave planning
- d. Changes clause

Guidance: level 1

:: Quality management ::

In quality management system, a __________ is a document developed by management to express the directive of the top management with respect to quality. __________ management is a strategic item.

Exam Probability: **Medium**

3. *Answer choices:*

(see index for correct answer)

- a. Regulatory translation
- b. Quality management system
- c. European Quality in Social Services
- d. Quality policy

Guidance: level 1

:: Industrial organization ::

In economics, specifically general equilibrium theory, a perfect market is defined by several idealizing conditions, collectively called _________ . In theoretical models where conditions of _________ hold, it has been theoretically demonstrated that a market will reach an equilibrium in which the quantity supplied for every product or service, including labor, equals the quantity demanded at the current price. This equilibrium would be a Pareto optimum.

Exam Probability: **Low**

4. *Answer choices:*

(see index for correct answer)

- a. domestic system
- b. Industrial organization
- c. Perfect competition
- d. Organizational studies

Guidance: level 1

:: Inventory ::

The __________ is the level of inventory which triggers an action to replenish that particular inventory stock. It is a minimum amount of an item which a firm holds in stock, such that, when stock falls to this amount, the item must be reordered. It is normally calculated as the forecast usage during the replenishment lead time plus safety stock. In the EOQ model, it was assumed that there is no time lag between ordering and procuring of materials. Therefore the __________ for replenishing the stocks occurs at that level when the inventory level drops to zero and because instant delivery by suppliers, the stock level bounce back.

Exam Probability: **High**

5. *Answer choices:*

(see index for correct answer)

- a. Average cost method
- b. Reorder point
- c. Lower of cost or market
- d. Inventory control problem

Guidance: level 1

:: E-commerce ::

__________ is the activity of buying or selling of products on online services or over the Internet. Electronic commerce draws on technologies such as mobile commerce, electronic funds transfer, supply chain management, Internet marketing, online transaction processing, electronic data interchange , inventory management systems, and automated data collection systems.

Exam Probability: **High**

6. *Answer choices:*

(see index for correct answer)

- a. GS1 Sweden
- b. Optimize Capital Markets
- c. Yemeksepeti
- d. Yakala.co

Guidance: level 1

:: Computer memory companies ::

__________ Corporation is a Japanese multinational conglomerate headquartered in Tokyo, Japan. Its diversified products and services include information technology and communications equipment and systems, electronic components and materials, power systems, industrial and social infrastructure systems, consumer electronics, household appliances, medical equipment, office equipment, as well as lighting and logistics.

Exam Probability: **Low**

7. *Answer choices:*

(see index for correct answer)

- a. UMAX Technologies
- b. Princeton Technology

- c. Toshiba
- d. Mushkin

Guidance: level 1

:: Industrial processes ::

_________ is a technique involving the condensation of vapors and the return of this condensate to the system from which it originated. It is used in industrial and laboratory distillations. It is also used in chemistry to supply energy to reactions over a long period of time.

Exam Probability: **Low**

8. *Answer choices:*

(see index for correct answer)

- a. North East of England Process Industry Cluster
- b. Reflux
- c. Vacuum deposition
- d. Cathodic arc deposition

Guidance: level 1

:: Production and manufacturing ::

_________ is a production planning, scheduling, and inventory control system used to manage manufacturing processes. Most MRP systems are software-based, but it is possible to conduct MRP by hand as well.

Exam Probability: **Medium**

9. *Answer choices:*

(see index for correct answer)

- a. Maynard Operation Sequence Technique
- b. Material requirements planning
- c. Economic dispatch
- d. Report generator

Guidance: level 1

:: Management ::

In organizational studies, _________ is the efficient and effective development of an organization`s resources when they are needed. Such resources may include financial resources, inventory, human skills, production resources, or information technology and natural resources.

Exam Probability: **Low**

10. *Answer choices:*

(see index for correct answer)

- a. Social business model
- b. Dynamic enterprise modeling
- c. Operations research
- d. Resource management

Guidance: level 1

:: Production and manufacturing ::

_________ is a concept in purchasing and project management for securing the quality and timely delivery of goods and components.

Exam Probability: **Medium**

11. *Answer choices:*

(see index for correct answer)

- a. Economic dispatch
- b. Expediting
- c. Seweasy
- d. Contract manufacturer

Guidance: level 1

:: Industrial engineering ::

_________ , in its contemporary conceptualisation, is a comparison of perceived expectations of a service with perceived performance , giving rise to the equation SQ=P-E. This conceptualistion of _________ has its origins in the expectancy-disconfirmation paradigm.

Exam Probability: **Medium**

12. *Answer choices:*

(see index for correct answer)

- a. Institute of Industrial Engineers
- b. Design of experiments
- c. Standard time
- d. Bayesian experimental design

Guidance: level 1

:: Metals ::

A _________ is a material that, when freshly prepared, polished, or fractured, shows a lustrous appearance, and conducts electricity and heat relatively well. _________ s are typically malleable or ductile . A _________ may be a chemical element such as iron, or an alloy such as stainless steel.

Exam Probability: **High**

13. *Answer choices:*

(see index for correct answer)

- a. Light metal
- b. Metal
- c. Non-ferrous metal
- d. Metals in medicine

Guidance: level 1

:: ::

Catalysis is the process of increasing the rate of a chemical reaction by adding a substance known as a _________ , which is not consumed in the catalyzed reaction and can continue to act repeatedly. Because of this, only very small amounts of _________ are required to alter the reaction rate in principle.

Exam Probability: **Medium**

14. *Answer choices:*

(see index for correct answer)

- a. similarity-attraction theory
- b. hierarchical

- c. open system
- d. Catalyst

Guidance: level 1

:: Production and manufacturing ::

_________ is the process of determining the production capacity needed by an organization to meet changing demands for its products. In the context of _________ , design capacity is the maximum amount of work that an organization is capable of completing in a given period. Effective capacity is the maximum amount of work that an organization is capable of completing in a given period due to constraints such as quality problems, delays, material handling, etc.

Exam Probability: **High**

15. *Answer choices:*

(see index for correct answer)

- a. Fixed position assembly
- b. Transfer line
- c. Capacity planning
- d. Fab lab

Guidance: level 1

:: Business process ::

A committee is a body of one or more persons that is subordinate to a deliberative assembly. Usually, the assembly sends matters into a committee as a way to explore them more fully than would be possible if the assembly itself were considering them. Committees may have different functions and their type of work differ depending on the type of the organization and its needs.

Exam Probability: **Low**

16. *Answer choices:*

(see index for correct answer)

- a. Steering committee
- b. Business process validation
- c. Intention mining
- d. Knowledge process outsourcing

Guidance: level 1

:: Chemical reactions ::

A __________ is a process that leads to the chemical transformation of one set of chemical substances to another. Classically, __________ s encompass changes that only involve the positions of electrons in the forming and breaking of chemical bonds between atoms, with no change to the nuclei , and can often be described by a chemical equation. Nuclear chemistry is a sub-discipline of chemistry that involves the __________ s of unstable and radioactive elements where both electronic and nuclear changes can occur.

Exam Probability: **Low**

17. *Answer choices:*

(see index for correct answer)

- a. Chemical reaction
- b. Radiolysis
- c. Screaming jelly babies
- d. Salt metathesis reaction

Guidance: level 1

:: Sampling (statistics) ::

_________ uses statistical sampling to determine whether to accept or reject a production lot of material. It has been a common quality control technique used in industry. It is usually done as products leaves the factory, or in some cases even within the factory. Most often a producer supplies a consumer a number of items and a decision to accept or reject the items is made by determining the number of defective items in a sample from the lot. The lot is accepted if the number of defects falls below where the acceptance number or otherwise the lot is rejected.

Exam Probability: **Low**

18. *Answer choices:*

(see index for correct answer)

- a. Response rate
- b. Sample
- c. Acceptance sampling
- d. Selective recruitment

Guidance: level 1

:: Industrial equipment ::

__________s are heat exchangers typically used to provide heat to the bottom of industrial distillation columns. They boil the liquid from the bottom of a distillation column to generate vapors which are returned to the column to drive the distillation separation. The heat supplied to the column by the __________ at the bottom of the column is removed by the condenser at the top of the column.

Exam Probability: **High**

19. *Answer choices:*

(see index for correct answer)

- a. Single-ended recuperative burner
- b. Levelling stone
- c. Reboiler
- d. Impact mill

Guidance: level 1

:: Production and manufacturing ::

__________ is a set of techniques and tools for process improvement. Though as a shortened form it may be found written as 6S, it should not be confused with the methodology known as 6S .

Exam Probability: **Low**

20. *Answer choices:*

(see index for correct answer)

- a. Computer-aided process planning
- b. Changeover
- c. Pre-shipment inspection
- d. Six Sigma

Guidance: level 1

:: Outsourcing ::

__________ is an institutional procurement process that continuously improves and re-evaluates the purchasing activities of a company. In the services industry, __________ refers to a service solution, sometimes called a strategic partnership, which is specifically customized to meet the client`s individual needs. In a production environment, it is often considered one component of supply chain management. Modern supply chain management professionals have placed emphasis on defining the distinct differences between __________ and procurement. Procurement operations support tactical day-to-day transactions such as issuing Purchase Orders to suppliers, whereas __________ represents to strategic planning, supplier development, contract negotiation, supply chain infrastructure, and outsourcing models.

Exam Probability: **High**

21. *Answer choices:*

(see index for correct answer)

- a. Strategic sourcing
- b. Managed VoIP Service
- c. Application Management Services Framework
- d. Legal outsourcing

Guidance: level 1

:: Management ::

A __________ is an idea of the future or desired result that a person or a group of people envisions, plans and commits to achieve. People endeavor to reach __________ s within a finite time by setting deadlines.

Exam Probability: **High**

22. *Answer choices:*

(see index for correct answer)

- a. Goal
- b. Intelligent customer
- c. Marketing management
- d. Value migration

Guidance: level 1

:: Metal forming ::

_________ is a type of motion that combines rotation and translation of that object with respect to a surface , such that, if ideal conditions exist, the two are in contact with each other without sliding.

Exam Probability: **High**

23. *Answer choices:*

(see index for correct answer)

- a. Hot metal gas forming
- b. Rolling
- c. Electroforming
- d. Superplastic forming and diffusion bonding

Guidance: level 1

:: ::

__________ is the quantity of three-dimensional space enclosed by a closed surface, for example, the space that a substance or shape occupies or contains. __________ is often quantified numerically using the SI derived unit, the cubic metre. The __________ of a container is generally understood to be the capacity of the container; i. e., the amount of fluid that the container could hold, rather than the amount of space the container itself displaces.Three dimensional mathematical shapes are also assigned __________ s. __________ s of some simple shapes, such as regular, straight-edged, and circular shapes can be easily calculated using arithmetic formulas. __________ s of complicated shapes can be calculated with integral calculus if a formula exists for the shape`s boundary. One-dimensional figures and two-dimensional shapes are assigned zero __________ in the three-dimensional space.

Exam Probability: **Low**

24. *Answer choices:*

(see index for correct answer)

- a. deep-level diversity
- b. similarity-attraction theory
- c. Volume
- d. empathy

Guidance: level 1

:: Quality ::

The _________ , formerly the _________ Control , is a knowledge-based global community of quality professionals, with nearly 80,000 members dedicated to promoting and advancing quality tools, principles, and practices in their workplaces and communities.

Exam Probability: **Medium**

25. *Answer choices:*

(see index for correct answer)

- a. Quality by Design
- b. American Society for Quality
- c. Customer Service Excellence
- d. Dualistic Petri nets

Guidance: level 1

:: Quality assurance ::

Organizations that issue credentials or certify third parties against official standards are themselves formally accredited by _________ bodies ; hence they are sometimes known as "accredited certification bodies". The _________ process ensures that their certification practices are acceptable, typically meaning that they are competent to test and certify third parties, behave ethically and employ suitable quality assurance.

Exam Probability: **Medium**

26. *Answer choices:*

(see index for correct answer)

- a. Health tourism provider
- b. Hospital accreditation
- c. Technical Control Department
- d. Accreditation

Guidance: level 1

:: Natural resources ::

_________ s are resources that exist without actions of humankind. This includes all valued characteristics such as magnetic, gravitational, electrical properties and forces etc. On Earth it includes sunlight, atmosphere, water, land along with all vegetation, crops and animal life that naturally subsists upon or within the heretofore identified characteristics and substances.

Exam Probability: **Medium**

27. *Answer choices:*

(see index for correct answer)

- a. Exploitation of natural resources
- b. Natural resource

- c. Ferrallitisation
- d. Natural Resources Acts

Guidance: level 1

:: Project management ::

A _________ is a team whose members usually belong to different groups, functions and are assigned to activities for the same project. A team can be divided into sub-teams according to need. Usually _________ s are only used for a defined period of time. They are disbanded after the project is deemed complete. Due to the nature of the specific formation and disbandment, _________ s are usually in organizations.

Exam Probability: **Low**

28. *Answer choices:*

(see index for correct answer)

- a. Project team
- b. Opportunity management
- c. Burn down chart
- d. Float

Guidance: level 1

:: ::

_________ is a kind of action that occur as two or more objects have an effect upon one another. The idea of a two-way effect is essential in the concept of _________, as opposed to a one-way causal effect. A closely related term is interconnectivity, which deals with the _________ s of _________ s within systems: combinations of many simple _________ s can lead to surprising emergent phenomena. _________ has different tailored meanings in various sciences. Changes can also involve _________ .

Exam Probability: **Low**

29. *Answer choices:*

(see index for correct answer)

- a. Interaction
- b. hierarchical
- c. information systems assessment
- d. open system

Guidance: level 1

:: Quality awards ::

The _________ recognizes U.S. organizations in the business, health care, education, and nonprofit sectors for performance excellence. The Baldrige Award is the only formal recognition of the performance excellence of both public and private U.S. organizations given by the President of the United States. It is administered by the Baldrige Performance Excellence Program, which is based at and managed by the National Institute of Standards and Technology , an agency of the U.S. Department of Commerce.

Exam Probability: **Low**

30. *Answer choices:*

(see index for correct answer)

- a. Deming Prize
- b. European Quality Award
- c. The Deming Cup
- d. Rajiv Gandhi National Quality Award

Guidance: level 1

:: Lean manufacturing ::

__________ is a scheduling system for lean manufacturing and just-in-time manufacturing . Taiichi Ohno, an industrial engineer at Toyota, developed __________ to improve manufacturing efficiency. __________ is one method to achieve JIT. The system takes its name from the cards that track production within a factory. For many in the automotive sector, __________ is known as the "Toyota nameplate system" and as such the term is not used by some other automakers.

Exam Probability: **Low**

31. *Answer choices:*

(see index for correct answer)

- a. Lean product development

- b. Fixed Repeating Schedule
- c. Kanban
- d. Lean laboratory

Guidance: level 1

:: Supply chain management ::

__________ is a core supply chain function and includes supply chain planning and supply chain execution capabilities. Specifically, __________ is the capability firms use to plan total material requirements. The material requirements are communicated to procurement and other functions for sourcing. __________ is also responsible for determining the amount of material to be deployed at each stocking location across the supply chain, establishing material replenishment plans, determining inventory levels to hold for each type of inventory , and communicating information regarding material needs throughout the extended supply chain.

Exam Probability: **High**

32. *Answer choices:*

(see index for correct answer)

- a. Security risk
- b. Institute for Supply Management
- c. Intermediary
- d. OBS Logistics

Guidance: level 1

:: Marketing ::

__________ or stock control can be broadly defined as "the activity of checking a shop's stock." However, a more focused definition takes into account the more science-based, methodical practice of not only verifying a business` inventory but also focusing on the many related facets of inventory management "within an organisation to meet the demand placed upon that business economically." Other facets of __________ include supply chain management, production control, financial flexibility, and customer satisfaction. At the root of __________, however, is the __________ problem, which involves determining when to order, how much to order, and the logistics of those decisions.

Exam Probability: **Low**

33. *Answer choices:*

(see index for correct answer)

- a. Promo
- b. Cannibalization
- c. Food marketing
- d. Inventory control

Guidance: level 1

:: Unit operations ::

_________ is the process of separating the components or substances from a liquid mixture by using selective boiling and condensation. _________ may result in essentially complete separation , or it may be a partial separation that increases the concentration of selected components in the mixture. In either case, the process exploits differences in the volatility of the mixture`s components. In industrial chemistry, _________ is a unit operation of practically universal importance, but it is a physical separation process, not a chemical reaction.

Exam Probability: **High**

34. *Answer choices:*

(see index for correct answer)

- a. Distillation
- b. Solvent impregnated resin
- c. Homogenization
- d. Sedimentation coefficient

Guidance: level 1

:: Monopoly (economics) ::

_________ are "efficiencies formed by variety, not volume" . For example, a gas station that sells gasoline can sell soda, milk, baked goods, etc through their customer service representatives and thus achieve gasoline companies _________ .

Exam Probability: **High**

35. *Answer choices:*

(see index for correct answer)

- a. Revenue-cap regulation
- b. Sherman Antitrust Act
- c. Monopoly
- d. Economies of scope

Guidance: level 1

:: Management ::

_________ is the identification, evaluation, and prioritization of risks followed by coordinated and economical application of resources to minimize, monitor, and control the probability or impact of unfortunate events or to maximize the realization of opportunities.

Exam Probability: **High**

36. *Answer choices:*

(see index for correct answer)

- a. Change advisory board
- b. Supervisory board
- c. Risk management

- d. Radical transparency

Guidance: level 1

:: Product management ::

_________ is the state of being which occurs when an object, service, or practice is no longer wanted even though it may still be in good working order; however, the international standard EN62402 _________ Management - Application Guide defines _________ as being the "transition from availability of products by the original manufacturer or supplier to unavailability". _________ frequently occurs because a replacement has become available that has, in sum, more advantages compared to the disadvantages incurred by maintaining or repairing the original. Obsolete also refers to something that is already disused or discarded, or antiquated. Typically, _________ is preceded by a gradual decline in popularity.

Exam Probability: **Medium**

37. *Answer choices:*

(see index for correct answer)

- a. Dwinell-Wright Company
- b. Tipping point
- c. Promise Index
- d. Product manager

Guidance: level 1

:: Project management ::

A __________ is one of a series of numbered markers placed along a road or boundary at intervals of one mile or occasionally, parts of a mile. They are typically located at the side of the road or in a median or central reservation. They are alternatively known as mile markers, mileposts or mile posts . Mileage is the distance along the road from a fixed commencement point. Commonly the term " __________ " may also refer to markers placed at other distances, such as every kilometre.

Exam Probability: **Low**

38. *Answer choices:*

(see index for correct answer)

- a. Hammock activity
- b. Milestone
- c. Site survey
- d. Risk register

Guidance: level 1

:: Manufacturing ::

A _________ is an object used to extend the ability of an individual to modify features of the surrounding environment. Although many animals use simple _________ s, only human beings, whose use of stone _________ s dates back hundreds of millennia, use _________ s to make other _________ s. The set of _________ s needed to perform different tasks that are part of the same activity is called gear or equipment.

Exam Probability: **Medium**

39. *Answer choices:*

(see index for correct answer)

- a. Industrial Valley
- b. Tool
- c. Computer appliance
- d. Nails

Guidance: level 1

:: Product development ::

In business and engineering, _________ covers the complete process of bringing a new product to market. A central aspect of NPD is product design, along with various business considerations. _________ is described broadly as the transformation of a market opportunity into a product available for sale. The product can be tangible or intangible , though sometimes services and other processes are distinguished from "products." NPD requires an understanding of customer needs and wants, the competitive environment, and the nature of the market.Cost, time and quality are the main variables that drive customer needs. Aiming at these three variables, innovative companies develop continuous practices and strategies to better satisfy customer requirements and to increase their own market share by a regular development of new products. There are many uncertainties and challenges which companies must face throughout the process. The use of best practices and the elimination of barriers to communication are the main concerns for the management of the NPD .

Exam Probability: **High**

40. *Answer choices:*

(see index for correct answer)

- a. DFMA
- b. Minimum viable product
- c. New product development
- d. Design for assembly

Guidance: level 1

:: Project management ::

_________ is a process of setting goals, planning and/or controlling the organizing and leading the execution of any type of activity, such as.

Exam Probability: **Medium**

41. *Answer choices:*

(see index for correct answer)

- a. Collaborative planning software
- b. Karol Adamiecki
- c. Stages of project finance
- d. Association for Project Management

Guidance: level 1

:: Distribution, retailing, and wholesaling ::

The _________ is a distribution channel phenomenon in which forecasts yield supply chain inefficiencies. It refers to increasing swings in inventory in response to shifts in customer demand as one moves further up the supply chain. The concept first appeared in Jay Forrester`s Industrial Dynamics and thus it is also known as the Forrester effect. The _________ was named for the way the amplitude of a whip increases down its length. The further from the originating signal, the greater the distortion of the wave pattern. In a similar manner, forecast accuracy decreases as one moves upstream along the supply chain. For example, many consumer goods have fairly consistent consumption at retail but this signal becomes more chaotic and unpredictable as the focus moves away from consumer purchasing behavior.

Exam Probability: **Medium**

42. *Answer choices:*

(see index for correct answer)

- a. Fast Fiction
- b. Physical inventory
- c. Bullwhip effect
- d. Distribution center management system

Guidance: level 1

:: Information technology management ::

The term _________ is used to refer to periods when a system is unavailable. _________ or outage duration refers to a period of time that a system fails to provide or perform its primary function. Reliability, availability, recovery, and unavailability are related concepts.The unavailability is the proportion of a time-span that a system is unavailable or offline.This is usually a result of the system failing to function because of an unplanned event, or because of routine maintenance .

Exam Probability: **Medium**

43. *Answer choices:*

(see index for correct answer)

- a. Mobile business development

- b. Intelligent workload management
- c. Downtime
- d. Service Measurement Index

Guidance: level 1

:: Data management ::

_________ refers to a data-driven improvement cycle used for improving, optimizing and stabilizing business processes and designs. The _________ improvement cycle is the core tool used to drive Six Sigma projects. However, _________ is not exclusive to Six Sigma and can be used as the framework for other improvement applications.

Exam Probability: **Low**

44. *Answer choices:*

(see index for correct answer)

- a. Data access
- b. DMAIC
- c. Computer-aided software engineering
- d. Reactive business intelligence

Guidance: level 1

:: Management ::

__________ is a method of quality control which employs statistical methods to monitor and control a process. This helps to ensure that the process operates efficiently, producing more specification-conforming products with less waste . SPC can be applied to any process where the "conforming product" output can be measured. Key tools used in SPC include run charts, control charts, a focus on continuous improvement, and the design of experiments. An example of a process where SPC is applied is manufacturing lines.

Exam Probability: **Low**

45. *Answer choices:*

(see index for correct answer)

- a. Statistical process control
- b. Omnex
- c. Concept of operations
- d. Participative decision-making

Guidance: level 1

:: Production and manufacturing ::

__________ is the production under license of technology developed elsewhere. It is an especially prominent commercial practice in developing nations, which often approach __________ as a starting point for indigenous industrial development.

Exam Probability: **Low**

46. *Answer choices:*

(see index for correct answer)

- a. Subir Chowdhury
- b. Joint product
- c. Plant layout study
- d. Nesting

Guidance: level 1

:: Occupational safety and health ::

_________ is a chemical element with symbol Pb and atomic number 82. It is a heavy metal that is denser than most common materials. _________ is soft and malleable, and also has a relatively low melting point. When freshly cut, _________ is silvery with a hint of blue; it tarnishes to a dull gray color when exposed to air. _________ has the highest atomic number of any stable element and three of its isotopes are endpoints of major nuclear decay chains of heavier elements.

Exam Probability: **Medium**

47. *Answer choices:*

(see index for correct answer)

- a. Lead

- b. Kissing the shuttle
- c. Defensible space
- d. National Fire Fighter Near-Miss Reporting System

Guidance: level 1

:: Business ::

The seller, or the provider of the goods or services, completes a sale in response to an acquisition, appropriation, requisition or a direct interaction with the buyer at the point of sale. There is a passing of title of the item, and the settlement of a price, in which agreement is reached on a price for which transfer of ownership of the item will occur. The seller, not the purchaser typically executes the sale and it may be completed prior to the obligation of payment. In the case of indirect interaction, a person who sells goods or service on behalf of the owner is known as a _________ man or _________ woman or _________ person, but this often refers to someone selling goods in a store/shop, in which case other terms are also common, including _________ clerk, shop assistant, and retail clerk.

Exam Probability: **Low**

48. *Answer choices:*

(see index for correct answer)

- a. Sales
- b. The Social Contract with Business
- c. Employee experience management
- d. Ian McLeod

Guidance: level 1

:: Packaging materials ::

_________ is a thin material produced by pressing together moist fibres of cellulose pulp derived from wood, rags or grasses, and drying them into flexible sheets.It is a versatile material with many uses, including writing, printing, packaging, cleaning, decorating, and a number of industrial and construction processes. _________ s are essential in legal or non-legal documentation.

Exam Probability: **High**

49. *Answer choices:*

(see index for correct answer)

- a. Tear tape
- b. Greensulate
- c. Unica
- d. Paper

Guidance: level 1

:: Industrial engineering ::

The _________ is the design of any task that aims to describe or explain the variation of information under conditions that are hypothesized to reflect the variation. The term is generally associated with experiments in which the design introduces conditions that directly affect the variation, but may also refer to the design of quasi-experiments, in which natural conditions that influence the variation are selected for observation.

Exam Probability: **High**

50. *Answer choices:*

(see index for correct answer)

- a. Design of experiments
- b. Industrial ecology
- c. Response surface methodology
- d. Therblig

Guidance: level 1

:: Data management ::

_________ is an object-oriented program and library developed by CERN. It was originally designed for particle physics data analysis and contains several features specific to this field, but it is also used in other applications such as astronomy and data mining. The latest release is 6.16.00, as of 2018-11-14.

Exam Probability: **Low**

51. *Answer choices:*

(see index for correct answer)

- a. ROOT
- b. Reactive business intelligence
- c. Uniform data access
- d. datum

Guidance: level 1

:: Marketing techniques ::

A __________ is an award to be given to a person, a group of people like a sports team, or organization to recognise and reward actions or achievements. Official __________ s often involve monetary rewards as well as the fame that comes with them. Some __________ s are also associated with extravagant awarding ceremonies, such as the Academy Awards.

Exam Probability: **Medium**

52. *Answer choices:*

(see index for correct answer)

- a. Relevant space
- b. Prize
- c. Enterprise engagement
- d. Micromarketing

Guidance: level 1

:: Information technology management ::

__________ is the discipline of engineering concerned with the principles and practice of product and service quality assurance and control. In the software development, it is the management, development, operation and maintenance of IT systems and enterprise architectures with a high quality standard.

Exam Probability: **Low**

53. *Answer choices:*

(see index for correct answer)

- a. Drill down
- b. Quality Engineering
- c. Cable management
- d. HP ePrint

Guidance: level 1

:: Asset ::

In financial accounting, an __________ is any resource owned by the business. Anything tangible or intangible that can be owned or controlled to produce value and that is held by a company to produce positive economic value is an __________. Simply stated, __________s represent value of ownership that can be converted into cash . The balance sheet of a firm records the monetary value of the __________s owned by that firm. It covers money and other valuables belonging to an individual or to a business.

Exam Probability: **Low**

54. *Answer choices:*

(see index for correct answer)

- a. Current asset
- b. Fixed asset

Guidance: level 1

:: Metalworking ::

A __________ is a round object with various uses. It is used in __________ games, where the play of the game follows the state of the __________ as it is hit, kicked or thrown by players. __________s can also be used for simpler activities, such as catch or juggling. __________s made from hard-wearing materials are used in engineering applications to provide very low friction bearings, known as __________ bearings. Black-powder weapons use stone and metal __________s as projectiles.

Exam Probability: **High**

55. *Answer choices:*

(see index for correct answer)

- a. Traditional metal working in Mexico
- b. Ironwork
- c. Powder metallurgy
- d. Industrial finishing

Guidance: level 1

:: Process management ::

When used in the context of communication networks, such as Ethernet or packet radio, _________ or network _________ is the rate of successful message delivery over a communication channel. The data these messages belong to may be delivered over a physical or logical link, or it can pass through a certain network node. _________ is usually measured in bits per second , and sometimes in data packets per second or data packets per time slot.

Exam Probability: **High**

56. *Answer choices:*

(see index for correct answer)

- a. Conformance checking
- b. Value grid
- c. Six Sigma for ROI
- d. Throughput

Guidance: level 1

:: Commerce ::

A __________ is an employee within a company, business or other organization who is responsible at some level for buying or approving the acquisition of goods and services needed by the company. Responsible for buying the best quality products, goods and services for their company at the most competitive prices, __________ s work in a wide range of sectors for many different organizations. The position responsibilities may be the same as that of a buyer or purchasing agent, or may include wider supervisory or managerial responsibilities. A __________ may oversee the acquisition of materials needed for production, general supplies for offices and facilities, equipment, or construction contracts. A __________ often supervises purchasing agents and buyers, but in small companies the __________ may also be the purchasing agent or buyer. The __________ position may also carry the title "Procurement Manager" or in the public sector, "Procurement Officer". He or she can come from both an Engineering or Economics background.

Exam Probability: **Medium**

57. *Answer choices:*

(see index for correct answer)

- a. Customs broking
- b. Mail order
- c. Purchasing manager
- d. Social gravity

Guidance: level 1

:: Production and manufacturing ::

_________ was a management-led program to eliminate defects in industrial production that enjoyed brief popularity in American industry from 1964 to the early 1970s. Quality expert Philip Crosby later incorporated it into his "Absolutes of Quality Management" and it enjoyed a renaissance in the American automobile industry—as a performance goal more than as a program—in the 1990s. Although applicable to any type of enterprise, it has been primarily adopted within supply chains wherever large volumes of components are being purchased .

Exam Probability: **Medium**

58. *Answer choices:*

(see index for correct answer)

- a. Digital materialization
- b. Value-added agriculture
- c. ERPNEXT
- d. Zero Defects

Guidance: level 1

:: Alchemical processes ::

In chemistry, a _________ is a special type of homogeneous mixture composed of two or more substances. In such a mixture, a solute is a substance dissolved in another substance, known as a solvent. The mixing process of a _________ happens at a scale where the effects of chemical polarity are involved, resulting in interactions that are specific to solvation. The _________ assumes the phase of the solvent when the solvent is the larger fraction of the mixture, as is commonly the case. The concentration of a solute in a _________ is the mass of that solute expressed as a percentage of the mass of the whole _________. The term aqueous _________ is when one of the solvents is water.

Exam Probability: **High**

59. *Answer choices:*

(see index for correct answer)

- a. Fixation
- b. Unity of opposites
- c. Solution
- d. Putrefying bacteria

Guidance: level 1

Commerce

Commerce relates to "the exchange of goods and services, especially on a large scale." It includes legal, economic, political, social, cultural and technological systems that operate in any country or internationally.

:: Real property law ::

A _________ is the grant of authority or rights, stating that the granter formally recognizes the prerogative of the recipient to exercise the rights specified. It is implicit that the granter retains superiority , and that the recipient admits a limited status within the relationship, and it is within that sense that _________ s were historically granted, and that sense is retained in modern usage of the term.

Exam Probability: **Low**

1. *Answer choices:*

(see index for correct answer)

- a. Charter
- b. Scottish Land Court
- c. Life interest
- d. Structural encroachment

Guidance: level 1

:: E-commerce ::

The phrase _________ was originally coined in 1997 by Kevin Duffey at the launch of the Global _________ Forum, to mean "the delivery of electronic commerce capabilities directly into the consumer's hand, anywhere, via wireless technology." Many choose to think of _________ as meaning "a retail outlet in your customer's pocket."

Exam Probability: **Medium**

2. *Answer choices:*

(see index for correct answer)

- a. Virtual enterprise
- b. Mobile commerce

- c. Supply chain attack
- d. Great Online Shopping Festival

Guidance: level 1

:: Globalization-related theories ::

_________ is the process in which a nation is being improved in the sector of the economic, political, and social well-being of its people. The term has been used frequently by economists, politicians, and others in the 20th and 21st centuries. The concept, however, has been in existence in the West for centuries. "Modernization, "westernization", and especially "industrialization" are other terms often used while discussing _________ . _________ has a direct relationship with the environment and environmental issues. _________ is very often confused with industrial development, even in some academic sources.

Exam Probability: **Low**

3. *Answer choices:*

(see index for correct answer)

- a. postmodernism
- b. Capitalism
- c. Economic development

Guidance: level 1

:: Basic financial concepts ::

_________ is a sustained increase in the general price level of goods and services in an economy over a period of time. When the general price level rises, each unit of currency buys fewer goods and services; consequently, _________ reflects a reduction in the purchasing power per unit of money a loss of real value in the medium of exchange and unit of account within the economy. The measure of _________ is the _________ rate, the annualized percentage change in a general price index, usually the consumer price index, over time. The opposite of _________ is deflation.

Exam Probability: **Medium**

4. *Answer choices:*

(see index for correct answer)

- a. Inflation
- b. Leverage cycle
- c. Present value of benefits
- d. Forward guidance

Guidance: level 1

:: Management ::

_________ is the process of thinking about the activities required to achieve a desired goal. It is the first and foremost activity to achieve desired results. It involves the creation and maintenance of a plan, such as psychological aspects that require conceptual skills. There are even a couple of tests to measure someone's capability of _________ well. As such, _________ is a fundamental property of intelligent behavior. An important further meaning, often just called " _________ " is the legal context of permitted building developments.

Exam Probability: **High**

5. *Answer choices:*

(see index for correct answer)

- a. Planning
- b. Supply chain sustainability
- c. Total security management
- d. Decentralized decision-making

Guidance: level 1

:: Price fixing convictions ::

__________ is the flag carrier airline of the United Kingdom, headquartered at Waterside, Harmondsworth. It is the second largest airline in the United Kingdom, based on fleet size and passengers carried, behind easyJet. The airline is based in Waterside near its main hub at London Heathrow Airport. In January 2011 BA merged with Iberia, creating the International Airlines Group , a holding company registered in Madrid, Spain. IAG is the world`s third-largest airline group in terms of annual revenue and the second-largest in Europe. It is listed on the London Stock Exchange and in the FTSE 100 Index. __________ is the first passenger airline to have generated more than $1 billion on a single air route in a year .

Exam Probability: **Medium**

6. *Answer choices:*

(see index for correct answer)

- a. British Airways
- b. ThyssenKrupp
- c. Northwest Airlines
- d. Archer Daniels Midland

Guidance: level 1

:: Cryptography ::

In cryptography, _________ is the process of encoding a message or information in such a way that only authorized parties can access it and those who are not authorized cannot. _________ does not itself prevent interference, but denies the intelligible content to a would-be interceptor. In an _________ scheme, the intended information or message, referred to as plaintext, is encrypted using an _________ algorithm – a cipher – generating ciphertext that can be read only if decrypted. For technical reasons, an _________ scheme usually uses a pseudo-random _________ key generated by an algorithm. It is in principle possible to decrypt the message without possessing the key, but, for a well-designed _________ scheme, considerable computational resources and skills are required. An authorized recipient can easily decrypt the message with the key provided by the originator to recipients but not to unauthorized users.

Exam Probability: **High**

7. *Answer choices:*

(see index for correct answer)

- a. Electronic Signature
- b. Encryption
- c. cryptosystem
- d. backdoor

Guidance: level 1

:: ::

__________ is getting a diploma or academic degree or the ceremony that is sometimes associated with it, in which students become graduates. The date of __________ is often called __________ day. The __________ ceremony itself is also called commencement, convocation or invocation.

Exam Probability: **Low**

8. *Answer choices:*

(see index for correct answer)

- a. Graduation
- b. deep-level diversity
- c. co-culture
- d. similarity-attraction theory

Guidance: level 1

:: Generally Accepted Accounting Principles ::

Expenditure is an outflow of money to another person or group to pay for an item or service, or for a category of costs. For a tenant, rent is an __________. For students or parents, tuition is an __________. Buying food, clothing, furniture or an automobile is often referred to as an __________. An __________ is a cost that is "paid" or "remitted", usually in exchange for something of value. Something that seems to cost a great deal is "expensive". Something that seems to cost little is "inexpensive". " __________ s of the table" are __________ s of dining, refreshments, a feast, etc.

Exam Probability: **High**

9. *Answer choices:*

(see index for correct answer)

- a. Long-term liabilities
- b. Cash method of accounting
- c. Paid in capital
- d. Petty cash

Guidance: level 1

:: ::

A _________ , or also known as foreman, overseer, facilitator, monitor, area coordinator, or sometimes gaffer, is the job title of a low level management position that is primarily based on authority over a worker or charge of a workplace. A _________ can also be one of the most senior in the staff at the place of work, such as a Professor who oversees a PhD dissertation. Supervision, on the other hand, can be performed by people without this formal title, for example by parents. The term _________ itself can be used to refer to any personnel who have this task as part of their job description.

Exam Probability: **Medium**

10. *Answer choices:*

(see index for correct answer)

- a. similarity-attraction theory
- b. co-culture
- c. Character
- d. Supervisor

Guidance: level 1

:: Marketing by medium ::

__________, also called online marketing or Internet advertising or web advertising, is a form of marketing and advertising which uses the Internet to deliver promotional marketing messages to consumers. Many consumers find __________ disruptive and have increasingly turned to ad blocking for a variety of reasons. When software is used to do the purchasing, it is known as programmatic advertising.

Exam Probability: **Medium**

11. *Answer choices:*

(see index for correct answer)

- a. Social intelligence architect
- b. Online advertising
- c. Social video marketing
- d. Direct Text Marketing

Guidance: level 1

:: E-commerce ::

An ________ , or automated clearinghouse, is an electronic network for financial transactions, generally domestic low value payments. An ACH is a computer-based clearing house and settlement facility established to process the exchange of electronic transactions between participating financial institutions. It is a form of clearing house that is specifically for payments and may support both credit transfers and direct debits.

Exam Probability: **High**

12. *Answer choices:*

(see index for correct answer)

- a. GeBIZ
- b. UN/CEFACT
- c. Automated Clearing House
- d. Segundamano

Guidance: level 1

:: Real estate ::

________ s serve several societal needs – primarily as shelter from weather, security, living space, privacy, to store belongings, and to comfortably live and work. A ________ as a shelter represents a physical division of the human habitat and the outside .

Exam Probability: **High**

13. *Answer choices:*

(see index for correct answer)

- a. Conditional limitation
- b. Displaced sales
- c. Building
- d. Amortization

Guidance: level 1

:: Stock market ::

_________ is freedom from, or resilience against, potential harm caused by others. Beneficiaries of _________ may be of persons and social groups, objects and institutions, ecosystems or any other entity or phenomenon vulnerable to unwanted change by its environment.

Exam Probability: **High**

14. *Answer choices:*

(see index for correct answer)

- a. Primary shares
- b. Indian Depository Receipt
- c. Prime Standard

- d. Security

Guidance: level 1

:: Management ::

_________ is a process by which entities review the quality of all factors involved in production. ISO 9000 defines _________ as "A part of quality management focused on fulfilling quality requirements".

Exam Probability: **Medium**

15. *Answer choices:*

(see index for correct answer)

- a. Quality control
- b. Tacit knowledge
- c. One in, one out policy
- d. Mission critical

Guidance: level 1

:: Asset ::

In financial accounting, an __________ is any resource owned by the business. Anything tangible or intangible that can be owned or controlled to produce value and that is held by a company to produce positive economic value is an __________. Simply stated, __________s represent value of ownership that can be converted into cash . The balance sheet of a firm records the monetary value of the __________s owned by that firm. It covers money and other valuables belonging to an individual or to a business.

Exam Probability: **Medium**

16. *Answer choices:*

(see index for correct answer)

- a. Current asset
- b. Asset

Guidance: level 1

:: ::

A __________ is a person or firm who arranges transactions between a buyer and a seller for a commission when the deal is executed. A __________ who also acts as a seller or as a buyer becomes a principal party to the deal. Neither role should be confused with that of an agent—one who acts on behalf of a principal party in a deal.

Exam Probability: **Low**

17. *Answer choices:*

(see index for correct answer)

- a. empathy
- b. co-culture
- c. personal values
- d. Broker

Guidance: level 1

:: Generally Accepted Accounting Principles ::

In accounting, _________ is the income that a business have from its normal business activities, usually from the sale of goods and services to customers. _________ is also referred to as sales or turnover.Some companies receive _________ from interest, royalties, or other fees. _________ may refer to business income in general, or it may refer to the amount, in a monetary unit, earned during a period of time, as in "Last year, Company X had _________ of $42 million". Profits or net income generally imply total _________ minus total expenses in a given period. In accounting, in the balance statement it is a subsection of the Equity section and _________ increases equity, it is often referred to as the "top line" due to its position on the income statement at the very top. This is to be contrasted with the "bottom line" which denotes net income .

Exam Probability: **Low**

18. *Answer choices:*

(see index for correct answer)

- a. Revenue
- b. Earnings before interest and taxes
- c. Net profit
- d. Earnings before interest, taxes, depreciation, and amortization

Guidance: level 1

:: ::

An __________ is an area of the production, distribution, or trade, and consumption of goods and services by different agents. Understood in its broadest sense, 'The __________ is defined as a social domain that emphasize the practices, discourses, and material expressions associated with the production, use, and management of resources'. Economic agents can be individuals, businesses, organizations, or governments. Economic transactions occur when two parties agree to the value or price of the transacted good or service, commonly expressed in a certain currency. However, monetary transactions only account for a small part of the economic domain.

Exam Probability: **High**

19. *Answer choices:*

(see index for correct answer)

- a. Economy
- b. co-culture
- c. personal values
- d. imperative

Guidance: level 1

:: ::

_________ is the collaborative effort of a team to achieve a common goal or to complete a task in the most effective and efficient way. This concept is seen within the greater framework of a team, which is a group of interdependent individuals who work together towards a common goal. Basic requirements for effective _________ are an adequate team size , available resources for the team to make use of , and clearly defined roles within the team in order for everyone to have a clear purpose. _________ is present in any context where a group of people are working together to achieve a common goal. These contexts include an industrial organization , athletics , a school , and the healthcare system . In each of these settings, the level of _________ and interdependence can vary from low , to intermediate , to high , depending on the amount of communication, interaction, and collaboration present between team members.

Exam Probability: **High**

20. *Answer choices:*

(see index for correct answer)

- a. Character
- b. Teamwork
- c. information systems assessment
- d. Sarbanes-Oxley act of 2002

Guidance: level 1

:: Business law ::

A __________ is a business entity created by two or more parties, generally characterized by shared ownership, shared returns and risks, and shared governance. Companies typically pursue __________s for one of four reasons: to access a new market, particularly emerging markets; to gain scale efficiencies by combining assets and operations; to share risk for major investments or projects; or to access skills and capabilities.

Exam Probability: **Medium**

21. *Answer choices:*

(see index for correct answer)

- a. Personal Property Security Act
- b. Joint venture
- c. Output contract
- d. Economic torts

Guidance: level 1

:: ::

In law, an _________ is the process in which cases are reviewed, where parties request a formal change to an official decision. _________ s function both as a process for error correction as well as a process of clarifying and interpreting law. Although appellate courts have existed for thousands of years, common law countries did not incorporate an affirmative right to _________ into their jurisprudence until the 19th century.

Exam Probability: **Low**

22. *Answer choices:*

(see index for correct answer)

- a. similarity-attraction theory
- b. Appeal
- c. information systems assessment
- d. personal values

Guidance: level 1

:: ::

Business is the activity of making one`s living or making money by producing or buying and selling products . Simply put, it is "any activity or enterprise entered into for profit. It does not mean it is a company, a corporation, partnership, or have any such formal organization, but it can range from a street peddler to General Motors."

Exam Probability: **Low**

23. *Answer choices:*

(see index for correct answer)

- a. Character
- b. Firm
- c. interpersonal communication
- d. empathy

Guidance: level 1

:: ::

In Christian denominations that practice infant baptism, confirmation is seen as the sealing of Christianity created in baptism. Those being _________ are known as confirmands. In some denominations, such as the Anglican Communion and Methodist Churches, confirmation bestows full membership in a local congregation upon the recipient. In others, such as the Roman Catholic Church, Confirmation "renders the bond with the Church more perfect", because, while a baptized person is already a member, "reception of the sacrament of Confirmation is necessary for the completion of baptismal grace".

Exam Probability: **Low**

24. *Answer choices:*

(see index for correct answer)

- a. levels of analysis
- b. Confirmed

- c. information systems assessment
- d. corporate values

Guidance: level 1

:: Behavior modification ::

In psychotherapy and mental health, _________ has a positive sense of empowering individuals, or a negative sense of encouraging dysfunctional behavior.

Exam Probability: **Medium**

25. *Answer choices:*

(see index for correct answer)

- a. Enabling
- b. behavioural change

Guidance: level 1

:: ::

An _________ is a systematic and independent examination of books, accounts, statutory records, documents and vouchers of an organization to ascertain how far the financial statements as well as non-financial disclosures present a true and fair view of the concern. It also attempts to ensure that the books of accounts are properly maintained by the concern as required by law. _________ ing has become such a ubiquitous phenomenon in the corporate and the public sector that academics started identifying an " _________ Society". The _________ or perceives and recognises the propositions before them for examination, obtains evidence, evaluates the same and formulates an opinion on the basis of his judgement which is communicated through their _________ ing report.

Exam Probability: **Medium**

26. *Answer choices:*

(see index for correct answer)

- a. process perspective
- b. information systems assessment
- c. deep-level diversity
- d. corporate values

Guidance: level 1

:: Information technology ::

__________ is the use of computers to store, retrieve, transmit, and manipulate data, or information, often in the context of a business or other enterprise. IT is considered to be a subset of information and communications technology . An __________ system is generally an information system, a communications system or, more specifically speaking, a computer system – including all hardware, software and peripheral equipment – operated by a limited group of users.

Exam Probability: **Low**

27. *Answer choices:*

(see index for correct answer)

- a. United States v. Ivanov
- b. Software-defined data center
- c. Mobile file management
- d. 2080

Guidance: level 1

:: Business models ::

A __________, __________ company or daughter company is a company that is owned or controlled by another company, which is called the parent company, parent, or holding company. The __________ can be a company, corporation, or limited liability company. In some cases it is a government or state-owned enterprise. In some cases, particularly in the music and book publishing industries, subsidiaries are referred to as imprints.

Exam Probability: **High**

28. *Answer choices:*

(see index for correct answer)

- a. The India Way
- b. Parent company
- c. Small business
- d. Cooperative

Guidance: level 1

:: Marketing ::

__________ is a concept introduced in a book of the same name in 1999 by marketing expert Seth Godin. __________ is a non-traditional marketing technique that advertises goods and services when advance consent is given.

Exam Probability: **High**

29. *Answer choices:*

(see index for correct answer)

- a. Category management
- b. Permission marketing
- c. Blind credential
- d. Marketing channel

Guidance: level 1

:: Data interchange standards ::

_________ is the concept of businesses electronically communicating information that was traditionally communicated on paper, such as purchase orders and invoices. Technical standards for EDI exist to facilitate parties transacting such instruments without having to make special arrangements.

Exam Probability: **Low**

30. *Answer choices:*

(see index for correct answer)

- a. Electronic data interchange
- b. Data Interchange Standards Association
- c. Domain Application Protocol
- d. Interaction protocol

Guidance: level 1

:: ::

_________ is the amount of time someone works beyond normal working hours. The term is also used for the pay received for this time. Normal hours may be determined in several ways.

Exam Probability: **Medium**

31. *Answer choices:*

(see index for correct answer)

- a. co-culture
- b. Overtime
- c. information systems assessment
- d. hierarchical

Guidance: level 1

:: Scientific method ::

In the social sciences and life sciences, a _________ is a research method involving an up-close, in-depth, and detailed examination of a subject of study, as well as its related contextual conditions.

Exam Probability: **Low**

32. *Answer choices:*

(see index for correct answer)

- a. Causal research
- b. pilot project
- c. Preference test
- d. Case study

Guidance: level 1

:: Direct marketing ::

_________ is a form of advertising where organizations communicate directly to customers through a variety of media including cell phone text messaging, email, websites, online adverts, database marketing, fliers, catalog distribution, promotional letters, targeted television, newspapers, magazine advertisements, and outdoor advertising. Among practitioners, it is also known as direct response marketing.

Exam Probability: **High**

33. *Answer choices:*

(see index for correct answer)

- a. Tupperware Brands
- b. Rick Cesari
- c. Response Dynamics
- d. Specialty catalogs

Guidance: level 1

:: Business law ::

The ________ , first published in 1952, is one of a number of Uniform Acts that have been established as law with the goal of harmonizing the laws of sales and other commercial transactions across the United States of America through UCC adoption by all 50 states, the District of Columbia, and the Territories of the United States.

Exam Probability: **Medium**

34. *Answer choices:*

(see index for correct answer)

- a. European Patent Convention
- b. Complex structured finance transactions
- c. Oppression remedy
- d. Uniform Commercial Code

Guidance: level 1

:: ::

_________ or accountancy is the measurement, processing, and communication of financial information about economic entities such as businesses and corporations. The modern field was established by the Italian mathematician Luca Pacioli in 1494. _________ , which has been called the "language of business", measures the results of an organization's economic activities and conveys this information to a variety of users, including investors, creditors, management, and regulators. Practitioners of _________ are known as accountants. The terms " _________ " and "financial reporting" are often used as synonyms.

Exam Probability: **Medium**

35. *Answer choices:*

(see index for correct answer)

- a. corporate values
- b. levels of analysis
- c. hierarchical perspective
- d. empathy

Guidance: level 1

:: ::

A federation is a political entity characterized by a union of partially self-governing provinces, states, or other regions under a central _________ . In a federation, the self-governing status of the component states, as well as the division of power between them and the central government, is typically constitutionally entrenched and may not be altered by a unilateral decision of either party, the states or the federal political body. Alternatively, federation is a form of government in which sovereign power is formally divided between a central authority and a number of constituent regions so that each region retains some degree of control over its internal affairs. It is often argued that federal states where the central government has the constitutional authority to suspend a constituent state`s government by invoking gross mismanagement or civil unrest, or to adopt national legislation that overrides or infringe on the constituent states` powers by invoking the central government`s constitutional authority to ensure "peace and good government" or to implement obligations contracted under an international treaty, are not truly federal states.

Exam Probability: **High**

36. *Answer choices:*

(see index for correct answer)

- a. hierarchical
- b. corporate values
- c. surface-level diversity
- d. Federal government

Guidance: level 1

:: ::

__________ refers to a business or organization attempting to acquire goods or services to accomplish its goals. Although there are several organizations that attempt to set standards in the __________ process, processes can vary greatly between organizations. Typically the word " __________ " is not used interchangeably with the word "procurement", since procurement typically includes expediting, supplier quality, and transportation and logistics in addition to __________ .

Exam Probability: **High**

37. *Answer choices:*

(see index for correct answer)

- a. Purchasing
- b. functional perspective
- c. empathy
- d. personal values

Guidance: level 1

:: Marketing ::

A __________ is an overall experience of a customer that distinguishes an organization or product from its rivals in the eyes of the customer. __________ s are used in business, marketing, and advertising. Name __________ s are sometimes distinguished from generic or store __________ s.

Exam Probability: **Low**

38. *Answer choices:*

(see index for correct answer)

- a. Product churning
- b. Object Value
- c. Brand
- d. Customer to customer

Guidance: level 1

:: ::

According to the philosopher Piyush Mathur , "Tangibility is the property that a phenomenon exhibits if it has and/or transports mass and/or energy and/or momentum".

Exam Probability: **Low**

39. *Answer choices:*

(see index for correct answer)

- a. surface-level diversity
- b. similarity-attraction theory
- c. Tangible
- d. hierarchical perspective

Guidance: level 1

:: Accounting source documents ::

A __________ is a commercial document and first official offer issued by a buyer to a seller indicating types, quantities, and agreed prices for products or services. It is used to control the purchasing of products and services from external suppliers. __________ s can be an essential part of enterprise resource planning system orders.

Exam Probability: **High**

40. *Answer choices:*

(see index for correct answer)

- a. Remittance advice
- b. Purchase order
- c. Bank statement
- d. Credit memorandum

Guidance: level 1

:: Organizational structure ::

An __________ defines how activities such as task allocation, coordination, and supervision are directed toward the achievement of organizational aims.

Exam Probability: **High**

41. *Answer choices:*

(see index for correct answer)

- a. Organization of the New York City Police Department
- b. Automated Bureaucracy
- c. Blessed Unrest
- d. Followership

Guidance: level 1

:: Commercial item transport and distribution ::

In a contract of carriage, the _________ is the entity who is financially responsible for the receipt of a shipment. Generally, but not always, the _________ is the same as the receiver.

Exam Probability: **Low**

42. *Answer choices:*

(see index for correct answer)

- a. Pallet
- b. Consignee
- c. SkyCat
- d. MC Freight Systems

Guidance: level 1

:: Summary statistics ::

__________ is the number of occurrences of a repeating event per unit of time. It is also referred to as temporal __________ , which emphasizes the contrast to spatial __________ and angular __________ . The period is the duration of time of one cycle in a repeating event, so the period is the reciprocal of the __________ . For example: if a newborn baby's heart beats at a __________ of 120 times a minute, its period—the time interval between beats—is half a second . __________ is an important parameter used in science and engineering to specify the rate of oscillatory and vibratory phenomena, such as mechanical vibrations, audio signals , radio waves, and light.

Exam Probability: **High**

43. *Answer choices:*

(see index for correct answer)

- a. Quartile
- b. Decile
- c. Frequency
- d. Location parameter

Guidance: level 1

:: ::

__________ is a marketing communication that employs an openly sponsored, non-personal message to promote or sell a product, service or idea. Sponsors of __________ are typically businesses wishing to promote their products or services. __________ is differentiated from public relations in that an advertiser pays for and has control over the message. It differs from personal selling in that the message is non-personal, i.e., not directed to a particular individual. __________ is communicated through various mass media, including traditional media such as newspapers, magazines, television, radio, outdoor __________ or direct mail; and new media such as search results, blogs, social media, websites or text messages. The actual presentation of the message in a medium is referred to as an advertisement, or "ad" or advert for short.

Exam Probability: **Medium**

44. *Answer choices:*

(see index for correct answer)

- a. Advertising
- b. open system
- c. cultural
- d. hierarchical

Guidance: level 1

:: ::

In marketing jargon, product lining is offering several related products for sale individually. Unlike product bundling, where several products are combined into one group, which is then offered for sale as a units, product lining involves offering the products for sale separately. A line can comprise related products of various sizes, types, colors, qualities, or prices. Line depth refers to the number of subcategories a category has. Line consistency refers to how closely related the products that make up the line are. Line vulnerability refers to the percentage of sales or profits that are derived from only a few products in the line.

Exam Probability: **Low**

45. *Answer choices:*

(see index for correct answer)

- a. interpersonal communication
- b. Product line
- c. functional perspective
- d. personal values

Guidance: level 1

:: ::

In marketing jargon, product lining is offering several related products for sale individually. Unlike product bundling, where several products are combined into one group, which is then offered for sale as a units, product lining involves offering the products for sale separately. A line can comprise related products of various sizes, types, colors, qualities, or prices. Line depth refers to the number of subcategories a category has. Line consistency refers to how closely related the products that make up the line are. Line vulnerability refers to the percentage of sales or profits that are derived from only a few products in the line.

Exam Probability: **High**

46. *Answer choices:*

(see index for correct answer)

- a. Product mix
- b. personal values
- c. empathy
- d. Character

Guidance: level 1

:: ::

_________ is the principled guide to action taken by the administrative executive branches of the state with regard to a class of issues, in a manner consistent with law and institutional customs.

Exam Probability: **Medium**

47. *Answer choices:*

(see index for correct answer)

- a. hierarchical perspective
- b. functional perspective
- c. empathy
- d. Public policy

Guidance: level 1

:: International trade ::

An _________ is a good brought into a jurisdiction, especially across a national border, from an external source. The party bringing in the good is called an _________ er. An _________ in the receiving country is an export from the sending country. _________ ation and exportation are the defining financial transactions of international trade.

Exam Probability: **High**

48. *Answer choices:*

(see index for correct answer)

- a. OPEC
- b. Development theory

- c. GlobalTrade.net
- d. Franz Oppenheimer

Guidance: level 1

:: Commercial item transport and distribution ::

A _________ , forwarder, or forwarding agent, also known as a non-vessel operating common carrier , is a person or company that organizes shipments for individuals or corporations to get goods from the manufacturer or producer to a market, customer or final point of distribution. Forwarders contract with a carrier or often multiple carriers to move the goods. A forwarder does not move the goods but acts as an expert in the logistics network. These carriers can use a variety of shipping modes, including ships, airplanes, trucks, and railroads, and often do utilize multiple modes for a single shipment. For example, the _________ may arrange to have cargo moved from a plant to an airport by truck, flown to the destination city, then moved from the airport to a customer`s building by another truck.

Exam Probability: **Low**

49. *Answer choices:*

(see index for correct answer)

- a. Freight forwarder
- b. Green logistics
- c. Third-party logistics
- d. Standard Carrier Alpha Code

Guidance: level 1

:: ::

Advertising is a marketing communication that employs an openly sponsored, non-personal message to promote or sell a product, service or idea. Sponsors of advertising are typically businesses wishing to promote their products or services. Advertising is differentiated from public relations in that an advertiser pays for and has control over the message. It differs from personal selling in that the message is non-personal, i.e., not directed to a particular individual.Advertising is communicated through various mass media, including traditional media such as newspapers, magazines, television, radio, outdoor advertising or direct mail; and new media such as search results, blogs, social media, websites or text messages. The actual presentation of the message in a medium is referred to as an _________ , or "ad" or advert for short.

Exam Probability: **High**

50. *Answer choices:*

(see index for correct answer)

- a. cultural
- b. deep-level diversity
- c. Advertisement
- d. process perspective

Guidance: level 1

:: ::

_________ Holdings, Inc. is an American company operating a worldwide online payments system that supports online money transfers and serves as an electronic alternative to traditional paper methods like checks and money orders. The company operates as a payment processor for online vendors, auction sites, and many other commercial users, for which it charges a fee in exchange for benefits such as one-click transactions and password memory. _________ `s payment system, also called _________ , is considered a type of payment rail.

Exam Probability: **High**

51. *Answer choices:*

(see index for correct answer)

- a. functional perspective
- b. deep-level diversity
- c. Sarbanes-Oxley act of 2002
- d. hierarchical perspective

Guidance: level 1

:: ::

_________ s are formal, sociotechnical, organizational systems designed to collect, process, store, and distribute information. In a sociotechnical perspective, _________ s are composed by four components: task, people, structure , and technology.

Exam Probability: **High**

52. *Answer choices:*

(see index for correct answer)

- a. Sarbanes-Oxley act of 2002
- b. open system
- c. Character
- d. empathy

Guidance: level 1

:: ::

_________ is the provision of service to customers before, during and after a purchase. The perception of success of such interactions is dependent on employees "who can adjust themselves to the personality of the guest". _________ concerns the priority an organization assigns to _________ relative to components such as product innovation and pricing. In this sense, an organization that values good _________ may spend more money in training employees than the average organization or may proactively interview customers for feedback.

Exam Probability: **Medium**

53. *Answer choices:*

(see index for correct answer)

- a. information systems assessment
- b. functional perspective
- c. Customer service
- d. levels of analysis

Guidance: level 1

:: Accounting source documents ::

An _________ , bill or tab is a commercial document issued by a seller to a buyer, relating to a sale transaction and indicating the products, quantities, and agreed prices for products or services the seller had provided the buyer.

Exam Probability: **Low**

54. *Answer choices:*

(see index for correct answer)

- a. Air waybill
- b. Parcel audit
- c. Superbill
- d. Bank statement

Guidance: level 1

:: ::

_________ refers to the overall process of attracting, shortlisting, selecting and appointing suitable candidates for jobs within an organization. _________ can also refer to processes involved in choosing individuals for unpaid roles. Managers, human resource generalists and _________ specialists may be tasked with carrying out _________, but in some cases public-sector employment agencies, commercial _________ agencies, or specialist search consultancies are used to undertake parts of the process. Internet-based technologies which support all aspects of _________ have become widespread.

Exam Probability: **Medium**

55. *Answer choices:*

(see index for correct answer)

- a. corporate values
- b. functional perspective
- c. personal values
- d. Recruitment

Guidance: level 1

:: Goods ::

In most contexts, the concept of _________ denotes the conduct that should be preferred when posed with a choice between possible actions. _________ is generally considered to be the opposite of evil, and is of interest in the study of morality, ethics, religion and philosophy. The specific meaning and etymology of the term and its associated translations among ancient and contemporary languages show substantial variation in its inflection and meaning depending on circumstances of place, history, religious, or philosophical context.

Exam Probability: **High**

56. *Answer choices:*

(see index for correct answer)

- a. Neutral good
- b. Good
- c. excludable
- d. Necessity good

Guidance: level 1

:: Income ::

In business and accounting, net income is an entity`s income minus cost of goods sold, expenses and taxes for an accounting period. It is computed as the residual of all revenues and gains over all expenses and losses for the period, and has also been defined as the net increase in shareholders` equity that results from a company`s operations. In the context of the presentation of financial statements, the IFRS Foundation defines net income as synonymous with profit and loss. The difference between revenue and the cost of making a product or providing a service, before deducting overheads, payroll, taxation, and interest payments. This is different from operating income .

Exam Probability: **Medium**

57. *Answer choices:*

(see index for correct answer)

- a. Meetup fee
- b. Bottom line
- c. Stipend
- d. Mandatory tipping

Guidance: level 1

:: Price fixing convictions ::

_________ AG is a German multinational conglomerate company headquartered in Berlin and Munich and the largest industrial manufacturing company in Europe with branch offices abroad.

Exam Probability: **Medium**

58. *Answer choices:*

(see index for correct answer)

- a. United States v. Archer Daniels Midland Co.
- b. Asahi Glass Co.
- c. Siemens
- d. SK Foods

Guidance: level 1

:: Management ::

A _________ is an idea of the future or desired result that a person or a group of people envisions, plans and commits to achieve. People endeavor to reach _________ s within a finite time by setting deadlines.

Exam Probability: **High**

59. *Answer choices:*

(see index for correct answer)

- a. Design leadership
- b. Performance management
- c. middle manager
- d. Value migration

Guidance: level 1

Business ethics

Business ethics (also known as corporate ethics) is a form of applied ethics or professional ethics, that examines ethical principles and moral or ethical problems that can arise in a business environment. It applies to all aspects of business conduct and is relevant to the conduct of individuals and entire organizations. These ethics originate from individuals, organizational statements or from the legal system. These norms, values, ethical, and unethical practices are what is used to guide business. They help those businesses maintain a better connection with their stakeholders.

The __________ was a severe worldwide economic depression that took place mostly during the 1930s, beginning in the United States. The timing of the __________ varied across nations; in most countries it started in 1929 and lasted until the late-1930s. It was the longest, deepest, and most widespread depression of the 20th century. In the 21st century, the __________ is commonly used as an example of how intensely the world's economy can decline.

Exam Probability: **Low**

1. *Answer choices:*

(see index for correct answer)

- a. Great Depression
- b. similarity-attraction theory
- c. corporate values
- d. levels of analysis

Guidance: level 1

:: Financial regulatory authorities of the United States ::

The __________ is an agency of the United States government responsible for consumer protection in the financial sector. CFPB's jurisdiction includes banks, credit unions, securities firms, payday lenders, mortgage-servicing operations, foreclosure relief services, debt collectors and other financial companies operating in the United States.

Exam Probability: **Medium**

2. *Answer choices:*

(see index for correct answer)

- a. Internal Revenue Service
- b. U.S. Securities and Exchange Commission
- c. Commodity Futures Trading Commission
- d. Federal Deposit Insurance Corporation

Guidance: level 1

:: ::

A __________ is the ability to carry out a task with determined results often within a given amount of time, energy, or both. __________s can often be divided into domain-general and domain-specific __________s. For example, in the domain of work, some general __________s would include time management, teamwork and leadership, self-motivation and others, whereas domain-specific __________s would be used only for a certain job. __________ usually requires certain environmental stimuli and situations to assess the level of __________ being shown and used.

Exam Probability: **Medium**

3. *Answer choices:*

(see index for correct answer)

- a. Skill
- b. similarity-attraction theory

- c. functional perspective
- d. personal values

Guidance: level 1

:: United States federal trade legislation ::

The _________ of 1914 established the Federal Trade Commission. The Act, signed into law by Woodrow Wilson in 1914, outlaws unfair methods of competition and outlaws unfair acts or practices that affect commerce.

Exam Probability: **Medium**

4. *Answer choices:*

(see index for correct answer)

- a. Tariff of 1857
- b. Federal Trade Commission Act
- c. Carriage of Goods by Sea Act
- d. African Growth and Opportunity Act

Guidance: level 1

:: ::

The __________ is an American stock exchange located at 11 Wall Street, Lower Manhattan, New York City, New York. It is by far the world`s largest stock exchange by market capitalization of its listed companies at US$30.1 trillion as of February 2018. The average daily trading value was approximately US$169 billion in 2013. The NYSE trading floor is located at 11 Wall Street and is composed of 21 rooms used for the facilitation of trading. A fifth trading room, located at 30 Broad Street, was closed in February 2007. The main building and the 11 Wall Street building were designated National Historic Landmarks in 1978.

Exam Probability: **Low**

5. *Answer choices:*

(see index for correct answer)

- a. New York Stock Exchange
- b. Character
- c. levels of analysis
- d. interpersonal communication

Guidance: level 1

:: ::

A __________ is an organization, usually a group of people or a company, authorized to act as a single entity and recognized as such in law. Early incorporated entities were established by charter . Most jurisdictions now allow the creation of new __________ s through registration.

Exam Probability: **High**

6. *Answer choices:*

(see index for correct answer)

- a. Corporation
- b. corporate values
- c. process perspective
- d. similarity-attraction theory

Guidance: level 1

:: Advertising techniques ::

The __________ is a story from the Trojan War about the subterfuge that the Greeks used to enter the independent city of Troy and win the war. In the canonical version, after a fruitless 10-year siege, the Greeks constructed a huge wooden horse, and hid a select force of men inside including Odysseus. The Greeks pretended to sail away, and the Trojans pulled the horse into their city as a victory trophy. That night the Greek force crept out of the horse and opened the gates for the rest of the Greek army, which had sailed back under cover of night. The Greeks entered and destroyed the city of Troy, ending the war.

Exam Probability: **Medium**

7. *Answer choices:*

(see index for correct answer)

- a. Transfer
- b. Testimonial
- c. Trojan horse
- d. Advertainment

Guidance: level 1

:: Renewable energy ::

_________ is the conversion of energy from sunlight into electricity, either directly using photovoltaics , indirectly using concentrated _________ , or a combination. Concentrated _________ systems use lenses or mirrors and tracking systems to focus a large area of sunlight into a small beam. Photovoltaic cells convert light into an electric current using the photovoltaic effect.

Exam Probability: **Low**

8. *Answer choices:*

(see index for correct answer)

- a. National Solar Conference and World Renewable Energy Forum 2012
- b. Renewable energy debate
- c. Solar power
- d. Market transformation

Guidance: level 1

:: Corporations law ::

A normal _________ consists of various departments that contribute to the company's overall mission and goals. Common departments include Marketing, [Finance, [[Operations managementOperations, Human Resource, and IT. These five divisions represent the major departments within a publicly traded company, though there are often smaller departments within autonomous firms. There is typically a CEO, and Board of Directors composed of the directors of each department. There are also company presidents, vice presidents, and CFOs.There is a great diversity in corporate forms as enterprises may range from single company to multi-corporate conglomerate. The four main _________ s are Functional, Divisional, Geographic, and the Matrix.Realistically, most corporations tend to have a "hybrid" structure, which is a combination of different models with one dominant strategy.

Exam Probability: **High**

9. *Answer choices:*

(see index for correct answer)

- a. Non-stock corporation
- b. Company and Securities Law Journal
- c. Corporate structure
- d. Prest v Petrodel Resources Ltd

Guidance: level 1

:: Electronic waste ::

__________ or e-waste describes discarded electrical or electronic devices. Used electronics which are destined for refurbishment, reuse, resale, salvage, recycling through material recovery, or disposal are also considered e-waste. Informal processing of e-waste in developing countries can lead to adverse human health effects and environmental pollution.

Exam Probability: **Low**

10. *Answer choices:*

(see index for correct answer)

- a. Computer liquidator
- b. Global waste trade
- c. ReGlobe
- d. World Reuse, Repair and Recycling Association

Guidance: level 1

:: Carbon finance ::

The __________ is an international treaty which extends the 1992 United Nations Framework Convention on Climate Change that commits state parties to reduce greenhouse gas emissions, based on the scientific consensus that global warming is occurring and it is extremely likely that human-made CO2 emissions have predominantly caused it. The __________ was adopted in Kyoto, Japan on 11 December 1997 and entered into force on 16 February 2005. There are currently 192 parties to the Protocol.

Exam Probability: **High**

11. *Answer choices:*

(see index for correct answer)

- a. FirstCarbon Solutions
- b. Kyoto Protocol
- c. Western Climate Initiative
- d. Carbon retirement

Guidance: level 1

:: Monopoly (economics) ::

A _________ is a form of intellectual property that gives its owner the legal right to exclude others from making, using, selling, and importing an invention for a limited period of years, in exchange for publishing an enabling public disclosure of the invention. In most countries _________ rights fall under civil law and the _________ holder needs to sue someone infringing the _________ in order to enforce his or her rights. In some industries _________ s are an essential form of competitive advantage; in others they are irrelevant.

Exam Probability: **Low**

12. *Answer choices:*

(see index for correct answer)

- a. Privatization
- b. Building block model
- c. Patent
- d. Practice of law

Guidance: level 1

:: ::

The Federal National Mortgage Association , commonly known as _________ , is a United States government-sponsored enterprise and, since 1968, a publicly traded company. Founded in 1938 during the Great Depression as part of the New Deal, the corporation's purpose is to expand the secondary mortgage market by securitizing mortgage loans in the form of mortgage-backed securities , allowing lenders to reinvest their assets into more lending and in effect increasing the number of lenders in the mortgage market by reducing the reliance on locally based savings and loan associations . Its brother organization is the Federal Home Loan Mortgage Corporation , better known as Freddie Mac. As of 2018, _________ is ranked #21 on the Fortune 500 rankings of the largest United States corporations by total revenue.

Exam Probability: **Low**

13. *Answer choices:*

(see index for correct answer)

- a. imperative
- b. co-culture
- c. functional perspective

- d. Fannie Mae

Guidance: level 1

:: ::

Revenge is a form of justice enacted in the absence or defiance of the norms of formal law and jurisprudence. Often, revenge is defined as being a harmful action against a person or group in response to a grievance, be it real or perceived . It is used to punish a wrong by going outside the law. Francis Bacon described revenge as a kind of "wild justice" that "does... offend the law [and] putteth the law out of office." Primitive justice or retributive justice is often differentiated from more formal and refined forms of justice such as distributive justice and divine judgment.

Exam Probability: **Medium**

14. *Answer choices:*

(see index for correct answer)

- a. personal values
- b. Retaliation
- c. empathy
- d. corporate values

Guidance: level 1

:: ::

_________ is a bundle of characteristics, including ways of thinking, feeling, and acting, which humans are said to have naturally. The term is often regarded as capturing what it is to be human, or the essence of humanity. The term is controversial because it is disputed whether or not such an essence exists. Arguments about _________ have been a mainstay of philosophy for centuries and the concept continues to provoke lively philosophical debate. The concept also continues to play a role in science, with neuroscientists, psychologists and social scientists sometimes claiming that their results have yielded insight into _________ . _________ is traditionally contrasted with characteristics that vary among humans, such as characteristics associated with specific cultures. Debates about _________ are related to, although not the same as, debates about the comparative importance of genes and environment in development .

Exam Probability: **Low**

15. *Answer choices:*

(see index for correct answer)

- a. similarity-attraction theory
- b. Human nature
- c. information systems assessment
- d. Sarbanes-Oxley act of 2002

Guidance: level 1

:: Water law ::

The __________ is the primary federal law in the United States governing water pollution. Its objective is to restore and maintain the chemical, physical, and biological integrity of the nation's waters; recognizing the responsibilities of the states in addressing pollution and providing assistance to states to do so, including funding for publicly owned treatment works for the improvement of wastewater treatment; and maintaining the integrity of wetlands. It is one of the United States' first and most influential modern environmental laws. As with many other major U.S. federal environmental statutes, it is administered by the U.S. Environmental Protection Agency , in coordination with state governments. Its implementing regulations are codified at 40 C.F.R. Subchapters D, N, and O .

Exam Probability: **High**

16. *Answer choices:*

(see index for correct answer)

- a. The Helsinki Rules on the Uses of the Waters of International Rivers
- b. Correlative rights doctrine
- c. Return flow
- d. Clean Water Act

Guidance: level 1

:: ::

_________ is the study and management of exchange relationships. _________ is the business process of creating relationships with and satisfying customers. With its focus on the customer, _________ is one of the premier components of business management.

Exam Probability: **Low**

17. *Answer choices:*

(see index for correct answer)

- a. Sarbanes-Oxley act of 2002
- b. personal values
- c. interpersonal communication
- d. deep-level diversity

Guidance: level 1

:: ::

_________ was a philosopher during the Classical period in Ancient Greece, the founder of the Lyceum and the Peripatetic school of philosophy and Aristotelian tradition. Along with his teacher Plato, he is considered the "Father of Western Philosophy". His writings cover many subjects – including physics, biology, zoology, metaphysics, logic, ethics, aesthetics, poetry, theatre, music, rhetoric, psychology, linguistics, economics, politics and government. _________ provided a complex synthesis of the various philosophies existing prior to him, and it was above all from his teachings that the West inherited its intellectual lexicon, as well as problems and methods of inquiry. As a result, his philosophy has exerted a unique influence on almost every form of knowledge in the West and it continues to be a subject of contemporary philosophical discussion.

Exam Probability: **High**

18. *Answer choices:*

(see index for correct answer)

- a. information systems assessment
- b. Character
- c. surface-level diversity
- d. process perspective

Guidance: level 1

:: Dutch inventions ::

The Fairtrade certification initiative was created to form a new method for economic trade. This method takes an ethical standpoint, and considers the producers first.

Exam Probability: **Low**

19. *Answer choices:*

(see index for correct answer)

- a. Dijkstra's algorithm
- b. Fair Trade Certified

Guidance: level 1

:: ::

The Ethics & Compliance Initiative was formed in 2015 and consists of three nonprofit organizations: the Ethics Research Center, the Ethics & Compliance Association, and the Ethics & Compliance Certification Institute. Based in Arlington, Virginia, United States, ECI is devoted to the advancement of high ethical standards and practices in public and private institutions, and provides research about ethical standards, workplace integrity, and compliance practices and processes.

Exam Probability: **Medium**

20. *Answer choices:*

(see index for correct answer)

- a. Ethics Resource Center
- b. information systems assessment
- c. similarity-attraction theory
- d. cultural

Guidance: level 1

:: Decentralization ::

__________ or sub __________ mainly refers to the unrestricted growth in many urban areas of housing, commercial development, and roads over large expanses of land, with little concern for urban planning. In addition to describing a particular form of urbanization, the term also relates to the social and environmental consequences associated with this development. In Continental Europe the term "peri-urbanisation" is often used to denote similar dynamics and phenomena, although the term __________ is currently being used by the European Environment Agency. There is widespread disagreement about what constitutes sprawl and how to quantify it. For example, some commentators measure sprawl only with the average number of residential units per acre in a given area. But others associate it with decentralization , discontinuity , segregation of uses, and so forth.

Exam Probability: **High**

21. *Answer choices:*

(see index for correct answer)

- a. Leopold Kohr

- b. Urban sprawl
- c. Somali Civil War
- d. Plurinationalism

Guidance: level 1

:: Business ::

_________ , or built-in obsolescence, in industrial design and economics is a policy of planning or designing a product with an artificially limited useful life, so that it becomes obsolete after a certain period of time. The rationale behind this strategy is to generate long-term sales volume by reducing the time between repeat purchases .

Exam Probability: **Medium**

22. *Answer choices:*

(see index for correct answer)

- a. Price-based selling
- b. Business partnering
- c. Vladislav Doronin
- d. Planned obsolescence

Guidance: level 1

:: United States law ::

The ABA __________ , created by the American Bar Association , are a set of rules that prescribe baseline standards of legal ethics and professional responsibility for lawyers in the United States. They were promulgated by the ABA House of Delegates upon the recommendation of the Kutak Commission in 1983. The rules are merely recommendations, or models, and are not themselves binding. However, having a common set of Model Rules facilitates a common discourse on legal ethics, and simplifies professional responsibility training as well as the day-to-day application of such rules. As of 2015, 49 states and four territories have adopted the rules in whole or in part, of which the most recent to do so was the Commonwealth of the Northern Mariana Islands in March 2015. California is the only state that has not adopted the ABA Model Rules, while Puerto Rico is the only U.S. jurisdiction outside of confederation has not adopted them but instead has its own Código de Ética Profesional.

Exam Probability: **High**

23. *Answer choices:*

(see index for correct answer)

- a. judgment notwithstanding the verdict
- b. Model Rules of Professional Conduct

Guidance: level 1

:: ::

In regulatory jurisdictions that provide for it , _________ is a group of laws and organizations designed to ensure the rights of consumers as well as fair trade, competition and accurate information in the marketplace. The laws are designed to prevent the businesses that engage in fraud or specified unfair practices from gaining an advantage over competitors. They may also provides additional protection for those most vulnerable in society. _________ laws are a form of government regulation that aim to protect the rights of consumers. For example, a government may require businesses to disclose detailed information about products—particularly in areas where safety or public health is an issue, such as food.

Exam Probability: **Medium**

24. *Answer choices:*

(see index for correct answer)

- a. Consumer Protection
- b. process perspective
- c. levels of analysis
- d. surface-level diversity

Guidance: level 1

:: Separation of investment and commercial banking ::

The _________ refers to § 619 of the Dodd–Frank Wall Street Reform and Consumer Protection Act . The rule was originally proposed by American economist and former United States Federal Reserve Chairman Paul Volcker to restrict United States banks from making certain kinds of speculative investments that do not benefit their customers. Volcker argued that such speculative activity played a key role in the financial crisis of 2007–2008. The rule is often referred to as a ban on proprietary trading by commercial banks, whereby deposits are used to trade on the bank`s own accounts, although a number of exceptions to this ban were included in the Dodd-Frank law.

Exam Probability: **Low**

25. *Answer choices:*

(see index for correct answer)

- a. Bank holding company
- b. Bank Holding Company Act
- c. Depository institution
- d. Independent Commission on Banking

Guidance: level 1

:: Culture ::

_________ is a society which is characterized by individualism, which is the prioritization or emphasis, of the individual over the entire group. _________ s are oriented around the self, being independent instead of identifying with a group mentality. They see each other as only loosely linked, and value personal goals over group interests. _________ s tend to have a more diverse population and are characterized with emphasis on personal achievements, and a rational assessment of both the beneficial and detrimental aspects of relationships with others. _________ s have such unique aspects of communication as being a low power-distance culture and having a low-context communication style. The United States, Australia, Great Britain, Canada, the Netherlands, and New Zealand have been identified as highly _________ s.

Exam Probability: **Low**

26. *Answer choices:*

(see index for correct answer)

- a. cultural framework
- b. High-context
- c. Individualistic culture
- d. Low-context culture

Guidance: level 1

:: Utilitarianism ::

__________ is a school of thought that argues that the pursuit of pleasure and intrinsic goods are the primary or most important goals of human life. A hedonist strives to maximize net pleasure . However upon finally gaining said pleasure, happiness may remain stationary.

Exam Probability: **High**

27. *Answer choices:*

(see index for correct answer)

- a. The Methods of Ethics
- b. Informed judge
- c. Utility monster
- d. Telishment

Guidance: level 1

:: Euthenics ::

__________ is an ethical framework and suggests that an entity, be it an organization or individual, has an obligation to act for the benefit of society at large. __________ is a duty every individual has to perform so as to maintain a balance between the economy and the ecosystems. A trade-off may exist between economic development, in the material sense, and the welfare of the society and environment, though this has been challenged by many reports over the past decade. __________ means sustaining the equilibrium between the two. It pertains not only to business organizations but also to everyone whose any action impacts the environment. This responsibility can be passive, by avoiding engaging in socially harmful acts, or active, by performing activities that directly advance social goals. __________ must be intergenerational since the actions of one generation have consequences on those following.

Exam Probability: **Medium**

28. *Answer choices:*

(see index for correct answer)

- a. Minnie Cumnock Blodgett
- b. Family and consumer science
- c. Social responsibility
- d. Euthenics

Guidance: level 1

:: Auditing ::

_________ refers to the independence of the internal auditor or of the external auditor from parties that may have a financial interest in the business being audited. Independence requires integrity and an objective approach to the audit process. The concept requires the auditor to carry out his or her work freely and in an objective manner.

Exam Probability: **Low**

29. *Answer choices:*

(see index for correct answer)

- a. Lease audit
- b. Audit planning
- c. Mainframe audit
- d. Audit Bureau of Circulations

Guidance: level 1

:: Fraud ::

In the United States, _________ is the claiming of Medicare health care reimbursement to which the claimant is not entitled. There are many different types of _________, all of which have the same goal: to collect money from the Medicare program illegitimately.

Exam Probability: **Medium**

30. *Answer choices:*

(see index for correct answer)

- a. Unconscious fraud
- b. Credit card kiting
- c. Lip-synching in music
- d. Medicare fraud

Guidance: level 1

:: Human resource management ::

_________ is the ethics of an organization, and it is how an organization responds to an internal or external stimulus. _________ is interdependent with the organizational culture. Although it is akin to both organizational behavior and industrial and organizational psychology as well as business ethics on the micro and macro levels, _________ is neither OB or I/O psychology, nor is it solely business ethics . _________ express the values of an organization to its employees and/or other entities irrespective of governmental and/or regulatory laws.

Exam Probability: **High**

31. *Answer choices:*

(see index for correct answer)

- a. Organizational ethics
- b. Internal communications

- c. Income bracket
- d. Human resource management in public administration

Guidance: level 1

:: Confidence tricks ::

A __________ is a business model that recruits members via a promise of payments or services for enrolling others into the scheme, rather than supplying investments or sale of products. As recruiting multiplies, recruiting becomes quickly impossible, and most members are unable to profit; as such, __________ s are unsustainable and often illegal.

Exam Probability: **Low**

32. *Answer choices:*

(see index for correct answer)

- a. Moving scam
- b. Pigeon drop
- c. Drop swindle
- d. Clip joint

Guidance: level 1

:: Office work ::

_________ is the process and behavior in human interactions involving power and authority. It is also a tool to assess the operational capacity and to balance diverse views of interested parties. It is also known as office politics and organizational politics.It is the use of power and social networking within an organization to achieve changes that benefit the organization or individuals within it. Influence by individuals may serve personal interests without regard to their effect on the organization itself. Some of the personal advantages may include access to tangible assets, or intangible benefits such as status or pseudo-authority that influences the behavior of others. On the other hand, organizational politics can increase efficiency, form interpersonal relationships, expedite change, and profit the organization and its members simultaneously.Both individuals and groups may engage in office politics which can be highly destructive, as people focus on personal gains at the expense of the organization. "Self-serving political actions can negatively influence our social groupings, cooperation, information sharing, and many other organizational functions." Thus, it is vital to pay attention to organizational politics and create the right political landscape. "Politics is the lubricant that oils your organization`s internal gears." Office politics has also been described as "simply how power gets worked out on a practical, day-to-day basis."

Exam Probability: **High**

33. *Answer choices:*

(see index for correct answer)

- a. Paperless office
- b. Service bureau
- c. Mobile office
- d. Executive suite

Guidance: level 1

:: Offshoring ::

A _________ is the temporary suspension or permanent termination of employment of an employee or, more commonly, a group of employees for business reasons, such as personnel management or downsizing an organization. Originally, _________ referred exclusively to a temporary interruption in work, or employment but this has evolved to a permanent elimination of a position in both British and US English, requiring the addition of "temporary" to specify the original meaning of the word. A _________ is not to be confused with wrongful termination. Laid off workers or displaced workers are workers who have lost or left their jobs because their employer has closed or moved, there was insufficient work for them to do, or their position or shift was abolished . Downsizing in a company is defined to involve the reduction of employees in a workforce. Downsizing in companies became a popular practice in the 1980s and early 1990s as it was seen as a way to deliver better shareholder value as it helps to reduce the costs of employers . Indeed, recent research on downsizing in the U.S., UK, and Japan suggests that downsizing is being regarded by management as one of the preferred routes to help declining organizations, cutting unnecessary costs, and improve organizational performance. Usually a _________ occurs as a cost cutting measure.

Exam Probability: **Low**

34. *Answer choices:*

(see index for correct answer)

- a. Advanced Contact Solutions
- b. Nearshoring
- c. Offshore outsourcing
- d. Layoff

Guidance: level 1

:: Minimum wage ::

A _________ is the lowest remuneration that employers can legally pay their workers—the price floor below which workers may not sell their labor. Most countries had introduced _________ legislation by the end of the 20th century.

Exam Probability: **Low**

35. *Answer choices:*

(see index for correct answer)

- a. Minimum Wage Fairness Act
- b. Working poor
- c. Guaranteed minimum income
- d. National Anti-Sweating League

Guidance: level 1

:: Social philosophy ::

The " _________ " is a method of determining the morality of issues. It asks a decision-maker to make a choice about a social or moral issue, and assumes that they have enough information to know the consequences of their possible decisions for everyone but would not know, or would not take into account, which person he or she is. The theory contends that not knowing one`s ultimate position in society would lead to the creation of a just system, as the decision-maker would not want to make decisions which benefit a certain group at the expense of another, because the decision-maker could theoretically end up in either group. The idea has been present in moral philosophy at least since the eighteenth century. The _________ is part of a long tradition of thinking in terms of a social contract that includes the writings of Immanuel Kant, Thomas Hobbes, John Locke, Jean Jacques Rousseau, and Thomas Jefferson. Prominent modern names attached to it are John Harsanyi and John Rawls.

Exam Probability: **Medium**

36. *Answer choices:*

(see index for correct answer)

- a. Veil of ignorance
- b. vacancy chain
- c. Invisible hand
- d. Freedom to contract

Guidance: level 1

:: Workplace ::

In business management, _________ is a management style whereby a manager closely observes and/or controls the work of his/her subordinates or employees.

Exam Probability: **High**

37. *Answer choices:*

(see index for correct answer)

- a. Workplace relationships
- b. Micromanagement
- c. Evaluation
- d. Workplace democracy

Guidance: level 1

:: ::

_________ in the United States is a federal and state program that helps with medical costs for some people with limited income and resources. _________ also offers benefits not normally covered by Medicare, including nursing home care and personal care services. The Health Insurance Association of America describes _________ as "a government insurance program for persons of all ages whose income and resources are insufficient to pay for health care." _________ is the largest source of funding for medical and health-related services for people with low income in the United States, providing free health insurance to 74 million low-income and disabled people as of 2017. It is a means-tested program that is jointly funded by the state and federal governments and managed by the states, with each state currently having broad leeway to determine who is eligible for its implementation of the program. States are not required to participate in the program, although all have since 1982. _________ recipients must be U.S. citizens or qualified non-citizens, and may include low-income adults, their children, and people with certain disabilities. Poverty alone does not necessarily qualify someone for _________ .

Exam Probability: **High**

38. *Answer choices:*

(see index for correct answer)

- a. Character
- b. Medicaid
- c. process perspective
- d. personal values

Guidance: level 1

:: United Kingdom labour law ::

The ________ was a series of programs, public work projects, financial reforms, and regulations enacted by President Franklin D. Roosevelt in the United States between 1933 and 1936. It responded to needs for relief, reform, and recovery from the Great Depression. Major federal programs included the Civilian Conservation Corps , the Civil Works Administration , the Farm Security Administration , the National Industrial Recovery Act of 1933 and the Social Security Administration . They provided support for farmers, the unemployed, youth and the elderly. The ________ included new constraints and safeguards on the banking industry and efforts to re-inflate the economy after prices had fallen sharply. ________ programs included both laws passed by Congress as well as presidential executive orders during the first term of the presidency of Franklin D. Roosevelt.

Exam Probability: **High**

39. *Answer choices:*

(see index for correct answer)

- a. Report of the committee of inquiry on industrial democracy
- b. Truck Acts
- c. New Deal
- d. Employment Information Directive

Guidance: level 1

:: Ethically disputed business practices ::

__________ is the trading of a public company's stock or other securities by individuals with access to nonpublic information about the company. In various countries, some kinds of trading based on insider information is illegal. This is because it is seen as unfair to other investors who do not have access to the information, as the investor with insider information could potentially make larger profits than a typical investor could make. The rules governing __________ are complex and vary significantly from country to country. The extent of enforcement also varies from one country to another. The definition of insider in one jurisdiction can be broad, and may cover not only insiders themselves but also any persons related to them, such as brokers, associates and even family members. A person who becomes aware of non-public information and trades on that basis may be guilty of a crime.

Exam Probability: **Medium**

40. *Answer choices:*

(see index for correct answer)

- a. Wrongful dismissal
- b. Intensive animal farming
- c. Insider trading
- d. Black market

Guidance: level 1

:: ::

A __________ is a form of business network, for example, a local organization of businesses whose goal is to further the interests of businesses. Business owners in towns and cities form these local societies to advocate on behalf of the business community. Local businesses are members, and they elect a board of directors or executive council to set policy for the chamber. The board or council then hires a President, CEO or Executive Director, plus staffing appropriate to size, to run the organization.

Exam Probability: **High**

41. *Answer choices:*

(see index for correct answer)

- a. Sarbanes-Oxley act of 2002
- b. corporate values
- c. surface-level diversity
- d. deep-level diversity

Guidance: level 1

:: Management ::

__________ or executive pay is composed of the financial compensation and other non-financial awards received by an executive from their firm for their service to the organization. It is typically a mixture of salary, bonuses, shares of or call options on the company stock, benefits, and perquisites, ideally configured to take into account government regulations, tax law, the desires of the organization and the executive, and rewards for performance.

Exam Probability: **High**

42. *Answer choices:*

(see index for correct answer)

- a. Executive compensation
- b. Twelve leverage points
- c. Mushroom management
- d. middle manager

Guidance: level 1

:: International trade ::

_________ involves the transfer of goods or services from one person or entity to another, often in exchange for money. A system or network that allows _________ is called a market.

Exam Probability: **High**

43. *Answer choices:*

(see index for correct answer)

- a. UNeDocs
- b. Trade
- c. Plaza Accord
- d. AgroEurasia

Guidance: level 1

:: Reputation management ::

_________ or image of a social entity is an opinion about that entity, typically as a result of social evaluation on a set of criteria.

Exam Probability: **Medium**

44. *Answer choices:*

(see index for correct answer)

- a. Infamy
- b. Trust metric
- c. Yasni
- d. Reputation

Guidance: level 1

:: Industrial ecology ::

__________ is a strategy for reducing the amount of waste created and released into the environment, particularly by industrial facilities, agriculture, or consumers. Many large corporations view P2 as a method of improving the efficiency and profitability of production processes by technology advancements. Legislative bodies have enacted P2 measures, such as the __________ Act of 1990 and the Clean Air Act Amendments of 1990 by the United States Congress.

Exam Probability: **Medium**

45. *Answer choices:*

(see index for correct answer)

- a. Design for the Environment
- b. Material flow management
- c. Waste hierarchy
- d. Pollution Prevention

Guidance: level 1

:: Business ethics ::

A __________ is a person who exposes any kind of information or activity that is deemed illegal, unethical, or not correct within an organization that is either private or public. The information of alleged wrongdoing can be classified in many ways: violation of company policy/rules, law, regulation, or threat to public interest/national security, as well as fraud, and corruption. Those who become __________ s can choose to bring information or allegations to surface either internally or externally. Internally, a __________ can bring his/her accusations to the attention of other people within the accused organization such as an immediate supervisor. Externally, a __________ can bring allegations to light by contacting a third party outside of an accused organization such as the media, government, law enforcement, or those who are concerned. __________ s, however, take the risk of facing stiff reprisal and retaliation from those who are accused or alleged of wrongdoing.

Exam Probability: **High**

46. *Answer choices:*

(see index for correct answer)

- a. Society for Business Ethics
- b. Accounting ethics
- c. Whistleblower
- d. Corruption of Foreign Public Officials Act

Guidance: level 1

:: ::

Oriental Nicety, formerly _________ , Exxon Mediterranean, SeaRiver Mediterranean, S/R Mediterranean, Mediterranean, and Dong Fang Ocean, was an oil tanker that gained notoriety after running aground in Prince William Sound spilling hundreds of thousands of barrels of crude oil in Alaska. On March 24, 1989, while owned by the former Exxon Shipping Company, and captained by Joseph Hazelwood and First Mate James Kunkel bound for Long Beach, California, the vessel ran aground on the Bligh Reef resulting in the second largest oil spill in United States history. The size of the spill is estimated to have been 40,900 to 120,000 m3 , or 257,000 to 750,000 barrels. In 1989, the _________ oil spill was listed as the 54th largest spill in history.

Exam Probability: **Medium**

47. *Answer choices:*

(see index for correct answer)

- a. similarity-attraction theory
- b. functional perspective
- c. Exxon Valdez
- d. personal values

Guidance: level 1

:: ::

_________ is an eight-block-long street running roughly northwest to southeast from Broadway to South Street, at the East River, in the Financial District of Lower Manhattan in New York City. Over time, the term has become a metonym for the financial markets of the United States as a whole, the American financial services industry , or New York–based financial interests.

Exam Probability: **High**

48. *Answer choices:*

(see index for correct answer)

- a. hierarchical perspective
- b. corporate values
- c. Wall Street
- d. cultural

Guidance: level 1

:: Anti-competitive behaviour ::

__________ is a secret cooperation or deceitful agreement in order to deceive others, although not necessarily illegal, as a conspiracy. A secret agreement between two or more parties to limit open competition by deceiving, misleading, or defrauding others of their legal rights, or to obtain an objective forbidden by law typically by defrauding or gaining an unfair market advantage is an example of __________. It is an agreement among firms or individuals to divide a market, set prices, limit production or limit opportunities.It can involve "unions, wage fixing, kickbacks, or misrepresenting the independence of the relationship between the colluding parties". In legal terms, all acts effected by __________ are considered void.

Exam Probability: **High**

49. *Answer choices:*

(see index for correct answer)

- a. Collusion
- b. Net Book Agreement
- c. Dividing territories
- d. Copyright misuse

Guidance: level 1

:: Commercial crimes ::

__________ is an agreement between participants on the same side in a market to buy or sell a product, service, or commodity only at a fixed price, or maintain the market conditions such that the price is maintained at a given level by controlling supply and demand.

Exam Probability: **Low**

50. *Answer choices:*

(see index for correct answer)

- a. Price fixing
- b. Fraudulent conveyance
- c. United States antitrust law
- d. FATF blacklist

Guidance: level 1

:: ::

The __________ is an institution of the European Union, responsible for proposing legislation, implementing decisions, upholding the EU treaties and managing the day-to-day business of the EU. Commissioners swear an oath at the European Court of Justice in Luxembourg City, pledging to respect the treaties and to be completely independent in carrying out their duties during their mandate. Unlike in the Council of the European Union, where members are directly and indirectly elected, and the European Parliament, where members are directly elected, the Commissioners are proposed by the Council of the European Union, on the basis of suggestions made by the national governments, and then appointed by the European Council after the approval of the European Parliament.

Exam Probability: **Medium**

51. *Answer choices:*

(see index for correct answer)

- a. levels of analysis
- b. European Commission
- c. deep-level diversity
- d. open system

Guidance: level 1

:: Trade unions ::

A __________ was a group formed of private citizens to administer law and order where they considered governmental structures to be inadequate. The term is commonly associated with the frontier areas of the American West in the mid-19th century, where groups attacked cattle rustlers and gangs, and people at gold mining claims. As non-state organizations no functioning checks existed to protect against excessive force or safeguard due process from the committees. In the years prior to the Civil War, some committees worked to free slaves and transport them to freedom.

Exam Probability: **Medium**

52. *Answer choices:*

(see index for correct answer)

- a. International Labour Sports Federation
- b. Ghent system
- c. Coordinating Committee of International Staff Unions and Associations of the United Nations System
- d. Craft unionism

Guidance: level 1

:: ::

Bernard Lawrence _________ is an American former market maker, investment advisor, financier, fraudster, and convicted felon, who is currently serving a federal prison sentence for offenses related to a massive Ponzi scheme. He is the former non-executive chairman of the NASDAQ stock market, the confessed operator of the largest Ponzi scheme in world history, and the largest financial fraud in U.S. history. Prosecutors estimated the fraud to be worth $64.8 billion based on the amounts in the accounts of _________ `s 4,800 clients as of November 30, 2008.

Exam Probability: **High**

53. *Answer choices:*

(see index for correct answer)

- a. levels of analysis
- b. functional perspective
- c. cultural
- d. Madoff

Guidance: level 1

:: Management ::

A _________ describes the rationale of how an organization creates, delivers, and captures value, in economic, social, cultural or other contexts. The process of _________ construction and modification is also called _________ innovation and forms a part of business strategy.

Exam Probability: **High**

54. *Answer choices:*

(see index for correct answer)

- a. Intopia
- b. Business model
- c. Manager Tools Podcast
- d. Quality, cost, delivery

Guidance: level 1

:: Public relations terminology ::

__________ , also called "green sheen", is a form of spin in which green PR or green marketing is deceptively used to promote the perception that an organization`s products, aims or policies are environmentally friendly. Evidence that an organization is __________ often comes from pointing out the spending differences: when significantly more money or time has been spent advertising being "green" , than is actually spent on environmentally sound practices. __________ efforts can range from changing the name or label of a product to evoke the natural environment on a product that contains harmful chemicals to multimillion-dollar marketing campaigns portraying highly polluting energy companies as eco-friendly.Publicized accusations of __________ have contributed to the term`s increasing use.

Exam Probability: **High**

55. *Answer choices:*

(see index for correct answer)

- a. Photo op
- b. Greenwashing
- c. Junk science
- d. PR Gallery

Guidance: level 1

:: Competition regulators ::

The _______ is an independent agency of the United States government, established in 1914 by the _______ Act. Its principal mission is the promotion of consumer protection and the elimination and prevention of anticompetitive business practices, such as coercive monopoly. It is headquartered in the _______ Building in Washington, D.C.

Exam Probability: **High**

56. *Answer choices:*

(see index for correct answer)

- a. Federal Trade Commission
- b. Fair Trade Commission
- c. Superintendency of Industry and Commerce
- d. National Board for Prices and Incomes

Guidance: level 1

:: Corporate scandals ::

_________ was a bank based in the Caribbean, which operated from 1986 to 2009 when it went into receivership. It was an affiliate of the Stanford Financial Group and failed when the its parent was seized by United States authorities in early 2009 as part of the investigation into Allen Stanford.

Exam Probability: **Medium**

57. *Answer choices:*

(see index for correct answer)

- a. Barings Bank
- b. Polly Peck
- c. Stanford International Bank
- d. Michael Bailey

Guidance: level 1

:: ::

The American Recovery and Reinvestment Act of 2009 , nicknamed the _________ , was a stimulus package enacted by the 111th U.S. Congress and signed into law by President Barack Obama in February 2009. Developed in response to the Great Recession, the ARRA`s primary objective was to save existing jobs and create new ones as soon as possible. Other objectives were to provide temporary relief programs for those most affected by the recession and invest in infrastructure, education, health, and renewable energy.

Exam Probability: **Low**

58. *Answer choices:*

(see index for correct answer)

- a. open system
- b. levels of analysis
- c. surface-level diversity
- d. co-culture

Guidance: level 1

:: ::

Competition law is a law that promotes or seeks to maintain market competition by regulating anti-competitive conduct by companies. Competition law is implemented through public and private enforcement. Competition law is known as " _________ law" in the United States for historical reasons, and as "anti-monopoly law" in China and Russia. In previous years it has been known as trade practices law in the United Kingdom and Australia. In the European Union, it is referred to as both _________ and competition law.

Exam Probability: **Low**

59. *Answer choices:*

(see index for correct answer)

- a. cultural
- b. imperative
- c. Antitrust
- d. functional perspective

Guidance: level 1

Accounting

Accounting or accountancy is the measurement, processing, and communication of financial information about economic entities such as businesses and corporations. The modern field was established by the Italian mathematician Luca Pacioli in 1494. Accounting, which has been called the "language of business", measures the results of an organization's economic activities and conveys this information to a variety of users, including investors, creditors, management, and regulators.

_________ is the income that is gained by governments through taxation. Taxation is the primary source of income for a state. Revenue may be extracted from sources such as individuals, public enterprises, trade, royalties on natural resources and/or foreign aid. An inefficient collection of taxes is greater in countries characterized by poverty, a large agricultural sector and large amounts of foreign aid.

Exam Probability: **Medium**

1. *Answer choices:*

(see index for correct answer)

- a. hierarchical
- b. cultural
- c. deep-level diversity
- d. process perspective

Guidance: level 1

:: Auditing ::

An _________ is a security-relevant chronological record, set of records, and/or destination and source of records that provide documentary evidence of the sequence of activities that have affected at any time a specific operation, procedure, or event. Audit records typically result from activities such as financial transactions, scientific research and health care data transactions, or communications by individual people, systems, accounts, or other entities.

Exam Probability: **High**

2. *Answer choices:*

(see index for correct answer)

- a. Control risk
- b. Audit trail
- c. Audit planning
- d. Lease audit

Guidance: level 1

:: Asset ::

In financial accounting, an _________ is any resource owned by the business. Anything tangible or intangible that can be owned or controlled to produce value and that is held by a company to produce positive economic value is an _________. Simply stated, _________ s represent value of ownership that can be converted into cash . The balance sheet of a firm records the monetary value of the _________ s owned by that firm. It covers money and other valuables belonging to an individual or to a business.

Exam Probability: **High**

3. *Answer choices:*

(see index for correct answer)

- a. Current asset

- b. Fixed asset

Guidance: level 1

:: Taxation ::

_________ refers to instances where a taxpayer can delay paying taxes to some future period. In theory, the net taxes paid should be the same. Taxes can sometimes be deferred indefinitely, or may be taxed at a lower rate in the future, particularly for deferral of income taxes.

Exam Probability: **Low**

4. *Answer choices:*

(see index for correct answer)

- a. Tax Freedom Day
- b. Tax Analysts
- c. Tax buoyancy
- d. Tax cap

Guidance: level 1

:: Stock market ::

__________ is a form of corporate equity ownership, a type of security. The terms voting share and ordinary share are also used frequently in other parts of the world; " __________ " being primarily used in the United States. They are known as Equity shares or Ordinary shares in the UK and other Commonwealth realms. This type of share gives the stockholder the right to share in the profits of the company, and to vote on matters of corporate policy and the composition of the members of the board of directors.

Exam Probability: **High**

5. *Answer choices:*

(see index for correct answer)

- a. stock price
- b. Intermarket sweep order
- c. Common stock
- d. Share price

Guidance: level 1

:: Inventory ::

__________ is the maximum amount of goods, or inventory, that a company can possibly sell during this fiscal year. It has the formula.

Exam Probability: **Low**

6. *Answer choices:*

(see index for correct answer)

- a. Cost of goods available for sale
- b. Stock obsolescence
- c. Ending inventory
- d. Periodic inventory

Guidance: level 1

:: Capital gains taxes ::

A _________ refers to profit that results from a sale of a capital asset, such as stock, bond or real estate, where the sale price exceeds the purchase price. The gain is the difference between a higher selling price and a lower purchase price. Conversely, a capital loss arises if the proceeds from the sale of a capital asset are less than the purchase price.

Exam Probability: **Low**

7. *Answer choices:*

(see index for correct answer)

- a. Capital Cost Allowance
- b. Capital gain
- c. Capital gains tax

Guidance: level 1

:: Land value taxation ::

_________ , sometimes referred to as dry _________ , is the solid surface of Earth that is not permanently covered by water. The vast majority of human activity throughout history has occurred in _________ areas that support agriculture, habitat, and various natural resources. Some life forms have developed from predecessor species that lived in bodies of water.

Exam Probability: **High**

8. *Answer choices:*

(see index for correct answer)

- a. Georgism
- b. Harry Gunnison Brown
- c. Land
- d. Land value tax

Guidance: level 1

:: Legal terms ::

__________ is a state of prolonged public dispute or debate, usually concerning a matter of conflicting opinion or point of view. The word was coined from the Latin controversia, as a composite of controversus – "turned in an opposite direction," from contra – "against" – and vertere – to turn, or versus , hence, "to turn against."

Exam Probability: **Low**

9. *Answer choices:*

(see index for correct answer)

- a. Controversy
- b. Merger clause
- c. Ambiguity
- d. Peremptory plea

Guidance: level 1

:: Business law ::

A __________ is a form of partnership similar to a general partnership except that while a general partnership must have at least two general partners , a __________ must have at least one GP and at least one limited partner.

Exam Probability: **Medium**

10. *Answer choices:*

(see index for correct answer)

- a. Limited partnership
- b. Economic torts
- c. Board of directors
- d. Fraudulent trading

Guidance: level 1

:: Shareholders ::

A __________ is a payment made by a corporation to its shareholders, usually as a distribution of profits. When a corporation earns a profit or surplus, the corporation is able to re-invest the profit in the business and pay a proportion of the profit as a __________ to shareholders. Distribution to shareholders may be in cash or, if the corporation has a __________ reinvestment plan, the amount can be paid by the issue of further shares or share repurchase. When __________s are paid, shareholders typically must pay income taxes, and the corporation does not receive a corporate income tax deduction for the __________ payments.

Exam Probability: **Low**

11. *Answer choices:*

(see index for correct answer)

- a. Majority interest
- b. UK Individual Shareholders Society
- c. Dividend

- d. non-controlling interest

Guidance: level 1

:: Generally Accepted Accounting Principles ::

In accounting, _________ is the income that a business have from its normal business activities, usually from the sale of goods and services to customers. _________ is also referred to as sales or turnover.Some companies receive _________ from interest, royalties, or other fees. _________ may refer to business income in general, or it may refer to the amount, in a monetary unit, earned during a period of time, as in "Last year, Company X had _________ of $42 million". Profits or net income generally imply total _________ minus total expenses in a given period. In accounting, in the balance statement it is a subsection of the Equity section and _________ increases equity, it is often referred to as the "top line" due to its position on the income statement at the very top. This is to be contrasted with the "bottom line" which denotes net income .

Exam Probability: **High**

12. *Answer choices:*

(see index for correct answer)

- a. Standard Business Reporting
- b. Petty cash
- c. Indian Accounting Standards
- d. Contributed capital

Guidance: level 1

:: Accounting terminology ::

Double-entry bookkeeping, in accounting, is a system of bookkeeping so named because every entry to an account requires a corresponding and opposite entry to a different account. The double entry has two equal and corresponding sides known as debit and credit. The left-hand side is debit and right-hand side is credit. For instance, recording a sale of $100 might require two entries: a debit of $100 to an account named "Stock" and a credit of $100 to an account named "Revenue."

Exam Probability: **Low**

13. *Answer choices:*

(see index for correct answer)

- a. General ledger
- b. Chart of accounts
- c. Internal auditing
- d. profit and loss statement

Guidance: level 1

:: Manufacturing ::

_________ s are goods that have completed the manufacturing process but have not yet been sold or distributed to the end user.

Exam Probability: **Low**

14. *Answer choices:*

(see index for correct answer)

- a. Finished good
- b. Distributed manufacturing
- c. Flexlink
- d. Automated guided vehicle

Guidance: level 1

:: ::

In the field of analysis of algorithms in computer science, the _________ is a method of amortized analysis based on accounting. The _________ often gives a more intuitive account of the amortized cost of an operation than either aggregate analysis or the potential method. Note, however, that this does not guarantee such analysis will be immediately obvious; often, choosing the correct parameters for the _________ requires as much knowledge of the problem and the complexity bounds one is attempting to prove as the other two methods.

Exam Probability: **Medium**

15. *Answer choices:*

(see index for correct answer)

- a. process perspective
- b. Accounting method
- c. open system
- d. deep-level diversity

Guidance: level 1

:: Tax avoidance ::

_________ s are any method of reducing taxable income resulting in a reduction of the payments to tax collecting entities, including state and federal governments. The methodology can vary depending on local and international tax laws.

Exam Probability: **Medium**

16. *Answer choices:*

(see index for correct answer)

- a. SUTA dumping
- b. Tax shelter
- c. Salary packaging
- d. Lagarde list

Guidance: level 1

:: Business ethics ::

In accounting and in most Schools of economic thought, _________ is a rational and unbiased estimate of the potential market price of a good, service, or asset. It takes into account such objectivity factors as.

Exam Probability: **Medium**

17. *Answer choices:*

(see index for correct answer)

- a. Fair value
- b. McJob
- c. Ethical consumerism
- d. Sustainability Accounting Standards Board

Guidance: level 1

:: Financial statements ::

__________ s - are the "Financial statements of a group in which the assets, liabilities, equity, income, expenses and cash flows of the parent company and its subsidiaries are presented as those of a single economic entity", according to International Accounting Standard 27 "Consolidated and separate financial statements", and International Financial Reporting Standard 10 " __________ s".

Exam Probability: **High**

18. *Answer choices:*

(see index for correct answer)

- a. Government financial statements
- b. Consolidated financial statement
- c. quarterly report
- d. Statement of retained earnings

Guidance: level 1

:: Real property law ::

A __________ or millage rate is an ad valorem tax on the value of a property, usually levied on real estate. The tax is levied by the governing authority of the jurisdiction in which the property is located. This can be a national government, a federated state, a county or geographical region or a municipality. Multiple jurisdictions may tax the same property. This tax can be contrasted to a rent tax which is based on rental income or imputed rent, and a land value tax, which is a levy on the value of land, excluding the value of buildings and other improvements.

Exam Probability: **Medium**

19. *Answer choices:*

(see index for correct answer)

- a. Cape
- b. Property tax
- c. Life interest
- d. Concurrent estate

Guidance: level 1

:: Accounting in the United States ::

The __________ is the source of generally accepted accounting principles used by state and local governments in the United States. As with most of the entities involved in creating GAAP in the United States, it is a private, non-governmental organization.

Exam Probability: **High**

20. *Answer choices:*

(see index for correct answer)

- a. Certified Public Accountant
- b. Accounting Today
- c. Association of Government Accountants

- d. Governmental Accounting Standards Board

Guidance: level 1

:: Types of business entity ::

A _________ is a partnership in which some or all partners have limited liabilities. It therefore can exhibit elements of partnerships and corporations. In a LLP, each partner is not responsible or liable for another partner`s misconduct or negligence. This is an important difference from the traditional partnership under the UK Partnership Act 1890, in which each partner has joint and several liability. In a LLP, some or all partners have a form of limited liability similar to that of the shareholders of a corporation. Unlike corporate shareholders, the partners have the right to manage the business directly. In contrast, corporate shareholders must elect a board of directors under the laws of various state charters. The board organizes itself and hires corporate officers who then have as "corporate" individuals the legal responsibility to manage the corporation in the corporation`s best interest. A LLP also contains a different level of tax liability from that of a corporation.

Exam Probability: **Medium**

21. *Answer choices:*

(see index for correct answer)

- a. Delaware statutory trust
- b. Proprietary company
- c. General partnership
- d. Value-added reseller

Guidance: level 1

:: Accounting in the United States ::

The __________ is a private-sector, nonprofit corporation created by the Sarbanes–Oxley Act of 2002 to oversee the audits of public companies and other issuers in order to protect the interests of investors and further the public interest in the preparation of informative, accurate and independent audit reports. The PCAOB also oversees the audits of broker-dealers, including compliance reports filed pursuant to federal securities laws, to promote investor protection. All PCAOB rules and standards must be approved by the U.S. Securities and Exchange Commission .

Exam Probability: **High**

22. *Answer choices:*

(see index for correct answer)

- a. American Institute of Certified Public Accountants
- b. Trueblood Committee
- c. Legal liability of certified public accountants
- d. Revolving fund

Guidance: level 1

:: Taxation ::

A _________ is a person or organization subject to pay a tax. _________ s have an Identification Number, a reference number issued by a government to its citizens.

Exam Probability: **Low**

23. *Answer choices:*

(see index for correct answer)

- a. Taxpayer
- b. Tax cut
- c. Payment in lieu of taxes
- d. Tax break

Guidance: level 1

:: ::

_________ is a costing method that identifies activities in an organization and assigns the cost of each activity to all products and services according to the actual consumption by each. This model assigns more indirect costs into direct costs compared to conventional costing.

Exam Probability: **Medium**

24. *Answer choices:*

(see index for correct answer)

- a. levels of analysis
- b. Activity-based costing
- c. empathy
- d. open system

Guidance: level 1

:: Financial ratios ::

Earnings per share is the monetary value of earnings per outstanding share of common stock for a company.

Exam Probability: **Low**

25. *Answer choices:*

(see index for correct answer)

- a. Debtor collection period
- b. P/B ratio
- c. CASA ratio
- d. Diluted earnings per share

Guidance: level 1

:: Foreign exchange market ::

A currency , in the most specific sense is money in any form when in use or circulation as a medium of exchange, especially circulating banknotes and coins. A more general definition is that a currency is a system of money in common use, especially for people in a nation. Under this definition, US dollars , pounds sterling , Australian dollars , European euros , Russian rubles and Indian Rupees are examples of currencies. These various currencies are recognized as stores of value and are traded between nations in foreign exchange markets, which determine the relative values of the different currencies. Currencies in this sense are defined by governments, and each type has limited boundaries of acceptance.

Exam Probability: **Medium**

26. *Answer choices:*

(see index for correct answer)

- a. Currency overlay
- b. Chiang Mai Initiative
- c. Petrodollar recycling
- d. Cent accounts

Guidance: level 1

:: Valuation (finance) ::

The __________ is one of three major groups of methodologies, called valuation approaches, used by appraisers. It is particularly common in commercial real estate appraisal and in business appraisal. The fundamental math is similar to the methods used for financial valuation, securities analysis, or bond pricing. However, there are some significant and important modifications when used in real estate or business valuation.

Exam Probability: **High**

27. *Answer choices:*

(see index for correct answer)

- a. Dividend discount model
- b. Cann v Willson
- c. Financial analysis
- d. Income approach

Guidance: level 1

:: ::

A work order is usually a task or a job for a customer, that can be scheduled or assigned to someone. Such an order may be from a customer request or created internally within the organization. Work orders may also be created as follow ups to Inspections or Audits. A work order may be for products or services.

Exam Probability: **Medium**

28. *Answer choices:*

(see index for correct answer)

- a. Job order
- b. levels of analysis
- c. similarity-attraction theory
- d. open system

Guidance: level 1

:: ::

__________ is the consumption and saving opportunity gained by an entity within a specified timeframe, which is generally expressed in monetary terms. For households and individuals, " __________ is the sum of all the wages, salaries, profits, interest payments, rents, and other forms of earnings received in a given period of time."

Exam Probability: **Medium**

29. *Answer choices:*

(see index for correct answer)

- a. open system
- b. similarity-attraction theory
- c. Income
- d. functional perspective

Guidance: level 1

:: Accounting source documents ::

_________ is a letter sent by a customer to a supplier to inform the supplier that their invoice has been paid. If the customer is paying by cheque, the _________ often accompanies the cheque. The advice may consist of a literal letter or of a voucher attached to the side or top of the cheque.

Exam Probability: **High**

30. *Answer choices:*

(see index for correct answer)

- a. Superbill
- b. Remittance advice
- c. Bank statement
- d. Air waybill

Guidance: level 1

:: Internal Revenue Code ::

The __________ , formally the __________ of 1986, is the domestic portion of federal statutory tax law in the United States, published in various volumes of the United States Statutes at Large, and separately as Title 26 of the United States Code . It is organized topically, into subtitles and sections, covering income tax , payroll taxes, estate taxes, gift taxes, and excise taxes; as well as procedure and administration. Its implementing agency is the Internal Revenue Service.

Exam Probability: **Low**

31. *Answer choices:*

(see index for correct answer)

- a. Johnson Amendment
- b. 475 fund
- c. Internal Revenue Code
- d. Casualty loss

Guidance: level 1

:: Generally Accepted Accounting Principles ::

Paid-in capital is capital that is contributed to a corporation by investors by purchase of stock from the corporation, the primary market, not by purchase of stock in the open market from other stockholders . It includes share capital as well as additional paid-in capital.

Exam Probability: **Low**

32. *Answer choices:*

(see index for correct answer)

- a. Standard Business Reporting
- b. Generally accepted accounting principles
- c. Statement of recommended practice
- d. Contributed capital

Guidance: level 1

:: E-commerce ::

A __________ is a plastic payment card that can be used instead of cash when making purchases. It is similar to a credit card, but unlike a credit card, the money is immediately transferred directly from the cardholder`s bank account when performing a transaction.

Exam Probability: **High**

33. *Answer choices:*

(see index for correct answer)

- a. Debit card
- b. Online locator service
- c. Mobile banking
- d. Open Market

Guidance: level 1

:: Financial accounting ::

In accounting, _________ is the value of an asset according to its balance sheet account balance. For assets, the value is based on the original cost of the asset less any depreciation, amortization or impairment costs made against the asset. Traditionally, a company's _________ is its total assets minus intangible assets and liabilities. However, in practice, depending on the source of the calculation, _________ may variably include goodwill, intangible assets, or both. The value inherent in its workforce, part of the intellectual capital of a company, is always ignored. When intangible assets and goodwill are explicitly excluded, the metric is often specified to be "tangible _________".

Exam Probability: **Medium**

34. *Answer choices:*

(see index for correct answer)

- a. Accounting identity
- b. Advance payment
- c. Book value
- d. SEC filing

Guidance: level 1

:: Financial accounting ::

__________ refers to any one of several methods by which a company, for `financial accounting` or tax purposes, depreciates a fixed asset in such a way that the amount of depreciation taken each year is higher during the earlier years of an asset's life. For financial accounting purposes, __________ is expected to be much more productive during its early years, so that depreciation expense will more accurately represent how much of an asset's usefulness is being used up each year. For tax purposes, __________ provides a way of deferring corporate income taxes by reducing taxable income in current years, in exchange for increased taxable income in future years. This is a valuable tax incentive that encourages businesses to purchase new assets.

Exam Probability: **Low**

35. *Answer choices:*

(see index for correct answer)

- a. Money measurement
- b. Asset recovery
- c. Accelerated depreciation
- d. Authorised capital

Guidance: level 1

:: Accounting systems ::

In accounting, the controlling account is an account in the general ledger for which a corresponding subsidiary ledger has been created. The subsidiary ledger allows for tracking transactions within the controlling account in more detail. Individual transactions are posted both to the controlling account and the corresponding subsidiary ledger, and the totals for both are compared when preparing a trial balance to ensure accuracy.

Exam Probability: **Medium**

36. *Answer choices:*

(see index for correct answer)

- a. Dome Publishing
- b. Inflation accounting
- c. Control account
- d. Off-balance sheet

Guidance: level 1

:: ::

The _________ of 1938 29 U.S.C. § 203 is a United States labor law that creates the right to a minimum wage, and "time-and-a-half" overtime pay when people work over forty hours a week. It also prohibits most employment of minors in "oppressive child labor". It applies to employees engaged in interstate commerce or employed by an enterprise engaged in commerce or in the production of goods for commerce, unless the employer can claim an exemption from coverage.

Exam Probability: **Low**

37. *Answer choices:*

(see index for correct answer)

- a. deep-level diversity
- b. Fair Labor Standards Act
- c. empathy
- d. levels of analysis

Guidance: level 1

:: Business ::

The seller, or the provider of the goods or services, completes a sale in response to an acquisition, appropriation, requisition or a direct interaction with the buyer at the point of sale. There is a passing of title of the item, and the settlement of a price, in which agreement is reached on a price for which transfer of ownership of the item will occur. The seller, not the purchaser typically executes the sale and it may be completed prior to the obligation of payment. In the case of indirect interaction, a person who sells goods or service on behalf of the owner is known as a _________ man or _________ woman or _________ person, but this often refers to someone selling goods in a store/shop, in which case other terms are also common, including _________ clerk, shop assistant, and retail clerk.

Exam Probability: **Low**

38. *Answer choices:*

(see index for correct answer)

- a. Sales
- b. Sustainopreneurship
- c. Signed number
- d. Gray ceiling

Guidance: level 1

:: United States Generally Accepted Accounting Principles ::

A _________ is a set of U.S. government financial statements comprising the financial report of a state, municipal or other governmental entity that complies with the accounting requirements promulgated by the Governmental Accounting Standards Board . GASB provides standards for the content of a CAFR in its annually updated publication Codification of Governmental Accounting and Financial Reporting Standards. The U.S. Federal Government adheres to standards determined by the Federal Accounting Standards Advisory Board .

Exam Probability: **Low**

39. *Answer choices:*

(see index for correct answer)

- a. Working Group on Financial Markets
- b. Comprehensive annual financial report
- c. Cost segregation study
- d. FIN 46

Guidance: level 1

:: International taxation ::

_________ is the levying of tax by two or more jurisdictions on the same declared income , asset , or financial transaction . Double liability is mitigated in a number of ways, for example.

Exam Probability: **High**

40. *Answer choices:*

(see index for correct answer)

- a. Spahn tax
- b. Tax equalization
- c. Controlled foreign corporation
- d. Foreign personal holding company

Guidance: level 1

:: ::

_________ is a means of protection from financial loss. It is a form of risk management, primarily used to hedge against the risk of a contingent or uncertain loss

Exam Probability: **Medium**

41. *Answer choices:*

(see index for correct answer)

- a. Sarbanes-Oxley act of 2002
- b. personal values
- c. information systems assessment
- d. empathy

Guidance: level 1

:: Types of business entity ::

A sole _________ , also known as the sole trader, individual entrepreneurship or _________ , is a type of enterprise that is owned and run by one person and in which there is no legal distinction between the owner and the business entity. A sole trader does not necessarily work `alone`—it is possible for the sole trader to employ other people.

Exam Probability: **Low**

42. *Answer choices:*

(see index for correct answer)

- a. Delaware General Corporation Law
- b. Proprietorship

- c. Proprietary company
- d. Privately held company

Guidance: level 1

:: Taxation and efficiency ::

_________ is the legal usage of the tax regime in a single territory to one`s own advantage to reduce the amount of tax that is payable by means that are within the law. Tax sheltering is very similar, although unlike _________ tax sheltering is not necessarily legal. Tax havens are jurisdictions which facilitate reduced taxes.

Exam Probability: **Low**

43. *Answer choices:*

(see index for correct answer)

- a. supply-side
- b. Tax exporting
- c. Excess burden of taxation
- d. Tax avoidance

Guidance: level 1

:: Money ::

In economics, _________ is money in the physical form of currency, such as banknotes and coins. In bookkeeping and finance, _________ is current assets comprising currency or currency equivalents that can be accessed immediately or near-immediately . _________ is seen either as a reserve for payments, in case of a structural or incidental negative _________ flow or as a way to avoid a downturn on financial markets.

Exam Probability: **Low**

44. *Answer choices:*

(see index for correct answer)

- a. Limping bimetallism
- b. Cash
- c. Green money
- d. Real de alerce

Guidance: level 1

:: Business law ::

A _________ is an arrangement where parties, known as partners, agree to cooperate to advance their mutual interests. The partners in a _________ may be individuals, businesses, interest-based organizations, schools, governments or combinations. Organizations may partner to increase the likelihood of each achieving their mission and to amplify their reach. A _________ may result in issuing and holding equity or may be only governed by a contract.

Exam Probability: **Medium**

45. *Answer choices:*

(see index for correct answer)

- a. Partnership
- b. Leave of absence
- c. Power harassment
- d. Vehicle leasing

Guidance: level 1

:: Generally Accepted Accounting Principles ::

The _________ principle is a cornerstone of accrual accounting together with the matching principle. They both determine the accounting period in which revenues and expenses are recognized. According to the principle, revenues are recognized when they are realized or realizable, and are earned , no matter when cash is received. In cash accounting – in contrast – revenues are recognized when cash is received no matter when goods or services are sold.

Exam Probability: **Low**

46. *Answer choices:*

(see index for correct answer)

- a. Statement of recommended practice
- b. Shares outstanding

- c. Revenue recognition
- d. Expense

Guidance: level 1

:: Generally Accepted Accounting Principles ::

_________ is a small amount of discretionary funds in the form of cash used for expenditures where it is not sensible to make any disbursement by cheque, because of the inconvenience and costs of writing, signing, and then cashing the cheque.

Exam Probability: **Low**

47. *Answer choices:*

(see index for correct answer)

- a. Gross income
- b. Normal balance
- c. Petty cash
- d. Management accounting principles

Guidance: level 1

:: Accounting software ::

__________ describes a type of application software that records and processes accounting transactions within functional modules such as accounts payable, accounts receivable, journal, general ledger, payroll, and trial balance. It functions as an accounting information system. It may be developed in-house by the organization using it, may be purchased from a third party, or may be a combination of a third-party application software package with local modifications. __________ may be on-line based, accessed anywhere at any time with any device which is Internet enabled, or may be desktop based. It varies greatly in its complexity and cost.

Exam Probability: **Medium**

48. *Answer choices:*

(see index for correct answer)

- a. ABLE
- b. Unit4
- c. Sage 50 Accounting
- d. FinanceWorks

Guidance: level 1

:: Accounting terminology ::

__________ or capital expense is the money a company spends to buy, maintain, or improve its fixed assets, such as buildings, vehicles, equipment, or land. It is considered a __________ when the asset is newly purchased or when money is used towards extending the useful life of an existing asset, such as repairing the roof.

Exam Probability: **High**

49. *Answer choices:*

(see index for correct answer)

- a. Accounts receivable
- b. Enterprise liquidity
- c. Double-entry accounting
- d. Capital expenditure

Guidance: level 1

:: Project management ::

_________ is the widespread practice of collecting information and attempting to spot a pattern. In some fields of study, the term " _________ " has more formally defined meanings.

Exam Probability: **High**

50. *Answer choices:*

(see index for correct answer)

- a. Stakeholder analysis
- b. Commissioning management systems
- c. Opportunity management
- d. Trend analysis

Guidance: level 1

:: Accounting source documents ::

An __________ , bill or tab is a commercial document issued by a seller to a buyer, relating to a sale transaction and indicating the products, quantities, and agreed prices for products or services the seller had provided the buyer.

Exam Probability: **Low**

51. *Answer choices:*

(see index for correct answer)

- a. Invoice
- b. Superbill
- c. Remittance advice
- d. Credit memo

Guidance: level 1

:: Supply chain management terms ::

In business and finance, _________ is a system of organizations, people, activities, information, and resources involved inmoving a product or service from supplier to customer. _________ activities involve the transformation of natural resources, raw materials, and components into a finished product that is delivered to the end customer. In sophisticated _________ systems, used products may re-enter the _________ at any point where residual value is recyclable. _________s link value chains.

Exam Probability: **High**

52. *Answer choices:*

(see index for correct answer)

- a. Supply chain
- b. Will call
- c. Widget
- d. inventory management

Guidance: level 1

:: Options (finance) ::

A _________ bond is a type of bond that allows the issuer of the bond to retain the privilege of redeeming the bond at some point before the bond reaches its date of maturity. In other words, on the call date, the issuer has the right, but not the obligation, to buy back the bonds from the bond holders at a defined call price. Technically speaking, the bonds are not really bought and held by the issuer but are instead cancelled immediately.

Exam Probability: **Medium**

53. *Answer choices:*

(see index for correct answer)

- a. Mountain range
- b. Turbo warrant
- c. Callable
- d. Interest rate guarantee

Guidance: level 1

:: ::

In accounting, the _________ is a measure of the number of times inventory is sold or used in a time period such as a year. It is calculated to see if a business has an excessive inventory in comparison to its sales level. The equation for _________ equals the cost of goods sold divided by the average inventory. _________ is also known as inventory turns, merchandise turnover, stockturn, stock turns, turns, and stock turnover.

Exam Probability: **Low**

54. *Answer choices:*

(see index for correct answer)

- a. similarity-attraction theory
- b. personal values

- c. co-culture
- d. Inventory turnover

Guidance: level 1

:: Actuarial science ::

The _________ is the greater benefit of receiving money now rather than an identical sum later. It is founded on time preference.

Exam Probability: **High**

55. *Answer choices:*

(see index for correct answer)

- a. Demography
- b. Lexis diagram
- c. Time value of money
- d. Maximum life span

Guidance: level 1

:: Management accounting ::

_________ , or dollar contribution per unit, is the selling price per unit minus the variable cost per unit. "Contribution" represents the portion of sales revenue that is not consumed by variable costs and so contributes to the coverage of fixed costs. This concept is one of the key building blocks of break-even analysis.

Exam Probability: **Medium**

56. *Answer choices:*

(see index for correct answer)

- a. Institute of Certified Management Accountants
- b. Responsibility center
- c. Contribution margin
- d. Management accounting in supply chains

Guidance: level 1

:: Financial ratios ::

The _________ is a financial ratio indicating the relative proportion of equity used to finance a company`s assets. The two components are often taken from the firm`s balance sheet or statement of financial position , but the ratio may also be calculated using market values for both, if the company`s equities are publicly traded.

Exam Probability: **Medium**

57. *Answer choices:*

(see index for correct answer)

- a. Put/call ratio
- b. Equity ratio
- c. Quick ratio
- d. Import ratio

Guidance: level 1

:: Cash flow ::

_________ s are narrowly interconnected with the concepts of value, interest rate and liquidity.A _________ that shall happen on a future day tN can be transformed into a _________ of the same value in t0.

Exam Probability: **Medium**

58. *Answer choices:*

(see index for correct answer)

- a. Cash flow statement
- b. Cash carrier
- c. Cash flow
- d. Cash flow loan

Guidance: level 1

:: Financial accounting ::

A _________ is an ownership interest in a corporation with enough voting stock shares to prevail in any stockholders` motion. A majority of voting shares is always a _________ . When a party holds less than the majority of the voting shares, other present circumstances can be considered to determine whether that party is still considered to hold a controlling ownership interest.

Exam Probability: **High**

59. *Answer choices:*

(see index for correct answer)

- a. Floating capital
- b. Controlling interest
- c. Finance charge
- d. Asset recovery

Guidance: level 1

INDEX: Correct Answers

Foundations of Business

1. d: Mission statement

2. c: Availability

3. c: Asset

4. b: Raw material

5. c: Resource management

6. b: Reputation

7. : Cash

8. d: Land

9. : Net income

10. : Debt

11. c: Number

12. a: Building

13. a: Revenue

14. a: Venture capital

15. a: Accounting

16. : Expense

17. a: Credit

18. : Empowerment

19. : Employment

20. : Accounts receivable

21. : Competition

22. : E-commerce

23. d: Analysis

24. b: Innovation

25. c: Law

26. d: Case study

27. b: Utility

28. : Problem

29. d: Sales

30. : Marketing research

31. : Good

32. : Bribery

33. b: Efficiency

34. d: Present value

35. b: Business

36. c: Cooperative

37. a: Market share

38. d: Partnership

39. b: Management

40. b: Planning

41. a: Economic Development

42. : Performance

43. a: Perception

44. : Brand

45. d: Bank

46. a: Balanced scorecard

47. c: Productivity

48. : Fraud

49. : Publicity

50. a: Firm

51. a: Common stock

52. a: Variable cost

53. c: Benchmarking

54. d: INDEX

55. a: Error

56. b: Outsourcing

57. b: Negotiation

58. : Inventory

59. a: Recession

Management

1. b: Shareholder

2. c: Linear programming

3. a: Budget

4. b: Job satisfaction

5. b: Chief executive

6. a: Ownership

7. : Risk management

8. b: Bureaucracy

9. b: Total quality management

10. b: Best practice

11. b: Sales

12. b: Feedback

13. d: Questionnaire

14. a: Ratio

15. b: Problem solving

16. a: Management system

17. b: Lead

18. d: 360-degree feedback

19. c: Project manager

20. a: Organization chart

21. : Organizational performance

22. b: Scientific management

23. d: Cost leadership

24. a: Restructuring

25. a: Customer

26. c: Partnership

27. d: Strategic planning

28. d: Recruitment

29. a: Standard deviation

30. c: Operations management

31. a: Explanation

32. d: Product design

33. a: Environmental scanning

34. b: Environmental protection

35. d: Size

36. a: Span of control

37. : Job enlargement

38. c: Affirmative action

39. a: Variable cost

40. a: Job description

41. : Centralization

42. d: Hotel

43. a: Perception

44. : Grievance

45. : Corporate governance

46. : Trade

47. a: Emotional intelligence

48. c: Quality circle

49. a: Cooperation

50. d: Training

51. c: Layoff

52. d: Job analysis

53. : Frequency

54. b: Offshoring

55. d: Philosophy

56. c: Decision-making

57. b: Meeting

58. c: Myers-Briggs type

59. b: Control chart

Business law

1. a: Real property

2. b: Requirements contract

3. d: Litigation

4. a: Consideration

5. : Warehouse receipt

6. d: Brand

7. c: Categorical imperative

8. c: Jury Trial

9. c: Policy

10. a: Arbitration

11. d: Adoption

12. : Trespass

13. c: Implied authority

14. b: Mediation

15. c: Berne Convention

16. c: Delegation

17. a: Output contract

18. : Broker

19. a: Apparent authority

20. b: Bill of lading

21. c: Regulation

22. d: Good faith

23. c: Board of directors

24. b: Authority

25. : Shareholder

26. a: Manufacturing

27. c: Eminent domain

28. d: Judicial review

29. d: Prohibition

30. c: Internal Revenue Service

31. b: Sexual harassment

32. d: Lease

33. b: Firm

34. d: Supreme Court

35. : Breach of contract

36. d: Management

37. a: Constitution

38. c: Summary judgment

39. d: Security

40. b: Statute of limitations

41. c: Operation of law

42. c: Corporation

43. a: Federal question

44. d: Subrogation

45. b: Duress

46. c: Personnel

47. d: Reasonable person

48. c: Marketing

49. : Advertising

50. d: Statute

51. d: Procedural law

52. : Real estate

53. b: Revocation

54. c: Joint venture

55. a: Constitutional law

56. b: Implied warranty

57. d: Criminal law

58. b: Market value

59. c: Affidavit

Finance

1. d: Bank of America

2. d: Creditor

3. c: Ending inventory

4. c: Operating leverage

5. : Pro forma

6. b: Exercise

7. c: Cost object

8. b: Call option

9. d: Long-term liabilities

10. a: Receipt

11. b: Matching principle

12. c: Capital expenditure

13. a: Public company

14. : Revenue

15. c: Book value

16. a: Par value

17. d: Factory

18. c: Subsidiary ledger

19. : Standard deviation

20. : Finance

21. b: Payment

22. d: Accounting

23. c: Finished good

24. : Accrued liabilities

25. d: Purchasing

26. c: Total cost

27. d: Treasury stock

28. : Operating Income

29. d: Net income

30. b: Inventory

31. d: Dividend yield

32. d: Bank statement

33. a: Accounts receivable

34. : Bank reconciliation

35. a: Equity method

36. b: Accounting method

37. d: Present value

38. d: Gross profit

39. c: Commercial paper

40. d: Cost allocation

41. d: Social security

42. a: Income tax

43. : Cost driver

44. : Journal entry

45. b: Absorption costing

46. : Derivative

47. a: Write-off

48. a: Economy

49. a: Ledger

50. b: Capital asset

51. : Net present value

52. d: Enron

53. b: Interest expense

54. : Debt-to-equity ratio

55. b: Fiscal year

56. : Financial ratio

57. : Coupon

58. a: Manufacturing

59. d: Policy

Human resource management

1. b: Task force

2. d: Skill

3. : Grievance

4. : Cafeteria plan

5. d: Strategic management

6. : Criterion validity

7. a: Goal setting

8. b: Deferred compensation

9. d: Unemployment

10. b: Content validity

11. : Intellectual capital

12. : Brainstorming

13. c: Merit pay

14. c: Human resource management

15. b: Love contract

16. b: Innovation

17. d: Knowledge worker

18. a: Reasonable person

19. c: Decentralization

20. a: Organizational justice

21. d: Human resources

22. b: Employee handbook

23. a: Officer

24. : Cost of living

25. a: Realistic job preview

26. c: Unemployment insurance

27. b: Bottom line

28. b: Social media

29. b: Wage curve

30. a: Applicant tracking system

31. b: Behavior modification

32. : Action learning

33. a: Case interview

34. d: Right to work

35. c: Expert power

36. b: Culture shock

37. b: Partnership

38. c: Balance sheet

39. d: Flexible spending account

40. a: Globalization

41. b: Sexual harassment

42. c: Impasse

43. c: Workforce

44. b: Conformity

45. c: Graveyard shift

46. : Job satisfaction

47. a: Departmentalization

48. b: UNITE HERE

49. b: Assessment center

50. : Total Reward

51. b: Cover letter

52. a: Employee stock

53. c: Stock appreciation right

54. c: Employee assistance program

55. : Professional employer organization

56. b: Bargaining unit

57. d: Minimum wage

58. : Worker Adjustment and Retraining Notification Act

59. : Restructuring

Information systems

1. a: Information systems

2. b: Utility computing

3. d: Usability

4. c: Online transaction processing

5. : American Express

6. d: Questionnaire

7. : Structured query language

8. c: Groupware

9. a: Enterprise systems

10. b: Mozy

11. c: Bit rate

12. c: Data security

13. : Freemium

14. a: ICANN

15. b: Sensitivity analysis

16. c: Reputation management

17. b: Geographic information system

18. b: Application software

19. a: Data model

20. b: Mass customization

21. c: Information management

22. c: Metadata

23. b: Social shopping

24. : Byte

25. : Random access

26. c: Availability

27. a: Input device

28. : Pop-up ad

29. b: Craigslist

30. d: Consumer-to-business

31. d: Query language

32. c: Innovation

33. c: Radio-frequency identification

34. : Strategic information system

35. c: Data center

36. c: Security management

37. b: Epicor

38. b: Zynga

39. b: Carnivore

40. c: Consumer-to-consumer

41. c: Cookie

42. c: Census

43. c: Mobile commerce

44. : Cybersquatting

45. : Google Maps

46. : Data redundancy

47. d: Text mining

48. c: Database model

49. b: Outsourcing

50. d: Search engine optimization

51. b: Content management

52. b: Analytics

53. : Local Area Network

54. a: Backup

55. : Open source

56. c: Transport Layer Security

57. b: Vertical integration

58. : Property

59. : Fault tolerance

Marketing

1. d: Monopoly

2. c: American Express

3. : Marketing management

4. d: Marketing strategy

5. : Firm

6. b: Preference

7. a: Business model

8. d: Information technology

9. d: Choice

10. c: Market research

11. d: Strategic planning

12. c: Gross domestic product

13. : Perception

14. : Adoption

15. b: Penetration pricing

16. c: Selling

17. c: Corporation

18. b: Sales promotion

19. b: Mass marketing

20. b: Trial

21. b: Green marketing

22. : Value proposition

23. c: Supply chain

24. : Trade association

25. b: Total Quality Management

26. b: Clayton Act

27. d: Public relations

28. : Mass customization

29. b: Marketing communications

30. c: Statistic

31. a: Department store

32. b: Customer retention

33. d: Total cost

34. d: Marketing research

35. c: Planning

36. d: Performance

37. d: E-commerce

38. b: Publicity

39. d: Audit

40. a: Pricing

41. d: Mobile marketing

42. a: Consideration

43. a: Brand extension

44. b: Contract

45. : Dimension

46. b: Fixed cost

47. d: Public

48. b: Globalization

49. d: Product manager

50. b: Product development

51. : Price

52. d: Advertisement

53. d: Quantitative research

54. d: Shares

55. b: New product development

56. a: Strategic alliance

57. b: Question

58. d: Health

59. : Customer satisfaction

Manufacturing

1. : Property

2. c: Rolling Wave planning

3. d: Quality policy

4. c: Perfect competition

5. b: Reorder point

6. : E-commerce

7. c: Toshiba

8. b: Reflux

9. b: Material requirements planning

10. d: Resource management

11. b: Expediting

12. : Service quality

13. b: Metal

14. d: Catalyst

15. c: Capacity planning

16. a: Steering committee

17. a: Chemical reaction

18. c: Acceptance sampling

19. c: Reboiler

20. d: Six Sigma

21. a: Strategic sourcing

22. a: Goal

23. b: Rolling

24. c: Volume

25. b: American Society for Quality

26. d: Accreditation

27. b: Natural resource

28. a: Project team

29. a: Interaction

30. : Malcolm Baldrige National Quality Award

31. c: Kanban

32. : Materials management

33. d: Inventory control

34. a: Distillation

35. d: Economies of scope

36. c: Risk management

37. : Obsolescence

38. b: Milestone

39. b: Tool

40. c: New product development

41. : Management process

42. c: Bullwhip effect

43. c: Downtime

44. b: DMAIC

45. a: Statistical process control

46. : Licensed production

47. a: Lead

48. a: Sales

49. d: Paper

50. a: Design of experiments

51. a: ROOT

52. b: Prize

53. b: Quality Engineering

54. c: Asset

55. : Ball

56. d: Throughput

57. c: Purchasing manager

58. d: Zero Defects

59. c: Solution

Commerce

1. a: Charter

2. b: Mobile commerce

3. c: Economic development

4. a: Inflation

5. a: Planning

6. a: British Airways

7. b: Encryption

8. a: Graduation

9. : Expense

10. d: Supervisor

11. b: Online advertising

12. c: Automated Clearing House

13. c: Building

14. d: Security

15. a: Quality control

16. b: Asset

17. d: Broker

18. a: Revenue

19. a: Economy

20. b: Teamwork

21. b: Joint venture

22. b: Appeal

23. b: Firm

24. b: Confirmed

25. a: Enabling

26. : Audit

27. : Information technology

28. : Subsidiary

29. b: Permission marketing

30. a: Electronic data interchange

31. b: Overtime

32. d: Case study

33. : Direct marketing

34. d: Uniform Commercial Code

35. : Accounting

36. d: Federal government

37. a: Purchasing

38. c: Brand

39. c: Tangible

40. b: Purchase order

41. : Organizational structure

42. b: Consignee

43. c: Frequency

44. a: Advertising

45. b: Product line

46. a: Product mix

47. d: Public policy

48. : Import

49. a: Freight forwarder

50. c: Advertisement

51. : PayPal

52. : Information system

53. c: Customer service

54. : Invoice

55. d: Recruitment

56. b: Good

57. b: Bottom line

58. c: Siemens

59. : Goal

Business ethics

1. a: Great Depression

2. : Consumer Financial Protection Bureau

3. a: Skill

4. b: Federal Trade Commission Act

5. a: New York Stock Exchange

6. a: Corporation

7. c: Trojan horse

8. c: Solar power

9. c: Corporate structure

10. : Electronic waste

11. b: Kyoto Protocol

12. c: Patent

13. d: Fannie Mae

14. b: Retaliation

15. b: Human nature

16. d: Clean Water Act

17. : Marketing

18. : Aristotle

19. b: Fair Trade Certified

20. a: Ethics Resource Center

21. b: Urban sprawl

22. d: Planned obsolescence

23. b: Model Rules of Professional Conduct

24. a: Consumer Protection

25. : Volcker Rule

26. c: Individualistic culture

27. : Hedonism

28. c: Social responsibility

29. : Auditor independence

30. d: Medicare fraud

31. a: Organizational ethics

32. : Pyramid scheme

33. : Workplace politics

34. d: Layoff

35. : Minimum wage

36. a: Veil of ignorance

37. b: Micromanagement

38. b: Medicaid

39. c: New Deal

40. c: Insider trading

41. : Chamber of Commerce

42. a: Executive compensation

43. b: Trade

44. d: Reputation

45. d: Pollution Prevention

46. c: Whistleblower

47. c: Exxon Valdez

48. c: Wall Street

49. a: Collusion

50. a: Price fixing

51. b: European Commission

52. : Vigilance committee

53. d: Madoff

54. b: Business model

55. b: Greenwashing

56. a: Federal Trade Commission

57. c: Stanford International Bank

58. : Recovery Act

59. c: Antitrust

Accounting

1. : Tax revenue

2. b: Audit trail

3. c: Asset

4. : Tax deferral

5. c: Common stock

6. a: Cost of goods available for sale

7. b: Capital gain

8. c: Land

9. a: Controversy

10. a: Limited partnership

11. c: Dividend

12. : Revenue

13. : Double-entry accounting

14. a: Finished good

15. b: Accounting method

16. b: Tax shelter

17. a: Fair value

18. b: Consolidated financial statement

19. b: Property tax

20. d: Governmental Accounting Standards Board

21. : Limited liability partnership

22. : Public Company Accounting Oversight Board

23. a: Taxpayer

24. b: Activity-based costing

25. d: Diluted earnings per share

26. : Monetary unit

27. d: Income approach

28. a: Job order

29. c: Income

30. b: Remittance advice

31. c: Internal Revenue Code

32. d: Contributed capital

33. a: Debit card

34. c: Book value

35. c: Accelerated depreciation

36. c: Control account

37. b: Fair Labor Standards Act

38. a: Sales

39. b: Comprehensive annual financial report

40. : Double taxation

41. : Insurance

42. b: Proprietorship

43. d: Tax avoidance

44. b: Cash

45. a: Partnership

46. c: Revenue recognition

47. c: Petty cash

48. : Accounting software

49. d: Capital expenditure

50. d: Trend analysis

51. a: Invoice

52. a: Supply chain

53. c: Callable

54. d: Inventory turnover

55. c: Time value of money

56. c: Contribution margin

57. b: Equity ratio

58. c: Cash flow

59. b: Controlling interest

CPSIA information can be obtained
at www.ICGtesting.com
Printed in the USA
LVHW041023301019
635717LV00002B/107/P

9 781538 86330